Library of
Davidson College

JURIES AND JUDGES

VERSUS THE LAW

Virginia's Provincial Legal

Perspective, 1783–1828

CONSTITUTIONALISM AND DEMOCRACY
KERMIT HALL AND DAVID O'BRIEN, EDITORS

Kevin T. McGuire
The Supreme Court Bar: Legal Elites in the Washington Community

Mark Tushnet, ed.
The Warren Court in Historical and Political Perspective

David N. Mayer
The Constitutional Thought of Thomas Jefferson

F. Thornton Miller
Juries and Judges versus the Law: Virginia's Provincial Legal Perspective, 1783–1828

Martin Edelman
Courts, Politics, and Culture in Israel

Tony Freyer
Producers versus Capitalists: Constitutional Conflict in Antebellum America

JURIES AND JUDGES
VERSUS THE LAW

*Virginia's Provincial Legal
Perspective, 1783–1828*

F. THORNTON MILLER

UNIVERSITY PRESS OF VIRGINIA

Charlottesville and London

THE UNIVERSITY PRESS OF VIRGINIA

Copyright © 1994 by the Rector and Visitors
of the University of Virginia

FIRST PUBLISHED 1994

Library of Congress Cataloging-in-Publication Data
Miller, Frederick Thornton.
    Juries and judges versus the law : Virginia's provincial legal perspective, 1783–1828 / F. Thornton Miller.
       p. cm. — (Constitutionalism and democracy)
    Includes bibliographical references and index.
    ISBN 0-8139-1486-8 (cloth)
    1. Justice, Administration of—Virginia—History. 2. Jury—Virginia—History. 3. Sociological jurisprudence. 4. State rights. I. Title. II. Series.
KFV2478.M55 1994
340'.115'09755—dc20   93-39426
                                                                 CIP

PRINTED IN THE UNITED STATES OF AMERICA

*For Sandra,
my children, my parents,
and Mamma*

CONTENTS

Tables, Map   viii

Preface   ix

Introduction   1

1 Against the Madisonian Round of Reform   12

2 A Power and Privilege Called Liberty and Right: Debtors and Trial by Jury   34

3 The Interposition of 1798 and the Emergence of the Old Republicans   47

4 A Shield of Liberty: Pendleton's and Roane's Court of Appeals   63

5 The Fairfax Litigation: A Model in Anti-Constitutional Law   74

6 Against the "Era of Good Feelings" Round of Reform   87

7 Virginia's Plea for a Separate Realm   113

Notes   123

Bibliography   141

Index   163

TABLES AND MAP

Tables

1. Appeals from county courts to state district courts, 1789–1806   7
2. Percentage of forms of legal action in civil suits, 1785–1825   36
3. Reappraising plaintiff win-loss ratios, 1789–92   37
4. Special motions in jury trials, 1785–1825   101

Map

Virginia, 1792–1828   14

PREFACE

This is a study of what can be called the other side of the law, not anarchy or illegality or even civil disobedience, but an undercurrent against the establishment of a supreme law of the land enforced by one Supreme Court. It studies the attempt in Virginia to conserve a traditional and provincial legal perspective that involved the preference for local justice, the power of juries vis-à-vis judges, and the opposition to a centralization of power that was beyond the control of rural, agrarian interests.

This work runs counter to the view of the law during the early Republic from works—most importantly Morton J. Horwitz, *The Transformation of American Law, 1780–1860* (Cambridge, Mass.: Harvard University Press, 1977)—that, by concentrating on New York and New England sources, have contended that America moved from an agrarian and amateur or popular law to a commercial and professional law allied to business interests. But the common law was not uniform in its development. Later sectional differences in America were foreshadowed in the diversity within the common-law tradition. Even if Morton Horwitz is right that the law became a means for transforming society and developing the economy in New York and New England, the evidence indicates that this sort of transformation was not occurring in Virginia, even in internal improvements (such as improving river navigation and building canals). This is not to say that Virginia lacked reform-minded lawyers, judges, and politicians. I believe, however, that not only were they frustrated, their very attempt at reform helped to bring about a conservative reaction against them.

The South has long been associated with the state-sovereignty constitutional doctrine. But, from the first, Northern and Southern judges did not just disagree on their views of the Constitution. They also differed on the law. Virginia's judges were not trying to instigate a Horwitz-style use of the law to transform society and the economy while they advanced the state sovereignty theory. Instead, they were developing a Southern jurisprudence. The Southern constitutional theory has been amply studied; Virginia's Southern jurisprudence has not. The two were connected. The common law practiced in Virginia's rural county courthouses and the jurisprudence of Edmund Pendleton and Spencer Roane were related, as was the defense of local juries and the opposition to a distant and "foreign" federal appellate jurisdiction. This work connects Virginia's socioeconomic history with the development of a political and constitutional states' rights doctrine, developments in the common law, and the principles and practices of judges, lawyers, and juries.

This work will also show that the development of the Southern jurisprudence model, as well as of the states' rights doctrine, predated the defense of slavery. It has often been assumed that in response to Northern criticism of the institution, Southerners looked around for weapons, for constitutional tools of defense, and took their stand advocating the strict construction of the Constitution and states' rights. There has been a popular tendency to take a post-1820 perspective, but the conservative legal perspective described in this work was well established before the Missouri crisis made slavery a political issue. Nonetheless, the Missouri crisis, as well as the panic of 1819, Marshall Court opinions, and the end of the Virginia Dynasty all added to Virginians' sense of decline and their lack of confidence in being able to influence the direction of America.

This work studies both those who advocated reform and the conservative reaction in Virginia and, in doing so, reveals a close relationship between law and society. The most important aspect of Virginia's socioeconomic history during the early Republic was the state's economic decline. For many, agriculture was closely linked with indebtedness, and this connection would influence views of the law, courts, and government. Certain interests and areas of the state advanced the conservative and provincial and localist legal perspective. The opponents of reform feared the justice of distant courts. Patrick Henry and the Anti-Federalists, for example, had real concerns when they opposed the Constitution, and not just hypothetical ones. At the federal and the state levels, they hoped that any appellate system would be decentralized through the use of local juries. They looked to the "country," the trial by a jury of one's peers, to temper the law—especially in debt cases—through the jury's control of facts, verdicts, and damages. (It should be noted that although there was continuity regarding specific interest groups and geographic areas of the state, there was a complex factionalism in Virginia, with shifting alignments.

No stable party system or political organizations spanned the period of this study.)

By studying the relationship of ideas to socio-economic interests, this work avoids a historiographical tendency to view the more ideologically vocal Virginians as impractical ideologues who criticized the people who did what was necessary to successfully administer a government. From Anti-Federalists to Old Republicans, these individuals were experienced in government at the state and local levels and wanted power to remain at those levels. Far from being removed from power, they often were trying to defend their power from what they perceived as outside threats to weaken it. When they spoke of liberty and rights, they often meant a protection of their local interests.

Both in relation to the antagonism within Virginia over legal reform and in relation to the federal-state division of power, localist and provincial conservatives often described the law as a "foreign" threat to their liberty. For them, the law could be a dangerous force, like a whirlpool, that both expanded in size and drew all to its center. Against a threat at two levels, federal and state, supporters of power at the local and state levels combined to oppose federal power, and there was also an in-state local conservative reaction against reform. Despite the ratification of the Constitution, the creation of state and federal appellate court systems, and Supreme Court precedents, both state reform and federal appellate jurisdiction were frustrated in Virginia politically and through the courts. In showing this, the work provides the background for, analyzes, and interprets several key Virginia appellate court opinions as well as two sets of litigation that went to the Supreme Court.

This study presents a new perspective on two landmark Supreme Court cases, *Ware v. Hylton* (1796) and *Martin v. Hunter's Lessee* (1816), by analyzing their impact. *Ware v. Hylton* was in practice reversed by local juries who frustrated British creditors to the point that they left the courts. *Martin* was one of a number of John Marshall's famous exercises, from *Marbury v. Madison* to *Worcester v. Georgia*, in trading practical defeats for, he hoped, theoretical future victories. It was a precedent for the Supreme Court's appellate jurisdiction over state courts but had no effect in Virginia law. Instead of being conclusive, it helped set the stage for a dispute that not only involved a debate over how to interpret the Constitution but dealt with the practical enforcement of federal law. Under the leadership of Spencer Roane, by 1814 the Virginia Supreme Court of Appeals acted as a bulwark to protect Virginians against outside interference by the federal judiciary. Marshall viewed these actions by the Virginia court as a continuation of the ratification controversy of 1788. He believed that Roane—the son-in-law of Patrick Henry—was still an Anti-Federalist and was trying to undermine the effectiveness of the national government by challenging the supreme law of the land. He believed that the Supreme Court and the federal government had to win in this conflict if the nation was to survive. Those who sought to establish an undisputed supreme law of the land achieved no clear victory, however. Instead, a balance existed between the law of the highest court and its enforcement at the lowest level.

There was a division among Virginia's politicians and jurists, who sought throughout the period of this study to lead the state in two different directions. George Wythe and St. George Tucker sought legal and constitutional reform and the development of legal professionalism. Like other jurists such as Joseph Story, they wanted the common law to be scientific, with principles that were universal. Edmund Pendleton and Spencer Roane led the conservatives, who wanted Virginia to have a separate common law based on custom and tradition, not science. The reformers had some success within Virginia, but the appellate court system that developed was, at best, a compromise. The local gentry elites and justices of the peace were able to maintain their power, and law remained mostly that of country lawyers practicing in county courthouses before local juries, while in the appellate court system, the legal perspective of Pendleton and Roane prevailed. It was based on the acceptance of British notions of the unwritten constitution, local court practice, and common-law traditions rather than on natural law or a scientific common law derived from reason, on a theory of structural checks and balances, or on the sovereign will of the people. This jurisprudence called for keeping power limited and decentralized and for protecting the rights and interests of states and local communities. It did not sanction the use of law to build a nation or empire, to reform government and society, and to compromise property rights to develop the economy. It was provincial, conservative, elitist, and libertarian: it upheld those fundamental rights that had passed the test of time.

The jury was at the heart of Virginia's conservative legal perspective, its Southern jurisprudence. It represented the local, the familiar, and, supposedly, the common-sense aspects of Virginia's common law system. The preservation of local control, the protection of local debtors from distant creditors, the state and local check in appellate court systems, the resistance to state centralization for economic development, and the security for the power of the gentry elites were all tied up in the significant role played by the jury. No other work has shown the important position held by the jury in Virginia law during this period.

Virginia's influence on the development of a Southern states' rights constitutional doctrine has been amply explored, but its influence on state common law has not. In studying the Virginia model for a Southern jurisprudence—particularly important for Southern states where power was located in the county courthouse—this work presents a significant contrast to the legal history of the period written on states north of Virginia.

The research has included, along with a study of published federal and state court reports, an analysis of the records of the federal circuit court in Virginia, the Virginia Supreme Court of Appeals, state district and superior courts, and county and city hustings courts. Because existing records of the state's courts are incomplete, no comprehensive study can be made even for a limited period. But, there are enough records to take a sample of terms from county and state courts in different regions of the state for the same period. I have done this approximately every ten years (1785, 1795, 1805, 1815, and 1825). The sample includes over forty-five hundred civil suits. I have also analyzed the legislative votes on legal and constitutional issues throughout the period of my study. Other sources include statutes, newspapers and other contemporary publications, and correspondence, published and manuscript.

This project began with my Ph.D. dissertation directed by Forrest McDonald. I thank him for his continued guidance and support. In expanding the work, I have had the benefit of the advice, insight, and constructive criticism on portions of the manuscript from a number of scholars including: W. Hamilton Bryson, Tony Freyer, Charles Hobson, Peter Hoffer, R. Kent Newmyer, A. Gregg Roeber, Philip Schwarz, E. Lee Shepard, and Peter Wallenstein. In getting the manuscript in final form, I wish to thank Richard Holway and Cynthia H. Foote at the University Press of Virginia, the series editors, Kermit L. Hall and David M. O'Brien, and an anonymous reader.

I am grateful to the Virginia Historical Society for a research fellowship and assistance from their library and archival staff. I also wish to thank Nelson D. Lankford and the *Virginia Magazine of History and Biography* for giving me permission to use my article, "John Marshall versus Spencer Roane: A Reevaluation of *Martin v. Hunter's Lessee*," 96 (1988):297–314.

JURIES AND JUDGES
VERSUS THE LAW

*Virginia's Provincial Legal
Perspective, 1783–1828*

Introduction

The Virginia Doctrine

In 1816, Supreme Court Justice Joseph Story handed down the opinion in *Martin v. Hunter's Lessee*. The Court claimed appellate jurisdiction over state courts on all matters touching federal law, and asserted the authority to reverse Virginia's highest court on a question concerning state law.[1] This was one of the most important precedents for nationalism set down by the Marshall Court. But, it was denounced in Virginia, where the judiciary refused to carry out the decision. The state's highest court declared that the Supreme Court did not have appellate jurisdiction over state courts, and the state legislature agreed. This was interposition. The state government interposed itself between the people of Virginia and a federal government that, it declared, was engaged in unconstitutional acts. The Marshall Court had made a pronouncement that it could not carry out. It was acting in a vacuum. The opinion of the Supreme Court in *Martin v. Hunter's Lessee* was of no force. This was a powerful precedent in its own right. This act began Virginia's renewed assertion of states' rights and state sovereignty. The doctrine set forth would be directly drawn upon for nullification and secession.

A number of Virginians were important in developing what became known as the Virginia Doctrine, including William Branch Giles, Thomas Jefferson, James Madison, Edmund Pendleton, John Randolph, Spencer Roane, and John Taylor. Taylor summed up the interpretation in his *New Views of the Constitution* (1823). Virginia's ancient constitution remained, though modified by Independence and confederation with the other sovereign republics. The Constitution itself was only the written agreement of those sovereign states, like a treaty. There were real constitutions, unwritten ones, and Virginia had one. But what good was the federal contract if it was being misinterpreted? That 1787 document was of little value if it was used to justify nationalism. As it was liable to contrary interpretations, Taylor seriously questioned its utility. He believed that the Articles of Confederation had been a better statement of the terms of the confederation.[2]

Taylor and the other espousers of the Virginia Doctrine, who called themselves the Old Republicans, feared that, even if nationalists such as John Marshall knew there had been no American nation in 1787, they were using the Constitution and federal law to create one. Instead of the people in a country deriving a common law, Marshall and the Supreme Court were going to establish the law first, then build the country around it. The people of the states in convention had not created an American nation but had agreed to a constitution. Could the Constitution, as interpreted by the Marshall Court, create that nation?[3]

The union existed, as did the principles that guided all good republics. But, the Old Republicans would contend, the Constitution and federal law should not be allowed to destroy those principles in order to turn the union into a nation or an empire. If that was how the Constitution was going to be used, then it would be better to discard it. It had created unnecessary confusion and grounds for antagonism within the union. John Randolph announced the firm resolution of the Old Republicans on the Constitution: they had never honored it, and in time they felt confident and defiant enough to publicly declare that it was superseded by the Virginia Doctrine. The states were independent and sovereign. The Old Republicans told Virginians that they could not expect the Constitution or federal law to protect them. Instead, the parchment document of 1787 was being used to justify their enemies. Federal law was being used to encroach upon and to threaten the liberties and rights of the states. The good citizens of the Old Dominion must be prepared to look elsewhere for protection. They must look to their own traditions and institutions.[4]

Randolph, Taylor, and other Old Republicans wrote about the principles of Virginia's government, the traditions of their unwritten constitution, and the legal rights and practices derived from the common law, which, they claimed, had its origins in the colonial period. The most fundamental part of their government was the county court. Justice was local, and the jury preserved the rights of the people. Of course, Virginia had not remained the same as in the colonial era. Some things had to be invented or modified before they could be conserved. But, a conservatism had developed. Virginians of the old school were anxious to preserve and to pass on their traditions.

During the period from the 1780s to the 1820s, the main socio-economic story in Virginia was the declining economy, especially due to the continuously depressed tobacco market. Indebted tobacco planters were the first to face this economic reality. In their plight, they faced continued debt litigation throughout the period. They looked to juries and to lenient justice or left the state. The panic of 1819, along with other problems, such as the end of the Virginia Dynasty, made Virginians doubt their ability to continue playing a leading role in America. Virginians of the gentry, of the county elites, concerned about the future, romanticized the past.[5] Their institutions, traditions, and former leaders were revered.

Characteristic of this was the glorification of country culture, of country gentlemen and country lawyers. Most Virginians were living as their ancestors had, on the land; if trying to pursue a profession—and the two favorite were law and politics—they were still connected to the land; and even in the few cities, the country gentleman remained the ideal. This old standard remained the model for would-be lawyers and politicians to pursue. Part of the romanticizing of Virginia's great men of the generation of America's founders was the elevation of Patrick Henry. In politics, Henry would always be remembered for "Give me liberty, or give me death." In the law, he would be remembered for his stand against the British creditors. During the British debt cases, the common law worked as a protection for citizens. With a simple man of the people—of the country—at the bar, with twelve good, honest neighbors in the jury, the farmers of Virginia were guarded by the shield of liberty. Henry was increasingly perceived by Virginians as the model country lawyer.[6]

Even advocates of legal education were well aware of the attraction of being a Henry-style country lawyer, especially in provincial areas. William Wirt's 1817 biography of Henry was very important in establishing his image. Wirt consulted a host of lawyers and judges who had known Henry or knew the stories of his feats: William Brockenbrough, William H. Cabell, Dabney Carr, Francis Walker Gilmer, Thomas Jefferson, John Page, Spencer Roane, Henry St. George Tucker, St. George Tucker, and John Tyler. It was almost a community production, with several, including Roane, writing almost pamphlet-length responses to assist Wirt in a work so important to Virginia. What follows is a sketch of how Henry was being portrayed. He had studied men, not books. He knew that in practice the common law was what the jury believed it was. Even if he lost on points of law to more knowledgeable legal rivals, he would win the jury and the verdict and the damages. Henry always addressed the jurors, became familiar with each one, and could see in their eyes where to go in his argument, what to say, and what not to say. Always speaking in general terms and appealing to emotions, he never wearied the jury with details and analysis.[7]

Henry lacked refinement, formal education, and, in some ways, ambition, but that only endeared him more to his neighbors, the planters and farmers of the Southside and the lower Piedmont. It made him more like them, and made it easier for him to understand them and to speak to them—be they jurors or voters—and to represent them. There was perhaps an advantage in seeing without "the spectacles of books." He was moved, not by theory, but by an understanding of his constituents.[8]

Patrick Henry's Virginia was a land of good, simple farmers and country gentlemen, of principle and tradition, where the center of legal and political activity remained at the county courthouse and where the watchword was liberty—and this was the Virginia that the Old Republicans looked back to and wanted so much to preserve. After John Randolph was elevated to the United States Senate, he was followed there by another states' rights advocate, Littleton Waller Tazewell. Governor William Branch Giles became the leader of the old school. He and the political faithful busied themselves teaching the young men what must be preserved, to secure their liberty and rights and to protect the interests of their country, Virginia. They had to preserve the Virginia Doctrine.

They passed down a kind of politics, a philosophical resistance to social change, an ideology and way of construing the Constitution and federal system, and a legal tradition. Beyond just ideological rhetoric and essays on states' rights, these Virginia politicians, judges, and lawyers left a way of viewing the law, a Southern jurisprudence. It was conservative and provincial—a law for country lawyers. It was the legal dimension to the Virginia Doctrine, appropriate for farmers, including a good many indebted tobacco planters, who were not sure they wanted change and progress. It was a law for a gentry who prided themselves on their liberty and independence.

Origins in Unwritten Law

Men such as Patrick Henry, Spencer Roane, and John Taylor, and those whom they led and represented, would be remembered in history as opponents of the Constitution and federal law and as defenders of weak government. They were also defenders of law, however, and would continue to be so, and they would go on to be great defenders of the constitution, although not the written Constitution of 1787. Instead, they wished to preserve the principles of government, the common law, and the unwritten constitution that had developed over the centuries.

The principles of the ancient constitution were the basis of an unwritten law the basic aspects of which were well known and agreed upon, and that, in practical terms, provided a real protection for rights and liberty: the common law. It originated in custom and was sanctioned through the courts. It began more as a set of principles and rules of procedure than as a process of following precedents. In practice in the colonial courts, the common law was more of an understanding aided by handbooks for lawyers and justices of the peace than a process in which judges expected lawyers to make arguments based on previously reported cases. With common-law courts in every county, this was the common law literally for the country—for country gentlemen who, in addition to farming, practiced law or were justices of the peace. Emphasis was placed on common sense and on a consensus on general principles and rules of law, government, and society.

During the colonial period, George Webb, in his manual for a Virginia justice of the peace, stated that he presented rules and maxims instead of making references to lawbooks, laws, and particular cases; dealt with practice and not speculation; and used language that was not difficult, but plain, clear, and easy to understand. He wrote for those who had been diverted from studying law by the necessity of managing their plantations and the "innocent pleasures of a country life." Other manuals followed for attorneys, county court clerks, and freeholders in general. Two of these were companion volumes: one instructed the planter on his property rights and how to transact his legal business at court, and the other instructed him on managing his plantation and improving his fields.[9]

The manual for a Virginia justice of the peace was brought up to date by Richard Starke and by William Waller Hening (the latter with four editions from 1795 to 1825). Hening stated that his main guides were common sense and legal principles. In his 1825 edition, he stated that the commonwealth had grown with the development of the justices of the peace, that "meritorious class of men." While much of the government changed during the Revolution, the county court system had remained intact because of how well it worked. The major function of the justice of the peace was to keep the peace by preventing quarrels between neighbors and by punishing those who were violent. In civil suits, the justice was to arbitrate and provide a setting for settling disputes. He was also expected to punish those who continuously instigated lawsuits with their neighbors. The goal was to have peace among the citizens both in the court and in the country.[10]

Anglo-American conceptions of property rights and of liberty were based on the common law, and it was regarded as a protection against arbitrary and tyrannical government. English citizens of the seventeenth century and Americans of the eighteenth century conceived of the common law as a sanctuary, a fortress, and described the jury-trial aspect of that law as the great jewel of liberty and the envy of the world. The trial by jury was perceived as a shield against any form of governmental tyranny that might deprive the citizen of life, liberty, or property. Thus it was a right insisted upon by English citizens under Stuart kings, by Americans under British rule, by Anti-Federalists against the federal government, and by local citizens against imperial, federal, or state jurisdictions. There was a happy security in being tried by twelve of one's neighbors. Juries decided something more important than legislative statutes or the decisions of a court of appeals. Regardless of the judge's determinations upon the legal issues, the jury studied the facts of the case, delivered the verdict, and determined the damages in civil suits. They served as a check on the judge and on superior courts, judicial precedents, and legislation, and could thus make a tyrannical law ineffective and an unpopular law unenforceable.[11]

Of course, the law, liberty, property rights, interests, and power were all tied together. Debt cases were the perfect example of this. The British and Loyalists charged, during the Revolution, that the Patriot cause was a way for tobacco planters, who wanted to be economically as well as politically free of Britain, to renege on their debts. As Virginians put up obstacles for British creditors to collect the debts, and as Patrick Henry and his party generally secured legislation in the 1780s that favored the debtor interest, James Madison and his reform party continued the charge that Henry's party lacked a respect for law and property rights—though both groups consisted of landowners and slaveholders.[12] Both sides in the dispute spoke of the right to protect one's property. The rights of a farmer to land, which provided for him and his family and was the basis of his liberty, was opposed to the rights of a creditor to receive repayment of debts plus interest or to gain property by collecting upon defaulting accounts. Which was nobler? Which should be protected by the law? Henry chose the property rights of farmers over the profits of merchants. He and his following saw themselves, not as being lawless, but as looking to fundamental principles.

In common-law trials in civil suits, when the plaintiffs were seen as threatening the interest of the locale, the jury was to play the role of its protector. In debtor-creditor suits, the juries were expected to favor the debtors. The local jury provided an indebted farmer facing a merchant creditor with protection from a "foreign" law. From the Revolution into the nineteenth century, the preeminent debtor-creditor concern brought before Virginia courts was the debts owed to British merchants. In these suits, there proved to be a substantial as well as an ideologically rhetorical basis for the idea that juries were favorable to defendant-debtors. Neither local partisanship nor crass self-interests completely broke down Virginia's system of justice. Even British merchants often won the principal owed them. But, juries denied the merchants their reason for being creditors, their profit, their interests. Indebted farmers were tried by their peers, twelve honest, indebted farmers.[13]

The common law of England had been brought to America and had developed separately in each of the colonies. The common law was the law common to a realm—to the customs, the rules of procedure developed by the courts, and the statutory modifications by the legislature of that realm. The statutes of Parliament modified the common law in England, and each of the colonial legislatures modified it in their own spheres. Each colony, then state, had slowly developed its own common law, and constituted its own legal realm. Under the law, the Virginians' commonwealth was their country.

The preference in Virginia for the traditions of the English unwritten constitution and the common law had an ideological dimension. There was a shared concern in the Country, republican ideology to protect principles and rights. By the Revolution, Americans had borrowed the Court-Country paradigm from England to explain to themselves and the world what they feared and why they resisted the imperial government. The concept of the Country had originated in a provincial outlook toward London and the central government; in a distinction between the people in the country and the king's court, his ministers and noble and wealthy courtiers; and in a belief that there was a division between the best interests of all and the self-interests of those in power in London. After the seventeenth-century conflict between the Crown and Parliament, it appeared that the Country had won with the Glorious Revolution of 1688. But, William III and the Whigs had their financial revolution, the English banking system was developed, and the national debt became an institution. Bankers and financial speculators were added to the list of those at Court who wished to grow wealthy by robbing the Country. The creation of a new Court party was completed under the leadership of Robert Walpole. A Country opposition arose again and claimed that a corrupt and tyrannical system of government had emerged, and that it altered the checks and balances, violated the ancient English constitution, and would soon end all English liberty—unless opposed. From this ideological perspective, Americans during the Revolution had waged a successful Country opposition and had won independence. If this was the case, to what extent would the Country, republican ideological tradition continue? Where? And among whom? In rural, agricultural Virginia, it took root well.[14]

In the 1780s, Henry and his following continued the cause. They believed that Madison and his party of legal and constitutional reformers were trying to reverse the results of the Revolution and to reestablish a government ruled by a Court party. In drawing upon the ideas of the Country, republican ideology, Henry and his party, however, were not founders of a republic of virtue. Henry, Taylor, Randolph, and Roane were not philosophes of the Continental Enlightenment trying to devise the ideal society. They saw themselves engaged in a fight, a continuous contest, to preserve their greatest treasure, their liberty. Liberty, not virtue, was their watchword. They were not democrats who believed in the virtue of the people. They were agrarians who believed in the right of independent farmers to protect their property. They appealed to an ancient, unwritten, and agrarian protection against the forces of centralization, royal courts and courtiers, the monied interest, and corruption. Ever sensitive to the least threat to their privileges, these country gentlemen invoked the shield of the law and the constitution as they prepared to fight for home and honor and the manly rights to liberty and independence.

The ideological and common-law traditions were drawn upon by Henry and his following—now called the "Anti-Federalists"—as they opposed the Constitution, and sought to protect themselves and to conserve the commonwealth from the outside world and from a superior centralized government. One reason they opposed the Constitution was because it did not deal with common-law rights, such as the right to jury trials in civil suits—because the Constitution expressly guaranteed jury trials only in criminal cases. Their opposition was based on far more than theoretical conjectures and mere prophesies of future evils that would come from the ratification of the Constitution. They had already fought the British to uphold trial by jury and common-law rights, and had been opposing the efforts of Madison's legal reform party in the state. British creditors waited anxiously to be able to open litigation, and the Constitution, without amendments, made possible the establishment of a federal judiciary that, in civil suits, could do without juries.

Henry, in essence, held up the written Constitution of 1787 to the ancient constitution and found it seriously wanting in the preservation of liberty. In the Virginia ratifying convention, the Federalists—supporters of the Constitution—took jabs at Henry for venerating the British constitution while he criticized the work of the Philadelphia Convention. Did he prefer a monarchical, unwritten, and uncertain constitution to the written, republican Constitution? Henry of course was not calling for American royalty and titled nobles; indeed, he was afraid that the new national government might establish a monarchical presidency and an aristocratic Senate. He wished to preserve that facet of the English unwritten law that protected the liberty of the people. There was no long, well-established tradition that could be called an "American constitution." "Americans," or rather, the people of the states, had a history, traditions, charters, rights, and an unwritten law, but it developed separately in each colony, then in each state. Henry believed that Americans would have to look to their states for the shield of liberty.[15]

After the Constitution was ratified, Henry's party went on to deny that it was the fundamental law. The ambivalence of *constitution* and *Constitution* would be used to advantage. With little respect for the latter, one could wholeheartedly serve the former. One could speak on behalf of the latter, could even come forward as its defender, when it conformed to the former. Taylor, for example, became one of America's most persistent, devoted, protectors of constitutional sanctity; he was thinking more in terms of the principles that a constitution should embody, however, rather than of the actual Constitution. He would test the Constitution, interpretations of it, and federal administration of it by how well they adherred to the principles of the unwritten constitution.[16] Such testing would be a subject for discussion in the state legislature.

Just as Parliament had instructed the king concerning his constitutional wrongdoing and as the colonial assembly had been a forum for grievances and for drawing up resolutions of protest against unconstitutional activity by the British government, so too would the Virginia General Assembly instruct Congress concerning constitutional wrongdoing. In the seventeenth century, the Crown had claimed that Parliament had no right to protest against its authority, and in the eighteenth century, Parliament claimed that the American colonial assemblies had no right to protest. The national government would claim the states had no right to protest in the nineteenth century. But, for states' righters, representatives of a people did not need the permission of a king, Parliament, or Congress to meet, discuss their grievances, petition, and pass resolutions of protest. It was, instead, one of the ancient rights of citizens that no government could rightfully take away.

In 1790, the representatives of the people of Virginia met to air their grievances, and they did so again in 1798–99 and in 1819–21. They petitioned Congress to repeal legislation. They proclaimed to everyone the impropriety of acts of the national government. They reviewed Hamiltonianism, the Alien and Sedition Acts, the appellate jurisdiction claimed by the Marshall Court over the state courts, and the Missouri Compromise, and declared them all to be unconstitutional. But, what kind of constitutionality was involved here? The written Constitution as interpreted by a party in power, the laws of Congress, and the decisions of the Supreme Court were all changeable and lacked the fundamental nature of an ancient custom. The common-law rights of liberty and independence were fundamental.

The unwritten-law perspective did not consider the distinction between statutory law and a written constitution to be important—although, to Madison and John Marshall, that distinction was one of America's great accomplishments, which separated America from the British with their absolute, sovereign Parliament. To those espousing the common-law tradition, however, the great distinction remained that between written and unwritten law. The fact that state conventions met and ratified the Constitution never altered the other fact that it was a new, written law, like legislation. What could not be accepted was the idea that a fundamental right—such as trial by jury—could cease to be a right because of its not being secured in the 1787 Constitution. Could such a right be suspended by the ratification of the Constitution, or by a later amendment, or by a ruling of the Supreme Court? Amendments and judicial decisions only pertained to and changed the Constitution, which, like all legislation, was alterable. Neither the Philadelphia Convention, Congress, nor the Supreme Court could alter the essential point that jury trial was a sacred, immemorial right and that it was fundamental, original, and, in this sense, constitutional in a way that the laws of Congress, the rulings of the Supreme Court, and the written Constitution were not.[17]

1

Against the Madisonian Round of Reform

The Threat at the Federal Level

After Independence, after the Patriots had ended the British rule of Virginia, Thomas Jefferson and James Madison led a group that hoped to cleanse the state of all things European, aristocratic, and feudal. They sought a disestablishment of the church, legal reform, the development of public education, and the revision of the state constitution to provide for a true separation and balance of powers between the branches and to curb the power of the local governments run by the county elites. Eventually, the reformers' agenda included a new federal constitution and supreme law to be imposed upon their fellow Virginians.[1] Was this the freedom the Patriots had fought for in the Revolution? To many, it appeared to be an attempt to reimpose a foreign rule upon them. In the 1780s, the Patriots of 1776 parted from each other. When it was realized that republican virtue did not necessarily follow from independence and liberty, most settled for the latter goals. This was especially true after it was seen who would benefit and who would lose from further reforms. Provincial farmers doubted whether Jefferson, Madison, and the reformers were necessarily the better for their cosmopolitanism.

Virginians were divided between the reform party, led by Madison, and Henry and his following, who wished to keep things as they were. The geographic base of Madison and his following was in the northern Valley, the Northern Neck—the area between the Potomac and the Rappahannock rivers—and, just below the Rappahannock, in the central Piedmont. Included in this group were Francis Corbin, Zachariah Johnson, John Marshall, George Mason, Wilson Cary Nicholas, Edmund Randolph, Archibald Stuart, George Washington, Alexander White, and most of the Lee family. After being frustrated at the state level, they sought reform at the federal level. In helping to draft the Constitution, Madison hoped that a federal government could be established that would check the activities of such states as Virginia led by such provincial-minded men as Henry. In "Vices of the Political System of the United States," written on the eve of the Philadelphia Convention, Madison revealed that his chief complaints concerned, not the lack of a strong federal government, but the actions of state governments. Further, most of the essay concerned the law. He was disturbed by the lack of permanence of the legislation passed by the state legislatures, by the volume of legislation, and especially by the kind of legislation. He suspected that laws were passed merely to satisfy the interests of a majority. This would lead him through the Virginia Plan to *The Federalist*, where he would explain that in an extended republic, with a national government representing the people, there would be such a diversity that no single interest could be in the majority and infringe on the rights of others.[2]

Henry's party refused to accept the Madisonian vision of America as a nation of several well-established and competing interests. There should only be one dominant interest, the one nearly all Americans were connected with, agriculture. That party gathered support from rural farmers; the agrarian ideologues, mainly from the Tidewater; and the tobacco planters—up the James River valley, in the Piedmont, and through the Southside—who included many potential defendants in debt suits in federal courts. Included in Henry's party were Isaac Coles, John Dawson, Joseph Jones, James Monroe, Josiah Parker, Spencer Roane, Edmund Ruffin; Meriwether Smith, French Strother, John Taylor, and various Harrisons and Randolphs. They also included many of the county justices of the peace. The justices provided local leadership and often represented their county—and the interests of local government—in the legislature. From their votes in the ratifying

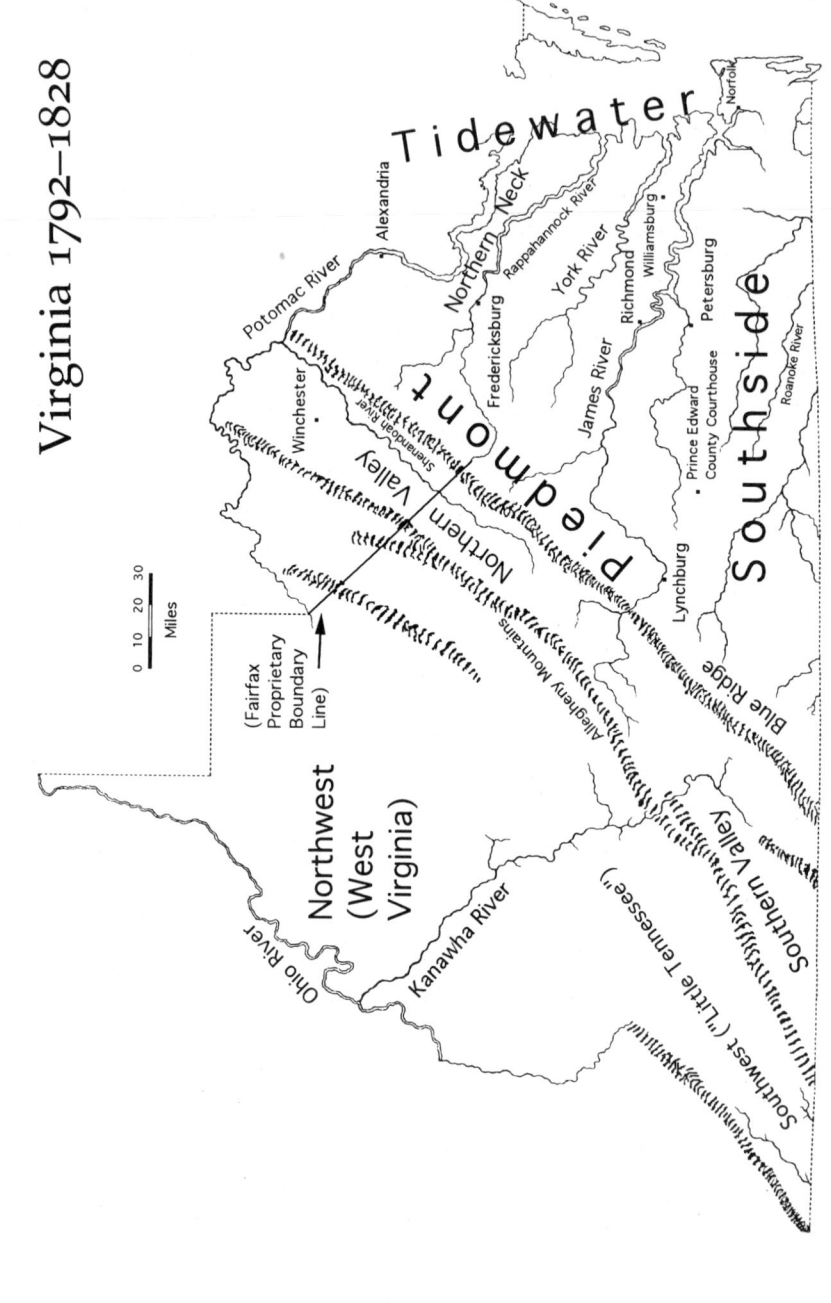

convention, it can safely be said that the Constitution would never have been ratified if its fate had been left to the men who dealt out law and justice in Virginia.[3] It was a challenge to their authority. But, even if they could have been persuaded that there would be no consolidation of the federal and state judiciaries, that they would continue to hold their offices, and that local courts would continue to handle the vast bulk of all judicial business, they were aware of the threat posed by this new superior law and federal judiciary that could act directly upon Virginians.

Madison hoped that the national government could check the states, and, in the Philadelphia Convention, he proposed that the new government have a veto over state legislation. In essence, he was proposing that the national government have the kind of power that the British imperial government had claimed before the Revolution (though he believed the use of this power by the new central government would be made viable by direct representation and checks and balances). Was Madison being republican to try to impose upon his fellow Virginians a law that transcended their interests and control and was, therefore, foreign to them? In arguing for an extended republic, he had assumed the existence of an American people. At the very beginning, before the Constitution was written (much less ratified), the stage was set for a debate over a law of the people of a state versus the law of the American people as a whole. The latter was a new kind of law altogether. It was not the common law modified by the legislature that represented the people. It was both a superior law and a distant one that Virginians did not create, and that, in ways, was as foreign to them as the law that had been made in London. This was how Henry viewed the matter. At the center of his debate with Madison were two very different conceptions of the law. While Henry was thinking in negative terms—of the protection secured by the common law, of the liberties and principles of the ancient, unwritten constitution—Madison was thinking in positive terms, of what could be done to solve problems through a new written Constitution.

There was an interesting difference of opinion between the Federalists and the Anti-Federalists concerning which side was favoring more government. The Federalists saw their role as reacting to, and hopefully establishing a government that could check, the Anti-Federalist–dominated state governments that catered to the popular will. The Federalists claimed they were not so much seeking to expand government at the federal level as they were reacting against too much government by the states. As the Virginia Anti-Federalists saw it, however, they had not encouraged large armies, high taxes, and hordes of bureaucrats. And, in fact, their use of government had been negative. Through stay laws and setting up installments for debt payments, for example, they had aided debtors by encouraging the lack of government: state judiciaries were closed to the debt cases or were restricted in being able to handle them. The commonwealth aided debtors by refusing to give creditors the means of holding debtors accountable. If there was anything excessive in the government, it was the legislators' disregard for the kind of law and judicial system that the Federalists demanded, one that would uphold the property rights of creditors and would enforce the obligation of contracts. This situation is what Madison and the Federalists would try to remedy through their proposed new superior law. From the Anti-Federalist perspective, the Federalists were trying to expand government, not to reduce it, especially at the federal level.

After the Constitution was drafted and submitted to the states, the battle in Virginia continued along much the same lines, with Madison leading the Federalists, the friends of the Constitution, and Henry leading the Anti-Federalists, its opponents. There was also a group in the middle, however, begun by George Mason and Governor Edmund Randolph (whose position became increasingly ambivalent)—both formerly part of Madison's reform party. Both had been at the Philadelphia Convention, wanted to discard the Articles of Confederation, and generally favored the Constitution. But, they would not support it without a bill of rights. In the ratifying convention, Mason allied with Henry.[4]

Henry displayed his famous oratory in the convention, spoke the most often and the longest, and, at times, appeared to be taking on the whole Federalist phalanx single-handedly. He and the Anti-Federalists were disturbed by the size and potential power of the new government. The old Confederation Congress had been merely a federal government deriving its powers from, representing, and acting through the sovereign states. The Constitution would set up a national government that would derive its power from, represent, and act directly upon the people of the states. The Anti-Federalists believed that this government would have too great a jurisdiction to be safe. The people of a single state could not feel secure in their rights, interests, and power, because they would be unable to control the national government and to prevent it from interfering in their internal affairs. Were they to trust the checks and balances in the Constitution? Henry had nothing to do with Madison's "rope-dancing, chain rattling, ridiculous ideal checks and contrivances." Great amounts of power should not be granted to a government with the expectation that, through an internal balance of powers, it would not grow corrupt. Power corrupts. Henry's solution to the problem of men being corrupted by power was not checks and balances but making government as weak as possible. If government was weak, then bad men could do little damage. Government, in other words, should remain as it was.[5]

The Anti-Federalists were not just "anti"—a negative force opposing the Federalists' Constitution. They were not just an opposition who had never been in power themselves. They were important at the state level and remained dominant in their counties. Indeed, in a sense, they were not opposing power so much as they were defending their own power. They were trying to conserve the society they had in the 1780s, in which most cultural, social, economic, political, and legal affairs took place at the county level. It was this image of America that they tried to preserve and would harken back to. They were concerned with the power a distant authority could have over them. The further removed a government was from their control, the more they wanted it to be limited. The more local the government, the less they were afraid of the evils of power. Of course, while they were strong in Virginia, they would be insignificant in Congress. Henry therefore wanted local interests to have the power to control their own affairs; he wanted Virginia farmers to be able to live with little interference from the rest of the world.[6]

But what was to control the power of the local elites? Anti-Federalists did not believe this should be a major concern. Were the gentry the instigators of dangerous innovations to rob people of their rights, their liberty, and their property? The justices of the peace gained nothing monetarily for their judicial services to the community. They did not favor changes in government, nor deny people due process of law, nor prevent the calling of juries, nor bar elections to the House of Delegates. Where was the loss of liberty within this local system? This government was not going to become progressive and expansive. There was little reason for it to be checked. The Virginia county was the model government: one so small and weak, and offering so little to the people who ran it, that there was little room for abuse. When liberty was the goal, strong state governments and a strong federal government and Constitution were not necessary. They would be necessary only if one had other objectives for Virginia and America.[7]

The provincial conservatives were aware of the benefits they were forsaking in holding on to an old order, but they believed that any such gains would be of little value compared to the harm that would be caused by the changing society. Much would be lost in interests and power as well as in rights. Through emulating the British, America could have banks, a great commerce, an empire, a navy, hordes of bureaucrats, a national debt, high taxes, and the loss of liberty. Henry warned his fellow Virginians that when people go "in search of grandeur, power and splendor," they become victims of their own folly and sacrifice their liberty. He reminded all good patriots that liberty was their object, not becoming "a great and mighty empire." Henry stated that his attachment to liberty may, "in these refined enlightened days, be deemed old fashioned." How could liberty be expanded by more government, whether larger or more energetic? Henry believed that expanding the jurisdiction and power of government would not protect liberty, but could only threaten it.[8]

Henry emphasized that the main question was over the revolution in government. The proposed Constitution was not a Virginian constitution but a foreign one, superseding the sovereignty of the state and creating a power that could intervene in local affairs. The ratification of the Constitution would create a law superior to state laws and provide for a judiciary to enforce that law directly on Virginians.[9]

The law was at the center of the debate. Not only was it an important issue inside the convention hall in Richmond, but it was the predominant issue on the outside. The main subjects discussed, such as the debts owed to the British, related to the power of the proposed federal judiciary. The Anti-Federalists knew that the major issue (or potential issue) of litigation was in civil suits to collect debts, much of which had been contracted to British merchants. They had to protect themselves from this threat. They looked to the tradition of the unwritten constitution and the legal rights of the common law. They stressed, most of all, trial by jury. They were familiar with the use of jury trials and knew how that institution could serve their purpose. It was easy enough for Henry to use the language of rights, and to speak of the debtor's right to jury trials, when the creditors were British.[10]

In the Anti-Federalists' attack on the Constitution, there were three interrelated issues regarding jury trials within the federal judiciary. All three involved rules practiced under the common law. First, juries needed to have jurisdiction over facts. The Anti-Federalists were particularly concerned with the appellate jurisdiction on fact as well as law given to the Supreme Court in Article Three of the Constitution. They did not accept the Federalist defense that this jurisdiction was necessary for matters of equity and admiralty law, since this distinction should have been stated in the Constitution. As it stood, in all cases, appellate court judges could allow the introduction of new evidence, reexamine the facts, or render a verdict without calling a jury. If the Anti-Federalists could secure jury control over facts, verdicts, and damages, then they would be more willing to accept federal judges determining the law. They could accept the jurisdiction over the abstract questions of the law held by judges, over whom they had no control, only on the condition that local juries, which acted through a consensus from shared common interests, controlled questions effecting a man's life, liberty, and property.[11]

The second issue involved juries being secured for civil suits. The Constitution only guaranteed jury trials for criminal cases, which meant that a plaintiff could instigate a suit in a federal court without the case having to be put before a jury. The Federalists had a good defense: there were different common-law procedures in different states on civil suits. Virginia Anti-Federalists would oppose anything that could erode those differences. But, they contended, some way had to be found to guarantee jury trial. Henry declared that if the Constitution was ratified, British creditors would tyrannize Virginia farmers. The farmers would be at the mercy of a cold, indifferent law without the protection of a jury. Henry, showing his agrarian bias, believed that local juries would understand better than federal judges that the liberty of farmers was of a higher value than mere business obligations.[12]

The third issue concerned the securing of provincial juries within the federal judiciary. As Henry explained to the convention, without this security, they could be hauled off to the center of the union, where jurors would be drawn from the corrupt inhabitants of the federal city, a New York or a Philadelphia or another "foreign" place, where they could not expect a sympathetic hearing. Jurors should meet the approval of and be drawn from the vicinity of the defendant. Ideally, they should know the accused. Anti-Federalists were criticized for equating the protection of individual rights with those of the community, or, in other words, for the preservation of local power. But, that was in the tradition of the common law and a justice system that involved familiarity with the defendant and community consensus. Henry praised the security that each person had in knowing that his neighbors would protect him. To guard themselves from foreigners, they wanted a guarantee in the Constitution that the federal judiciary would be established with a broad-based appellate system made up of circuit courts in each state—or preferably drawing upon state courts themselves—and using local juries.[13]

The Anti-Federalists succeeded in convincing a majority in the convention that the Constitution threatened their rights and interests and needed to be amended. They failed, however, to convince a majority to reject it altogether. Federalists circulated a compromise plan, first devised by the Massachusetts ratifying convention, and introduced in the Virginia convention by George Wythe, which called for ratifying the Constitution plus recommending amendments. Henry condemned the very idea of a compromise with one's liberty. He noted that when the good Patriots had risen up in 1776, it was all well and good then for them to talk of representation of the people, liberty, and the rights of man, and of less government. Now, however, this talk was out of fashion. What applied to colonies against the imperial government no longer applied to states against the proposed federal government. Principles once carried forth by all—including Washington, Jefferson, the Randolphs, and the Lees—were now being associated with the provincial-minded, who, it was claimed, sought to use these ideals to protect local power and interests. As Madison and Jefferson and the new lights convinced themselves of their moral purity when confronted with the less-sophisticated provincials, especially of the Southside, Henry knew his cause was in trouble. There would be just enough moderates to want to give the new government a chance. Henry argued in vain that all would be lost unless the state waited and ratified the Constitution after it was satisfactorily amended. A narrow majority in the convention favored ratification before amendments. The Anti-Federalists could only declare that, in their opinion, the ratification was conditional upon Congress's proposing amendments to the states.[14]

To the Anti-Federalists, a foreign law would now be established, one that Virginians could not control, one that could act directly upon them. There were three qualifications to the Anti-Federalist defeat in 1788. First, there was the promise of amendments. The Federalists had agreed to compromise and would be conciliatory in the Bill of Rights and the Judiciary Act of 1789. Second, there was little that Madison's reform party could do about the fact that most government would be at the state and local level, and that, in Virginia, the Anti-Federalists remained strong. Third, ways could be found to resist and weaken the new federal government, and a doctrine of state sovereignty could be developed. The state government could be used against the federal government, just as it had been used against the British.

Among the ratifying convention's recommendations for amending the Constitution were the following: that there would be a guarantee of trial by jury in civil suits; that the appellate jurisdiction of the Supreme Court should apply to matters of law only (except in equity and admiralty cases); that jurors should be drawn from a defendant's vicinage (and that the defendant could challenge jury members); and that the original jurisdiction of the federal judiciary should be limited to the Supreme Court and admiralty courts, so that most nonadmiralty cases would have to be initiated in state courts.[15]

Virginia had ratified only because amendments were expected. Madison and a majority of Federalists won seats in Congress by promising such amendments. In the First Congress, with a Federalist majority trying to soothe the opposition, Madison drafted and guided a set of amendments, the Bill of Rights, through the House—the bulk of which were the legal rights stressed by the Virginia Anti-Federalists, including the one pressed hardest: that of trial by jury in civil suits. Another right was affirmed, the common-law rule that juries determined facts and that facts would not be reexamined by appellate courts. And there was a guarantee of trial in the vicinity (and the defendant's right to challenge jurors).[16] The forming of a judicial system, left ambiguous and sketchy in the Constitution, was handled in a similar manner, conciliatory toward the opposition.

The subject of a judicial establishment was taken up in the United States Senate, where Virginia Anti-Federalists William Grayson and Richard Henry Lee advanced the idea—included in the Virginia convention's recommended amendments—that the original jurisdiction of the federal judiciary be restricted. This idea was rejected by the Senate for not conforming to Article Three of the Constitution. Still, what was passed, the Judiciary Act of 1789, went a long way toward satisfying the concern that justice be kept close to home. Although a federal court system was established, each state was made a district for district and circuit courts, and, within each such district, that state's rules applying to common-law trials would be used when in accordance with the United States Constitution and laws. Also, district judges had to reside in their districts. Questions of fact were to be tried by a jury, and appeals would be on the record as it stood from the lower court. (The district courts were given jurisdiction mainly over admiralty cases.) The circuit courts, which consisted of the federal judge of the district in which the court was held and two Supreme Court justices (who literally rode the circuit through their different districts), were given jurisdiction over civil suits where aliens or residents of different states were parties (and the disputed matter exceeded five hundred dollars). An appellate procedure was established within the federal judiciary leading to the Supreme Court.[17]

Although the Anti-Federalists were unable to get an amendment passed that would make the federal judiciary dependent on the state courts, they could find satisfaction in the legal rights guaranteed in the Bill of Rights and the Judiciary Act of 1789 regarding the use of local juries. A ruling on a question of law determined by the Supreme Court might in practice be canceled by the actions of a jury in a lower court as it judged the facts. Further, the Judiciary Act of 1789 not only established a decentralized federal judicial system with courts in each state, it also drew upon the services of the state courts. Some of the delegates in the Philadelphia Convention had found the Supremacy Clause suspect because of what it could imply for state authority. Anti-Federalists quickly realized how the Supremacy Clause could be used to support concurrent jurisdiction by state courts over federal and constitutional questions. Although section 25 of the judiciary act allowed for appeals from the states' highest courts to the Supreme Court on questions concerning the Constitution, treaty, and federal statute—and, in accord with this section, the Supremacy Clause could be used to support national legal uniformity—one could only speculate as to how well the federal appellate authority over the state judiciaries would work.

While moderate Anti-Federalists were being conciliated by the passage and ratification of the Bill of Rights, those who had been in Henry's party—who had opposed constitutional reform and had tried to prevent the establishment of a national government—not only counted on state courts and local juries to limit the law of the new government, they never gave up on the addition of radical amendments that would weaken it. In the House of Delegates, they pressed for resolutions critical of Congress for not considering all of the amendments proposed by the ratifying convention. They called for amendments through the 1790s, but, except for the passage of the Eleventh Amendment, it became obvious that they could place little hope in this mode of achieving their goals.[18]

During the 1790s, many Anti-Federalists joined Madison and Jefferson in their Republican opposition to drive Alexander Hamilton and the Federalists out of power. To counter the Federalists, the strict construction of the Constitution was devised by Madison and Jefferson. For the Anti-Federalists, this also served as a convenient means of restricting the administration of the federal government as much as possible. Extreme Anti-Federalists, however, did not want to be limited to just that approach. First, they still hoped to secure amendments to structurally undermine the government, and, second, they developed a constitutional interpretation that would limit the federal government further than a mere strict construction of its constitutionally granted powers. In Congress, John Page emerged as an early champion of the new interpretation, that the perpetual union specified in the Articles of Confederation had not been contradicted by the Constitution. Indeed, the 1787 document had been intended "to remedy the defects of the Confederation to a certain degree," but "without endangering the sovereignty and independence of the individual states." Congress was authorized to do certain things such as regulating interstate commerce, but should "leave their respective states in the full enjoyment of every right and privilege they held before their adoption of the new Constitution." These Anti-Federalists would view the Constitution as merely a revised Articles of Confederation, as if the events of 1787 and 1788 had never occurred. They ignored the national aspect of the central government and saw it as only a federal compact. In their opinion, the Constitution had been agreed to as separate governments would agree to a treaty.[19]

The origins of the later Virginia Doctrine lay in this interpretation, developed during the 1790s by the Anti-Federalists, that denied that the Constitution was the fundamental law of the land. For such a law, one had to look beyond written documents and legislation to the unwritten law and constitution.

The Threat at the State Level

As Henry noted in the ratifying convention, the enlightened ones must have their reforms, and the provincial ones must then find ways to control the machinery created by those reforms. Experiences at the state level gave the latter cause for hope as they assessed their situation vis-à-vis the federal government, for, at the state level, Henry and his faction were learning the art of compromise and how to minimize their losses in apparent defeats. They suffered two defeats in 1788. After the Constitution was ratified, Madison's reform party succeeded in passing legislation establishing a state district-court system.

Throughout the 1780s, Henry and his party voted in the legislature against judicial and constitutional reforms. They wanted to keep the Old Dominion decentralized, with the counties being practically states in a federal system, and with power being centered in the county courthouse on court day.[20] There was little to check the local courts. In their political and administrative capacity, which the district court reform did not touch upon, the justices of the peace ran the county governments.

Under Virginia's 1776 constitution, drafted when the Patriots were concerned about too much government, the legislature sketched the general objects of the government and left the administration of the laws to others, but not to the governor. Like other states in 1776, Virginia had established a weak executive branch, subservient to the legislature. The execution of the laws was mostly the province of the justices of the peace. Their jurisdiction covered practically every aspect of life in the state. They proved and recorded wills, deeds, bills of sale, and mortgages. Their patronage power included the appointment of the sheriff, county clerk, tax collectors, and all militia officers under division rank. They authorized the clearing of creeks and rivers that ran through their counties; the construction of roads, dams, and mills; and the establishment and location of ferries. They licensed taverns. They issued marriage licenses. At least by statute, they had the authority to regulate tavern rates for liquor, food, and lodging, and for stable, feed, and pasturage; the blue laws; hunting; and the maintenance of fences. They were also expected to enforce quarantining and inoculations for small pox and control diseases in herds; to enforce the rules governing servants and slaves; and to see to the inspection of items for sale including tobacco, flour, timber, pork, and beef. They determined how much the county government spent to perform its duties, and paid for it through collecting fines and taxes.[21]

The justices of the peace were elected neither by the people nor by the legislature. They were, for all practical purposes, self-perpetuating bodies (though formally they made nominations for replacements to the governor). Their membership was drawn from the local gentry elite. A powerful group in Virginia during the early Republic, they made up half of the membership of the House of Delegates. In Richmond, they could look after local interests. In their judicial capacity, making up the county courts, they had jurisdiction over (noncapital) criminal cases and civil suits. In the Virginia judiciary, beyond these county courts, there were, for most kinds of cases, only the General Court, which dealt with both civil suits and criminal cases, and the court of chancery or equity law. Eight judges presided over these two courts, and they (along with the three members of an admiralty court) made up a final court of appeals. These judges were unable to handle the volume of litigation, however, so plaintiffs were primarily dependent on county courts.[22]

Madison's reform party had long been calling for an expansion of the Virginia judiciary to make it more effective, to allow appeals away from the county courts and thus to check them, and to allow creditors to have courts above the county level in which to instigate suits. With the increase of courts, more litigation would be possible, which would aid plaintiffs trying to get around the backlog of cases on the county court and General Court dockets. It appeared that, with the introduction of the district court system, a major reform of the state judiciary had been achieved. The number of General Court judges was increased to twelve and, along with a term in Richmond, the judges would ride circuit through eighteen districts in the state, holding terms in each district. Madison's party could only hope that now the machinery was in place to assure a rational, systematic law. In the short run, however, Henry's faction held out for more debt-installment legislation. In the long run, not only did the reform leave the political power of the justices of the peace intact, there was still some question whether, despite the increased capacity to handle litigation, the decisions and verdicts of the district court system were going to be much different from the majority of those at the county-court level.[23]

When the state district court system got underway, much of its business was similar to the federal circuit court, due to the presence of British debt cases. In these suits, the defendant did not agree with the plaintiff on the facts—on the payment or the amount of the debt—so that the question was put before the defendant's "country," a jury. The result was nearly always a subtraction of interests, and the award, due to legislation—the last of which passed in conjunction with setting up the district court system—was paid by the defendant in installments, often not beginning until the next year (and paid in crops). If the plaintiff could sometimes win all he asked for, he could just as easily lose all, gaining neither principal nor interest and having to pay court costs. The court provided the opportunity for suits to be engaged and concluded through out-of-court settlements, but over half of the cases were taken to a jury trial.[24]

Virginia's district court system supplemented the county courts but did not supplant them. Most legal matters that property owners engaged in, such as the recording of deeds and wills, continued in the county courts. Most suits were still instigated at the county level, and the local courts did not become small-claims courts. One could enter a case in the district court if the suit was for more than a hundred dollars, but suits of higher value were tried in the county courts. Also, few county cases were appealed to the district courts. The direct check of the state judiciary overseeing county courts to aid the merchant-creditors never developed. The scenario of the plaintiffs going into the county courts, losing, and then appealing to the district courts was not played out. In fact, the few appeals from the county level were more likely to be brought by the defendant. (See table 1.) The state district court offered, instead, an alternative for instigating suits. It did not significantly lessen the business of the county courts, but it allowed more litigation to be conducted. As the debt cases clearly recorded, however, these were far from being plaintiffs' courts.[25]

What had happened to the court system that was to bring about Madison's reforms? Henry and his party only appeared to have lost in the creation of the state district-court system. It was a compromise that—besides being passed in conjunction with prodebtor legis-

TABLE 1 Appeals from county courts to the state district courts at Prince Edward County and Winchester, 1789–1806

Total cases on appeal	16%
Appeals by plaintiffs	4%
Appeals by defendants	96%
County court decision overturned	35%
County court decision upheld	65%

Sources: PED, 1:3–158; 2:1–50; 4:14–66; District Court at Winchester, OB, 1:41–205.

lation and besides perpetuating the political power of the justices of the peace—actually further decentralized the judiciary. Granted that the volume of business in the state General Court and the number of General Court judges were increased, the time the General Court was in a central session was reduced, and, much of the time, the General Court judges would be out riding the circuit between the district courts. Further, the districts were made up of geographical areas usually consisting of four or five counties. Someone from the western Southside, for example, might leave his county but not his area to go to the district-court session held in a neighboring county courthouse. Not only would the travel not be expensive or overly inconvenient, the jurors would be drawn from the area.[26]

As with the federal judiciary, the local juries in the state and county courts provided a very important protection. The jury served as a shield against outside interference. It was a simple enough rule in adversarial justice that lawyers and their clients would always want a jury when they thought it would better serve their chance of winning. When two locals went to court, however, it might not be advantageous for either to want a jury. The court then served as a forum for airing differences and a place to reconcile, to arbitrate, and to keep the peace. But when outside plaintiffs, especially creditors, were taking locals to trial, then the jury was called upon often to serve as a protector. At the county-court level—for example, in Cumberland County—defendants did not contest plaintiffs who had similar property holdings, but defendants who owned no property outside the county did contest plaintiffs who owned property outside the county. Only then did the defendant place his cause before the country, the jury, or the plaintiff might withdraw. This use of the jury as a tool for the defense would occur most in courts with larger jurisdictions, when the antagonists came from different locations in the state, or when the plaintiff was from outside the state. The jury would also serve as a local check in implementing appellate court decisions. Questions of law were determined by appellate court judges, but questions of fact, including the amount of damages, were determined by the jury. The jury was called upon to serve this purpose at the state district-court level and to an even greater extent at the federal level, where the plaintiffs were often British or American agents of British firms. It should be added that more-distant plaintiffs preferred the higher court levels. In debt cases in sessions from 1785 to 1795 in the Campbell, Frederick, and York county courts, jury trials made up 25 percent of the cases, but they were 50 percent of the debt cases in the District Court at Prince Edward County Courthouse and 100 percent of the British debt cases in the United States circuit court.[27]

Juries performed the same role whether they were in the county courts or in the state district-court system. As for the judges, there would not be a lot of difference between the old and the new state judiciary. The state judicial machinery was created and put in place only to be filled often by the very same people the reformers had opposed. Many had been appointed to the General Court in the 1780s by a legislature that Henry and his party had dominated and they continued to be able to control this body on particular issues. The lawyers also would not be too different from those who practiced in the county courts. Much depended upon the circuit. Who would want to practice in a circuit of district courts in the Piedmont and Southside or in one in the southern Valley? Without changing their ways, some of the same lawyers who had practiced in the counties in an area would take up practicing in the state district court in that area.

Prince Edward County courthouse was the location for one of the district courts. The district included the counties of the upper James River valley. This area was rural tobacco country, was highly indebted (to both domestic and British creditors), and had supported Henry, opposed judicial reform, and been Anti-Federalist. This location clearly demonstrates how an area that had opposed the reformers, an area that had the kinds of practices that the reformers wanted to correct, would be affected by the reforms—to show whether or not the reforms could, in themselves, produce a significant transformation of Virginia's legal culture. Here local conservatives in Henry country would watch as the reformed judiciary brought a new spirit of the law to bear upon them. But this was not Richmond. The courthouse was not even located in a town. The courtroom was not imposing, and the lawyers were known. One of the first men to offer his legal services in this new district court was Henry. The opponent of the court's establishment was there to help get it started. Henry practiced in the county courts in and around Prince Edward County and now added the District Court at Prince Edward County. His clients were mostly from the area.[28]

And who were the judges? Spencer Roane, Henry's son-in-law, was on this circuit, along with Henry Tazewell and John Tyler. Most of the eight judges who, in different sessions in the next several years, presided over the district court at Prince Edward County courthouse had been in Henry's party—which had opposed court reform.[29]

And who were the jurors? The jurors were similar to those who were drawn in the county courts, for both the petit and the grand juries. To qualify as a juror, one had to be a freeholder, but what was more revealing was that the holdings of those jurors called before the state district court that met at Prince Edward County courthouse who lived in Prince Edward County were equivalent to those of the average landholder in the county. This conformed to the tradition, on the one hand, of petit jurors being average citizens of the community. Grand jurors, on the other hand, were men of substance and estate, responsible and respected members of the community, and they owned over twice as much land in the county as the average freeholder or member of a petit jury. The judicial reform did not alter the social distinction in agrarian Virginia between farmers, who served on the petit juries, and the gentry or planters who served on the grand juries.[30]

The same men continuously sat on the grand juries. They were well-informed citizens of the community. Over a third of the members of grand juries in the state district court at Prince Edward County courthouse were justices of the peace; nearly as many were members of the House of Delegates. Gentry justice continued in the district-court system. All new state General Court judges were expected to get to know these country gentlemen. In terms of the success of both a judge's court and his career, it was even more important to know them than the local bar. The protectors of local justice thus also played a leading part in the judicial system of the state.[31]

Similar to the makeup of grand juries, the same people served on a number of petit juries in a session. They were called from the local communities and from those doing business at the courthouse. For example, at the District Court at Prince Edward County, two-thirds of the jurors had also served on other juries within the same court session. Over half of the jurors owned land in Prince Edward County. One-fourth of the jurors had some business going on during the same court session in which they were serving as jurors, and over half of those jurors were defendants, including jurors in debt cases who were also defendants in other debt cases. The ethics of all of this could be questioned by present-day professional legal standards, but this was trial by a jury of peers: which meant that debtors should be tried by a jury that could contain debtors. And it was a justice of familiarity, where the judges, the grand and petit jury members, the attorneys, and the litigants all knew each other.[32]

Local justices of the peace and other local freeholders drawn to this rural setting as jurors, men like Henry practicing law, and judges like Roane presiding—Was this what Madison and Jefferson had envisioned as the necessary reform of Virginia's legal system? Was this the kind of change that would instill confidence in potential plaintiffs? No wonder the British were so discouraged when Jefferson, as Washington's secretary of state, informed their minister that all was well, because they could carry their suits in Virginia as well as in federal courts.[33] The machinery itself, especially one so decentralized, would not necessarily alter the provincial character of the law in the countryside. The manner in which the law was practiced might not be legislated away so easily.

The district court system did not create an across-the-board transformation of the state's legal culture. But, it did provide more courts for a growing law profession. The profession grew in the cities and large towns and was attracted to the circuits that ran through the towns and the more populous areas, such as Richmond, Norfolk, Alexandria, Fredericksburg, and the Northern Neck. Richmond offered the court of appeals, the General Court in general session, and the federal circuit court as well. The judicial structure was not as important for the rising legal profession as the location of the courts.[34]

Although most county courts (or hustings courts in towns) continued their normal business—in both type and volume—after the district-court system was established, Fredericksburg provides an example of what could have resulted throughout the state from the change in the judicial machinery. After Fredericksburg was made the location of a district court, suits that would have been instigated in the town hustings court were opened instead in the district court. The hustings court, which had previously thrived, now saw its business vastly reduced. The district court was convenient for the town merchants, and they may well have preferred the larger jurisdiction. After all, much of their legal business would involve pursuing debtors who lived in the Fredericksburg area but outside of the town. This general movement of plaintiffs in Fredericksburg from the local court to the state court remained the exception, however.[35]

The rule in this predominantly rural state was continuity in the county courts and, regrettably for the reformers, a similarity between what occurred in the county courts and in the state district courts. There was some diversity and alternative courts and some increased professional opportunity for lawyers, but, in general, no new spirit had been infused into the law. The new machinery did not transform the law in the Old Dominion.

An additional change was made in the court system in 1808, however. The legislature again altered the state judiciary at the lower-court level, and the district court system was replaced by the superior court or circuit court system. This change actually decentralized the judiciary even further, however. Without a middle tier of appellate courts having been created, the state judiciary was to be located in each county. The General Court was only slightly expanded, by three judges, while the circuits were extended to include, not courts for districts that contained four or five counties, but a court for each county. This meant that the General Court judges were going to spend even more time riding the circuit, and any potential increase in the litigation that the courts could handle was compromised by the reduction from two to one judge presiding over each court.[36]

The decentralizing aspects of this legislation were increased by the requirement that the judges reside within their circuits and by the circuit courts using the county clerks who were appointed by the county court judges. As in the previous district-court system, many of the new circuits were remote from Richmond and the towns. This made them less attractive to anyone but country lawyers. Two of the thirteen circuits were in the Allegheny Mountains, two were in the Southside, one was in the southern Valley, one was in the upper James River valley—the area of the former district court held at Prince Edward County—and two covered part of the Piedmont and part of the Valley. (The remaining five ran through the Tidewater, the Northern Neck, and the area around Richmond.)[37]

All of these changes would only assure that most lawyers would still be practicing in an area of the state in two or three counties or at the state court in the area and, after 1808, could follow the state judge in his circuit through the counties in the area. The lawyers who, like the judges, spent a good amount of the year at their profession lived in the area, owned a farm, and needed it to supplement their income. Any hope of professionalization with the development of the state judiciary was compromised by its continuing decentralization. Indeed, splitting the General Court into district courts and then splitting the district courts into state courts for each county not only heightened the burden of the circuit-riding judges, not only made them more provincial than a centralized court, but decentralized the old bar of the General Court. There was speculation that less competition in a single state court worked to lower the quality of the bar and that majorities had been found in the legislature to support the reforms only because enough fathers and brothers of young men realized that the legislation would expand the number of lawyers who could practice in the state. The decentralization made opportunities for young lawyers who could begin their practice at the local level, but, because there was a greater number dividing the business, their chance of success had diminished.[38] The expanding state judiciary had assured the continuation of an ample number of country lawyers in the county courthouses, but they were quite different from the new, professional lawyers in the cities. Throughout much of the state, the development of the judiciary could not end the country character of Virginia law.

As for the hope that the appellate structure might remedy problems in the judicial system: an increase of courts at the bottom of the structure without any corresponding change above, such as a middle tier of courts, would not open up more appeals. There was a growing backlog in the court of appeals. From the district court system to the superior (or circuit) court system, Virginia had established only a limited appellate structure. The state's judiciary was a compromise with a provincial, county-oriented society. Guidelines for the law were set at the upper level, but the vast bulk of litigation in the state judiciary was handled by the superior courts, which kept justice close to home, where most legal business in the commonwealth continued to be transacted: in the county courthouse.

2

A Power and Privilege
Called Liberty and Right

Debtors and Trial by Jury

By the middle of the eighteenth century, Virginia's colonial economy and debtor status had locked the tobacco culture into a way of seeing the world that would remain long afterward. No cotton prosperity would rescue Virginia from having to come to terms with its decline. Tobacco would not return to its former glory, and much of the James River valley and, increasingly, the Southside was connected to that staple. Indebtedness, which may have partly caused the Revolution, did not end with it and became an integral part of Virginia agriculture. Economics, politics, and the law were intertwined.[1]

Debt cases made up most of the business of the courts in Virginia at all levels. Indebtedness colored how planters and farmers would view the law, the expansion of courts, and the growth in the cities of a legal profession with bankers and merchants as clients. For many, the law was seen as a way to lose one's property to creditors, who were considered leeches using the law and the courts as tools to live off the wealth of the land. There was an ambivalent attitude toward the law as enemy and as protector, with the former associated with the distant law of a foreign court, corrupt judges, and big-city lawyers and the latter associated with local justices of the peace, country lawyers, and juries made up of one's peers.

The situation is described well from the creditor's point of view by John Hook, from Scotland, who was a partner with David Ross in one of the larger mercantile firms in Virginia. Hook complained of his problems in getting debtors to sign bonds showing their indebtedness and obligation to repay. He saw a great amount of litigation ahead to recover debts, and was particularly concerned about those who "will stand out in hopes if juries will acquit them of Interests." He did not relish the legal fight ahead. Nonetheless, living among the planters and farmers and seeing the problems they had in making payments, he found himself sympathizing with them. He admitted that he had developed a "tenderness for the Debtors." Hook was becoming a "country banker," caught between Ross in Richmond and the local farmers. His sympathy for the debtors became costly as he in turn became indebted to Ross, and eventually Ross sued him to collect.[2]

Of the approximately ten kinds of common-law actions that generally occurred in the courts in civil suits, two types were predominant: debt and trespass on the case or "case." (See table 2.) Like the former action, the latter generally involved suits to recover debt. The debt action was used where there was a bond signed by a debtor admitting his indebtedness to a creditor. The "case" action was used when a creditor could only show that, according to his account books, a person was deficient in payment. The creditor claimed that there was a promise of payment and that the debtor had failed to live up to his promise. In the debt action, the creditor sued to recover the debt: principal plus interests. Through the "case" action, the creditor sued to show that the debtor had wronged him and that he, the creditor, had suffered damages: principal plus interests and sometimes punitive damages. A defendant made a plea of payment with the former action and of *non assumpsit* (not making a promise) with the latter if he wished to put the case before his "country," a petit jury.[3]

Debtors could look with hope to their local juries and judges. Plaintiffs often had to drop their suits when they saw they were going to lose before a jury (because only by dropping the suit could a plaintiff later begin another suit to collect from that defendant). It was common practice for the plaintiff's counsel to advise withdrawing the suit when

TABLE 2 Percentage of forms of legal action in civil suits, 1785–1825 (Campbell, Caroline, Cumberland, Frederick, Wythe, and York county courts, Fredericksburg and Richmond city hustings courts, and the state district and superior courts at Fredericksburg and Prince Edward County)

Common law	
Trover	0.25%
Slander	0.25
Ejectment	0.5
Covenant	1
Detinue	2
Assault and battery	3
Trespass	3
Bond	6
Trespass on the case ("case")	36
Debt	42
Chancery or equity law	6

Sources: Campbell County Court, OB, 2:1–77; 4–5:356–69; Caroline County Court, OB, 1804–5: 346–79; Cumberland County Court, OB, 1792–97: 313–30; 1824–26: 147–203; District Court at Fredericksburg, OB, 1806–7: 1–133; PED 1:3–158; 2:1–50; 1805: 14–66; Frederick County Court, OB, 19:99–145; 25:404–92; 36: 145–240; Fredericksburg City Hustings Court, OB, A: 195–202; C: 244; Fredericksburg and Spotsylvania Superior Court, OB, G: 87–103; H: 166–74; Prince Edward County Superior Court, District Court at Prince Edward County OB, 1804–31: 409–417, 533–38, 602; Richmond City Hustings Court, OB, 1:246–77; 3:324–58; Wythe County Court, OB, 1795–96: 1–15; 1805–8: 81–98; 1815–20: 20–31; 1822–26: 183–206; York County Court, OB, 5:150–72; 6:693–714; 8:72–78; 9:21–37; 11:1–23.

Note: Drawn from sessions of county and state courts from different regions of the state every ten years, 1785–1825. A total of 4,537 suits were classified.

a hostile verdict was expected.[4] In addition, out-of-court settlements generally involved the dropping of the interests. A victory in terms of the law, the judge, and even the jury's verdict was often compromised for plaintiffs who received only limited damages. In awarding damages, juries usually subtracted interests, thus depriving creditors of their profits. The amount of accumulated interests could often exceed the principal of the original debt. (Again, by statute, debts recovered were paid through installments in crops, and the defendant was usually given through the next harvest or a year to begin payments.) Because the interests was often dropped, defendants looked for justice in Virginia's courts. This was why reformers wanted to change the system. This part of the significance of the jury trial is lost if one merely counts judgments and verdicts in win-loss terms for the plaintiffs and defendants (see table 3).

The reforms of the state judiciary could do nothing to end the tobacco indebtedness or jurors' sympathies for indebted defendants. Increasing the decentralization of the judiciary in this rural society assured that justice in Virginia would remain in harmony with the interests of the local citizens. There remained more protection in the law than rational efficiency. Indeed, the process of securing agrarian interests and property rights through the common law only continued.

During the Revolution, and after 1788, many Virginians wanted to be protected from a foreign power and a distant law whether it was that of England or that of the federal government. The Anti-Federalists had not just raised a theoretical issue during the ratification debate. They were trying to defend themselves against a known enemy who would use the Constitution to threaten their interests. The debt cases that many had hoped to negate by the Revolution, that had been held at bay through the courts having been closed during the Revolution and the 1780s, soon began to be heard. The Loyalists and the British could now bring action against Virginians, who were to be held accountable by a new law, new courts, and new judges who were not Virginian.

A geographic dimension can be seen in the federal court records

TABLE 3 Reappraising plaintiff win-loss ratios, 1789–92, in the state district court at Prince Edward County

Simple win-loss verdict and judgment	
Plaintiffs won	83%
Defendants won	17%
Accounting for plaintiff withdrawals and reduced damages	
Plaintiffs withdrew	45%
Trial to judgment	55%
Plaintiffs won declared damages	16%
Plaintiffs received reduced damages (losing interests)	67%
Defendants won verdict	17%

Sources: PED, 1:3–56; District Court at Prince Edward County, Records at Large, 1789–92: 1–52.

that show those Virginians in debt to the British creditors. The area of greatest indebtedness included the river valleys of the James, York, and Rappahannock, from the Chesapeake to the Piedmont through the Southside. This was tobacco country. Henry's party in the General Assembly included the representatives of the indebted regions, who, voting their interests, had supported pro-debtor legislation and had opposed compliance with the treaty of 1783 (which recognized the claims of British merchants), ratification of the Constitution, and establishment of a judiciary—at the state or federal levels—wherein creditors could enter suits against their constituents.[5]

The British Debt Cases, as they were called, were Virginia's showcase litigation of the 1790s, and were important for a number of reasons. They provided ample proof that the Anti-Federalists had been right to believe that a non-Virginian Constitution and federal government would be used by foreigners to hurt them; it provided Henry with another opportunity to strike at the British oppressor and to stand for the cause of liberty and independence; and it revealed how the new federal system would work and whether or not Virginians of Henry's persuasion could find a way to make it work for them.

In 1790, the federal circuit court for the district of Virginia opened. After a session in Charlottesville and one in Williamsburg, the court was held in Richmond from then on. Its docket quickly filled with British debt cases, which, in the court's first three years, made up 88 percent of the total cases. Along with pleas to secure a trial by jury, the attorneys for the debtors put forward a number of special pleas raising questions of law that had to be decided by the judges before there could be a trial for repayment of the debt. The special pleas included: that acts of the General Assembly in 1779 and 1782 set up a process for the legal confiscation of British-enemy property, which included debts, and they barred suits in Virginia's courts by the British; that the treaty of 1783 was not in effect, since the British government had broken it by not returning slaves taken during the war and by not giving up posts held in American territory; and that the dissolution of the British government in Virginia, in 1776, annulled the contractual obligations, economic as well as political, between Britons and Virginians. Hearings began, in the circuit court, in Richmond, in 1791, on *Jones v. Walker*, a test case. Other similar suits were delayed until a decision was reached.[6]

In this defense of Virginia's debtors, Henry was center stage. While defending the poor indebted farmer, he added to his fame as an orator. He prepared for this defense as he had never done before as a politician or lawyer. He gave great performances to a packed courtroom. Though he spoke as a lawyer in a system of adversary justice, his defense of this particular debtor was also a defense of all debtors, himself, his party, and their actions since the Revolution. He attacked the conduct of the British while answering their charge that Virginians had revolted to avoid paying their debts. He reminded his audience that British tyranny had caused the Revolution, that not only had Americans fought for their liberty but, if they had lost the war, they could have lost their property and their lives. During the Revolution, when the bonds of the Anglo-American society were broken, all legal and financial connections between the two countries ended. Virginians became independent of the British economically as well as politically. After 1776, Virginia, as an independent nation, had the sovereign power to confiscate the debts owed to the British. Henry believed that a false sanctity had been given to these obligations. He contended that Virginia had rightly closed its courts to the British and that the British should remain barred from collecting the debts.[7]

Several of Henry's points appeared compromised by the treaty of 1783. Because it called for the clearing of all obstacles to the collection of the British debts, neither the breaking of the political bonds in 1776 nor the confiscation of British property during the war had abolished those debts. Henry challenged the treaty's validity: it was of no effect, since it had been broken by the British who had retained posts in American territory and had not returned or compensated the owners for the slaves taken off at the end of the war. If it was not in effect, then the British could not expect a repayment of the debts, and it mattered not that the Constitution made treaties the law of the land.[8]

No decision was reached in 1791; indeed, the case of *Jones v. Walker* was postponed until 1793 due to the absences, for over a year, of the two Supreme Court justices (because of a death in the family of one justice and the illness of the other) whose presence was necessary, along with that of the federal district court judge, to form a circuit court. (This kind of problem was resolved by Congress in a 1793 revision of the Judiciary Act of 1789. Only one Supreme Court justice would thereafter be necessary to conduct all the business of a circuit court if one or two of the other members were absent.) The plaintiff, William Jones, was the surviving partner of Farrel and Jones, one of the two largest British mercantile firms that brought suits against Virginia debtors in the circuit court. He died before the case resumed, which suspended that suit as well as his others. His administrator, John Tyndal Ware, reopened the suits. The first to be heard, the new test case, was *Ware v. Hylton* (which had originally entered the docket in 1791 as *Jones v. Hylton*). The suit was against Daniel Hylton & Co. and Francis Eppes (an executor, along with Jefferson, for John Wayles, Jefferson's father-in-law, who had been indebted to Farrel and Jones).[9]

Ware v. Hylton involved a partial payment of debt into the state loan office. To gain a revenue during the war, Virginia had allowed debtors to pay to the state the debt they owed to British creditors, the state then presumably taking responsibility for the debt. As a result, in addition to the other pleas, another special plea was put forward: that debt paid into the state loan office had been discharged and could not be collected by a British creditor.[10]

In 1793, in *Ware v. Hylton*, the federal circuit court, consisting of Chief Justice John Jay, Justice James Iredell, and Cyrus Griffin, the federal district court judge for the Virginia district, ruled for the plaintiff, the British firm. It rejected all of the defendants' special pleas except the one on payments into the loan office. The court was not swayed by the argument that events during the Revolution had ended the debts, because they were recognized as existing in the treaty of 1783. Nor would the court declare that the treaty had been broken by the British. The judiciary did not have the authority to make such a decision, for that was the domain of, first, the Confederation Congress, and then, under the Constitution, the president and the Senate; and, until the other branches declared otherwise, the judiciary must assume that a treaty was in effect. This decision meant that, for most debts, there was no legal bar to recovery.[11]

The victory of British creditors was made problematic, however, because they had to place their cause before Virginia juries. In *Ware v. Hylton*, after the circuit court had settled most of the questions of law, the plea of debt payment, as a question of fact, was put to a jury (on the part of the debt not paid into the loan office). The jury gave a verdict for the plaintiff—since there was ample evidence that Hylton was indebted to Ware—but the damages awarded were not what Ware had requested. Interests on the debt for the entire period of the war was subtracted. (Indeed, even if both the payments into the loan office and the interests during the war were not counted,

Ware only received about 40 percent of what he had sued to collect.) Subtracting the interests during the war became the dominant pattern for the cases that followed—at the state and federal levels—when the British creditor won a verdict. In 89 percent of the British debt cases, Virginia juries deducted the war interests. And, in 17 percent of the total cases, the subtraction of "war interests" was an understatement: the interests owed did not begin until the time of the trial.[12]

In *Ware v. Hylton*, Jay had instructed the jury that it should not subtract the war interests, but this area was a question of fact, the jurisdiction of juries and not of a federal chief justice. It was public knowledge that concerning the British debt cases, Jay disapproved of the juries' actions. Edmund Pendleton, the president of the Virginia court of appeals, came to their defense in his opinion in *McCall v. Turner*. In that case, the court of appeals upheld the following procedure, which had been developed in the state's courts: the defendant's counsel presented a plea to give evidence to the jury that the plaintiff was a British merchant who had been out of the country and had been unable to receive payments during the war, and that he was responsible, therefore, for the interests not having been paid.[13] Of course, actions by the state and its citizens had made it unwise for a British creditor to be in Virginia at that time, much less to try to collect interest payments, but this maneuver provided the legal ground for juries to withhold the war interests. The justification for this was like that given for refusing to repay the debts: mainly the violations of the treaty of 1783 by the British.

The British creditors had another problem. In *Ware v. Hylton*, the federal circuit court had ruled favorably on the plea that debts paid into the loan office were discharged. With Jay dissenting, Iredell declared that during the Revolution, Virginia, as a sovereign state, had the authority to confiscate British property, including debts, and the debts paid into the loan office were, in effect, confiscated by the state. To the debtor, the state had taken the place of the British creditor, and to the British creditor, the state had taken the place of the debtor. The state had the choice of paying the debts to the British or retaining them. Iredell agreed with the defendant's counsel that the treaty of 1783 had not been binding on the states. The circuit court recognized that until the ratification of the Constitution, sovereignty resided in the states. (The Supreme Court upheld this position in the appeal.) However, upon the ratification of the Constitution, the treaty became the law of the land. Though this obligated the debtors to the British merchants, it did not retroactively affect those who had discharged their debts through payments to the state. If the British wanted to collect the debts that had been paid into the loan office, then they would have to take that up with the state of Virginia.[14]

Iredell was not suggesting to the plaintiff the option of suing the state in the Supreme Court. He did not believe that Virginia could be sued. This was made clear in 1793 in his dissent in *Chisholm v. Georgia*. Iredell recognized that, according to Article Three of the Constitution, if a state and a citizen of another state were parties in a suit, it could only be heard in the Supreme Court; and, logically, it was possible for a state to be a defendant as well as a plaintiff in such a case. But, he asked, in what kind of suit could a sovereign state be a defendant? In *Chisholm v. Georgia*, the United States Constitution, treaties, and laws were not involved. The case was a common-law suit. Under the common law, a sovereign state could not be sued involuntarily. Without Georgia's permission, the Supreme Court did not have the jurisdiction to hear the case. Iredell said he was afraid of the consequences of the Court asserting this jurisdiction, and so were many others who passed and ratified the Eleventh Amendment, which excluded this kind of case from the jurisdiction of the Court. Iredell stated that, under the common law, an individual could only petition a sovereign government for redress.[15] From his opinion in *Chisholm v. Georgia*, it was clear that, in *Ware v. Hylton*, he was giving Ware and the British merchants a very impractical option in relation to the debts paid into the loan office: they could politely ask the state of Virginia to give back those debt payments. Given the history of the matter, they could expect that their petitions to the General Assembly would be rejected. Ware chose, instead, to appeal his case against Hylton to the Supreme Court. Until a decision was reached there, Virginians could continue to use in the courts the special plea of payment into the loan office to prevent the collection of those debts. With this exception, the suits could proceed.

The appeal of *Ware v. Hylton* was heard in 1796 before Justices Samuel Chase, William Paterson, James Wilson, William Cushing, and Iredell. Although Iredell did not vote on the appeal of the circuit court decision, he stated that his opinion had not changed. The opinions of the Supreme Court were given seriatim, each judge giving his opinion either in concurrence with or dissent from the majority decision. The majority of the Court affirmed Iredell's lower court opinion that, during the Revolution, Virginia had had the authority to confiscate British property, including debts; that payments into the loan office discharged debt; and that the treaty of 1783 was not clearly binding on the states until the ratification of the Constitution, when the treaty became the law of the land. But, the Court rejected Iredell's conclusion. The Constitution retroactively nullified state laws contrary to the treaty. This canceled Virginia's authorization of debt payments being made into the state loan office. Those who had paid into the loan office were still obligated for all their debt to their original creditor. The Supreme Court reversed the judgment of the circuit court and threw out the special plea that debts paid into the loan office were discharged.[16]

Ware v. Hylton was sent back to the circuit court for the decision to be carried out, which included calling a jury to try the issue of payment into the loan office as a question of fact.[17] This process, in the *Ware v. Hylton* cases, showed Anti-Federalist Virginians that the federal judiciary, through a broad-based appellate system, worked as they had hoped it would. The appeal to the Supreme Court was on a point of law, while the facts were tried by local juries at the circuit court level in Virginia. After the Supreme Court decision in this case, the most important legal question left regarding the British debts was a question, not of law, but of fact, the war interests. This placed the British creditors in the hands of Virginia juries.

The British merchants' frustrations in collecting debts and interests were part of a larger set of problems in Anglo-American relations during the 1780s and 1790s that, concerned violations of the treaty of 1783. The claim that the British had violated that treaty was used to defend the refusal to pay the debts and interests. On the subject of debts, the British minister told Secretary of State Jefferson in 1792 that Virginia was the only state causing them anxiety. The next year the General Assembly passed resolutions calling on Congress (through the state's congressmen) to suspend the treaty of 1783 and the litigation of British debts in the federal judiciary until the British complied with the other aspects of the treaty, specifically by surrendering the posts held on American territory and by returning the slaves. The abduction of the slaves was the major grievance Virginians held against the British. The British maintained that it would be immoral to return the freedmen to slavery. The Virginians could accept this but insisted upon compensation for their loss.[18]

It did not matter that—along with the moral question—there was a spurious element in connecting the debt question to that of the slaves. It was claimed that, in taking the slaves and in taking and destroying other property, the British had deprived the debtors of the means to pay their creditors. The indebted and those who had lost slaves and other property were generally not the same persons, however. Most of Virginia had had little direct contact with the war. Most of the Virginia area highly indebted to the British was spared the loss of property and slaves during the war. The Tidewater, especially in the James and York river valleys, was not a heavily indebted area but had suffered the greatest wartime property losses. In other words, the least-devastated area of the state included the most-indebted area, and one of the less-indebted areas was the most devastated. The debtors did have real problems caused by the war, which had brought a breakdown in the economy, making it exceedingly difficult for them to pay their debts, domestic or British.[19] But, abstract economic forces lacked the emotional quality of British "injustice," and so the taking of the slaves continued to be used as the rationale for resisting the collection of British debts and war interest.

After 1793, Anglo-American problems expanded beyond violations of the treaty of 1783 when the war between revolutionary France and the rest of Europe included a naval war that affected America's commerce. George Washington sent John Jay to London to negotiate. The result of the mission, the Jay Treaty, was opposed by Virginia's congressmen because of its lack of reciprocity. America made concessions to the British, but not vice versa. The treaty made little mention of British infractions of the treaty of 1783—there was no mention of compensation for the slaves abducted during the war—but there was to be complete payment of the British debts. In 1795 the Virginia General Assembly passed resolutions condemning the Jay Treaty and calling for constitutional amendments to prevent federal judges from going on diplomatic missions and to allow the House of Representatives to participate in the treaty-making process. Virginians in the House of Representatives were part of a futile attempt to stop the treaty from going into effect by refusing to appropriate the funds necessary to implement it.[20]

The inability of the British creditors to find satisfaction in America's courts, however, had led them to hope for a diplomatic alternative. Their government and Jay, who was sympathetic to them, provided an out-of-court solution to their problem. The Jay Treaty called for the establishment of a commission to hear the British debt claims. Even though the creditors had succeeded, by the Supreme Court case of *Ware v. Hylton,* in removing all the special pleas that had barred the collection of the debts, they were still being frustrated by the juries. Unable to obtain the war interests through the courts, the creditors now looked to the debt commission that began meeting in Philadelphia in 1797. The treaty stipulated that it be made up of two American and two British commissioners and a fifth who would be chosen by them, or, if they could not agree, would be determined by lot. The latter proved necessary, and the British won the choice. The British majority set rules of procedure that the Americans could not accept. The British insisted that demands for the payment of war interests be heard by the commission. The commission ceased when the Americans walked out.[21]

Not until Jefferson's presidency was a solution worked out, one that was satisfying to Virginians. By the Convention of 1802, the claims of the British creditors against Americans would be paid by the British government, which, in turn, would be compensated by the American government. Congress appropriated $2,664,000 to absorb the debts. Of course, only a portion of Americans actually owed the debt, mainly Virginians.[22] Nonetheless, the United States government would cover the debt claims made by the British government on behalf of the British creditors rather than take as its official position that they were canceled because of the Revolution.

Earlier, Henry and his party had tried to argue that the law that debtors had to pay back their debts was rendered invalid because of British tyranny and American losses during the Revolution—and they had failed. They had attempted to prevent the establishment of any court with jurisdiction to try the claims, and they had failed. The legal principle stood, and the national government would enforce it. Yet, the government assumed responsibility for private debts. It could be said that the rule of law on paying debts remained in force but special arrangements had been necessary due to outstanding circumstances; or, it could be said, Henry and the Virginia debtors had won. In the end, the use of delaying tactics through local courts and the obstinate refusal to submit proved successful. So, too, did the role of the juries. The law had been tempered. Sympathetic jurors had not allowed the plaintiffs to collect the interests on the debts, which would have ruined fellow Virginians and sent them moving out of the state south and west. They had denied British profits instead. This was how Anti-Federalists and provincial conservatives wanted the legal system to work. No distant or "foreign" law had tyrannized Virginians. The law as threat—creditor-plaintiffs pursuing Virginians in federal courts—was met by the law as protector through the local jury trial. Debtors put their fate in the hands of the "country," their neighbors.

As for indebtedness, there was no solution. From Independence to the Convention of 1802, from closing courts to withholding interests, the economic problems of the tobacco farmers were not resolved. The debtor-relief laws and sympathetic juries had not and could not end the problems. Again, a good example of the problems can be seen in John Hook's situation, where David Ross sued Hook for the debt Hook himself had failed to collect. Hook complained of the inability of his neighbors to pay him, and how hard it had been to settle his accounts and to bond the debtors. Beyond his original sympathy for them, he came to realize that he was, as he described it, "in the power of my Debtors." They would try to forestall him until past the statute of limitations. And they could bring social and economic pressure to bear upon him. They could all refuse to do business with him in the future. He had found that often all he could do—under the best compromise, out-of-court solution—was to accept the payment of principal minus the interests.[23]

Debt cases remained predominant in the courts of Virginia, and would continue to do so through the 1820s. How could it be otherwise as long as the economic problems continued in the state? It was seriously questioned whether the state could ever rid itself of its indebtedness. Eventually, the panic of 1819 and the depression that followed would supply the answer.[24]

3

The Interposition of 1798 and the Emergence of the Old Republicans

The Madisonian round of legal and constitutional reform in Virginia had been compromised by Henry's faction and by the legal and judicial realities of the state. Political realities would finish bringing the reform movement to a standstill. Attempts to decrease the power of the county judges lessened, the revision of the state constitution was tabled, and the political momentum behind reform ended as Madison and Jefferson called upon their former adversaries to help them put together the Republican party to counter Alexander Hamilton. During the 1790s, Madison and Jefferson formed an alliance with Anti-Federalists who were former followers of Henry; took up the agrarian cause against Hamiltonianism; drew upon the ideas of the Country, republican ideology, and, by the end of the decade, in the Virginia Resolutions of 1798, had taken their states' rights stand against the federal government. They were practical men who would achieve their political goal: the Federalists would be defeated. But William Branch Giles, Edmund Pendleton, John Randolph, Spencer Roane, John Taylor, and a host of Virginians calling themselves the Old Republicans would not let them forget the importance of the act of interposition in the Virginia Resolutions of 1798. It would be enshrined as the grand event in the formation of the Virginia Doctrine.

Earlier, in the 1780s, Henry had warned Virginians that the former power Britain had over them could be replaced by a central power in America. Soon after the new federal government was established, it appeared his prophesies were coming true. The new issues were associated with Hamiltonianism. From the perspective of the Country, republican ideology, Hamilton was attempting to bring Britain's corrupt governmental system to America.[1]

Henry would have enjoyed saying "I told you so," but, given the consensus of dislike for Hamilton's policies, Henry was unable to take political advantage of the situation in Virginia. In passing the Resolutions of 1790 in the General Assembly, he had to share leadership with Madison-party Federalists Henry Lee and Francis Corbin. The resolutions were a classic statement of Country opposition principles. The Virginia legislature instructed Congress that Hamilton's economic plan resembled the system in England, which included a perpetual debt, and that it gave the executive branch a corrupt influence over the rest of the government.[2]

Madison would spend most of his political career in support of the federal government, but in the 1790s he became an opposition man. Or rather, he and Jefferson sought to use opposition to gain power. In doing this, Madison broke with Hamilton—with whom, along with Jay, he had coauthored *The Federalist*—and divided the Federalists. He formed the Republican party in Congress and helped establish the *National Gazette* to counter Hamilton's policies. The core of his party in Congress came from Virginia's large delegation. Along with support from long-term associates Richard Bland Lee, Andrew Moore, and Alexander White, of the Northern Neck and the northern Valley, Madison relied on several of Henry's persuasion from the areas from the Tidewater to the Southside, including John Page, Josiah Parker, the young William Branch Giles, and, in the Senate, James Monroe and John Taylor.[3]

In Virginia, Madison and Jefferson had gained in popularity and outmaneuvered Henry by attracting many away from his faction. Madison, who had been the target of political abuse since the ratification of the Constitution, having been almost "Henrymandered" out of Congress, saw his standing in his home state improve with his drafting the Bill of Rights, and it improved further as he led the Virginia phalanx in the House of Representatives. Henry had prophesied evil consequences from the ratification of the Constitution, but he could never have envisioned that national issues would allow Madison to challenge him in influence and leadership within the state. With the stand he took against Hamiltonianism, Madison courted the Country party in his home state and won many of the legislators from the Tidewater to the James River valley. This area had tipped the scales in Henry's favor in the 1780s—joining with the Southside—and did so for Madison in the 1790s, joining with the Northern Neck. In each decade the area was won through an appeal to the values of agrarianism and the Country, republican ideology. It furnished the Republicans with their states' rights, former Anti-Federalist leaders, while the nationalist, former Federalist, or moderate Republican leaders came from the area from the central Piedmont to the Northern Neck.[4]

Henry's enemies had apparently won the state government, but the Republicans were compromised in two ways. First, they were in power only because of their opposition to the federal government and Hamiltonianism, and only because of an alliance with many of the Anti-Federalists who had been split away from Henry. Also, it should be noted, the Anti-Federalists were opposing the Federalists and Hamiltonianism, not endorsing party politics. Second, the Republicans were strong only at the state level, and most government still remained at the county level. The justices of the peace still ran the county governments, and their presence in the legislature continued undiminished. As earlier, as many as half the members of the House of Delegates at any given time were county judges. They came from all regions of the state and represented the range of socioeconomic differences there was among the legislators. Along with looking after their own socioeconomic, geographic, or political interests, they could also look after those of their local governments. Sitting in force in the legislature, they were the guardians of the existing constitution.[5]

Their allies gave Madison and Jefferson serious problems. First, the Republican ascendency at the state level did not lead to a change in the power of the county courts. The Republicans needed the support of the provincial and localist conservatives, who sought to preserve the veneration for the ancient, unchanging constitution and the common law and to keep Virginia's society, economy, and government fragmented and decentralized. A decentralized government dominated by local elites was what Jefferson, Madison, and the 1780s legal and constitutional reformers had hoped to end. Jefferson always lamented its continuation. But, to assure their political success, the Republicans had to suspend the goal of calling a constitutional convention to weaken local power or to establish a strong state executive. Although the Republicans could use another way to administer the state's legislation, by chartering corporations, no restrictions were placed on the domain of the county governments. Indeed, in the 1790s, their administrative role was expanded by the legislature.[6]

Second, the Republicans had trouble with their allies over the Constitution and the federal government. Whereas the Republicans, and the moderate Anti-Federalists who had been reconciled to the Constitution, opposed only the Federalist administration, not the government itself, and did not blame the Constitution for Hamilton's policies—they strictly construed the Constitution to constrain and to defeat the Federalists, but they did not seek changes in the Constitution—the extreme Anti-Federalists did not just want to defeat the Federalists. They continued to reject the Constitution as a fundamental law, and interpreted the Constitution as if it was a revised Articles of Confederation. They supported resolutions in the General Assembly that criticized Congress for not considering all the amendments proposed by the ratifying convention and continued to call for amendments that would weaken the national government. They blamed the Constitution for allowing the success of Hamiltonianism: indeed, its success proved that a tyranny could come from the government established by the Constitution. They understood that Hamilton could present a good argument to defend his actions based on a valid construction of the Constitution. There were and would be many ways to interpret that document. But, they believed, the true constitution or fundamental law could not be so construed. By it, Hamilton's corrupt actions were wrong, and his edifice should be torn down. All government must be returned to its original principles.[7]

The division within the Republican party into moderate and extreme wings corresponded to the continued political and geographic division within the state. In the House of Delegates, the areas of the Northern Neck to the central Piedmont to the northern Valley were in the majority that consistently voted against the Southside on further amendments to the Constitution.[8]

Along with having to deal with the extreme wing of their party, the moderate Republicans faced a growing number of Federalists in the commonwealth who were willing to defend George Washington's administration against their criticism. The Federalist party had their initial success in the towns, such as Richmond, Alexandria, and Norfolk. When Madison began courting the Country by opposing Hamiltonianism, he was aware of his loss of support from the towns, and among merchants, and professionals—including James Innes, the state attorney general, and leading members of the state bar—who were engaging in Court politics, and favored establishing banking in Virginia. Madison became concerned with the influence a Federalist monied interest could have within the state. Henry Lee, the governor, devised a way the Republicans could counter this potential influence and still hold the towns. The state could charter its own banks, pursue its own "Court-style" policies, while opposing Hamiltonianism and the federal government. In time this won the town interests over to the Republicans. While the power "center" for Henry's party in the 1780s—and for all of those who continued in the old school of Virginia politics—was the county courthouse, the power center, or the potential center, for those who wanted progress in the state was the capital. This change of role for the state government in the 1790s had been a major reason why Henry and many of his supporters, especially in the Southside, opposed the state government; these were the Anti-Federalists who did not ally themselves with the Republicans.[9]

In countering the Republicans, the emerging Federalists in Virginia were led by John Marshall, one of the few public figures in the state who had continuously supported the Washington administration, even voting against the Resolutions of 1790. In a series of essays, under the names of Aristides and Gracchus, he criticized the style and tactics of the Republicans. He argued against the Country-opposition approach to politics. Instead of its continuously being opposed, the national government should only be watched and allowed to prove itself. The best way to voice discontent with politics was through elections. The government that the Republicans countered, after all, was not a monarchy or an aristocracy but a representative democracy. It was elected by the sovereign people and should be viewed in a positive and friendly manner. Marshall pointed out the inconsistency of Republicans who, in the name of the people, opposed the government elected by the people.[10]

Earlier Federalists such as Henry Lee and Francis Corbin—who had gone into the opposition with Madison—went back into the Federalist fold after their alarm at the excesses of the French Revolution and the activities of both Edmond Genet, the French minister to the United States, and American supporters of France. The nationalism of Lee and Corbin and their desire for order were greater than their agrarianism. Lee, as governor, supported Washington's policy of neutrality and gladly accepted the command, in 1794, to lead the militia of the United States into the backwoods of Pennsylvania to put down the Whiskey Rebellion and to prevent revolution and anarchy from sweeping through the nation. Federalist support came from the Northern Neck and the northern Valley—which sent two Federalists to Congress including Henry Lee—and from the cities, with Richmond and Norfolk swinging their congressional districts to the Federalist side, thus assuring a congressional seat for Marshall.[11]

While the Republicans faced a growing Federalist party in the state, they still had to contend with Henry and his supporters as well. The more rural and provincial Southside was their base for opposition. As the Republicans pursued "Court" politics, creating state banking, Henry led the agrarian and Country opposition. Whereas there was a Republican and Anti-Federalist consensus in the vote on the Resolutions of 1790 against Hamiltonianism, the Northern Neck and the Southside went their separate ways over state banking, with the former in favor and the latter opposed. Only the Southside voted against "Court" policies at both the federal and the state levels. By the late 1790s, with the Republicans having trouble from Henry's Southside and losing the Northern Neck to the Federalists, an unusual north-south alliance developed within the state against the center.[12]

With the rise of a Federalist party, a two-party system evolved in the state, as it did at the national level. The Republicans remained dominant in the Old Dominion, but, as the decade of the 1790s progressed, their position was increasingly challenged. Worsening relations with France and the patriotism that accompanied the Quasi-War would give the critics of the national government cause for despair.

John Adams and the Federalists in Congress were at the height of their popularity and power, and as part of their wartime legislation, they enacted the Alien and Sedition Acts in 1798. The Sedition Act was highly controversial, making it a crime to write or to speak in "a false, scandalous and malicious" manner against the federal government or its officials. The Federalist federal judiciary upheld the laws. Ten Republican newspaper editors were tried and jailed. Was this the result of the Federalists' Constitution? Was the rule of law to be applied by Federalists against Republicans? This was just the kind of threat by a "foreign" law that Henry had prophesied. It appeared that the Federalists were as strong as ever; and Taylor advised disunion as the only solution.[13]

Jefferson and Madison decided to go on the offensive, with a public condemnation of the Federalists, to rally the opposition and to call Americans back to first principles. This resulted in the famous Kentucky and Virginia Resolutions of 1798, which declared that the Alien and Sedition Acts were unconstitutional. Jefferson and Madison used state legislatures as forums for making their public appeal. (Wilson Cary Nicholas got Jefferson's draft of resolutions to the Kentucky legislature, and Madison's resolutions were presented by Taylor in the House of Delegates.) The Republicans were drawing upon an English, colonial, and revolutionary tradition. The American Patriots had not been a people in arms against the government, but had been thirteen legislatures acting on behalf of the people of the colonies. The colonial legislatures had been the institutions where grievances could be heard, petitions could be made, and resolutions of protest could be drafted. In this tradition, instead of the people against government, the states could be used to counter the federal government.[14]

Far from reflecting a consensus, as Republicans later liked to remember, the Virginia Resolutions of 1798 inspired the greatest political debate in Virginia between the ratifying convention of 1788 and the state constitutional convention of 1829–30. In the House of Delegates, the leaders of the Republican side were John Taylor, Giles, and Nicholas; on the Federalist side were Henry Lee and George Keith Taylor, a brother-in-law of the Marshalls. The Republicans tried to focus attention upon the unconstitutionality of the Alien and Sedition Acts, but the Federalists demanded to know by what authority a state legislature could pass judgment upon an act of Congress. The debate that followed focused on these two issues.[15]

When the Republicans charged that the Sedition Act violated the First Amendment by imposing censorship on the press, Federalists responded that this was no innovation; most of the states had similar acts, all designed to protect themselves in times of danger; and the purpose of the act was not to prevent publication but to punish publications that printed libelous material against the government. This was in the Anglo-American common law tradition, and, the Federalists pointed out, the Sedition Act was an improvement upon it, since truth was made a defense. Republicans answered that it was easier to ascertain the truth of fact than of opinion and most cases would hinge upon the latter.[16] And, they asked whether the act was worth accepting as an improvement over the common law if the latter did not apply to the federal government.

Virginia Republicans vehemently denied that there was a federal common law, and declared this opinion in resolutions passed by the state legislature. They held that the English common law had been brought to the colonies and was modified by statute by the several colonial, then state, legislatures. There were, accordingly, as many common-law systems in America as there were states. Neither by the Articles of Confederation nor by the Constitution had the common law of England or the states been assumed by the federal government. Citizens of a state shared a common law with one another but not with citizens of the other states. All that the citizens of the different states shared together legally was the Constitution, treaties, and the statutes of Congress.[17]

Another reason the Republicans opposed the Sedition Act, and the Alien Acts as well, related to the other issue in the debate, that of the legislature's authority to pass the resolutions: police power and questions of public libel were exclusively the province of the states; and since all parts of government had the right to declare their opinions on matters that concerned their powers—the Republicans argued—then this justified Virginia's resolutions. The right of a state to declare its opinion regarding the Constitution was grounded upon the method that had been used for ratification.[18]

Madison's resolutions left two points unclear. First, was the legislature declaring acts of Congress to be null and void, or was it merely stating its opinion? Second, were the state governments, or the people of the states, or both, sovereign parties to the adoption of the Constitution? The differences between the extreme and moderate wings of the Republican party continued. When John Taylor presented Madison's resolutions to the House of Delegates, he took the liberty of editing them to read that the state governments alone were the parties to the ratification of the Constitution and that the Alien and Sedition Acts were "null and void." If the state governments were the creators of the Constitution and the federal government and could nullify federal law, then, in terms of sovereignty, the situation was unchanged from what had prevailed under the Articles of Confederation. The moderates prevailed in returning the resolutions to Madison's original wording.[19]

The results of the debate, for the Republicans, were far from promising. Unanimity was not established in the House of Delegates. The resolutions passed by a vote of 100 to 63, and the official publication of them was answered by an address published by the Federalist minority. The debate did not end with votes in the General Assembly but continued in the press into 1799. Federalist actions having blunted the effect of a united stand, the Republicans were further dismayed by the response from the rest of America. The resolutions were sent to the other states to facilitate their joining in the protest, but the reaction was a sharp rebuff. Not a single state supported Kentucky and Virginia and most responded with counterresolutions. Addressing themselves mostly to the extreme Republican view, the other state legislatures denied that America was a compact of sovereign state governments: the Articles of Confederation had been replaced.[20]

The debate over the Virginia Resolutions of 1798 continued into the 1799 elections in the commonwealth. Henry was going to reenter the legislature to lead the coalition against the Republican party. Madison decided he had better run as well, to be there to meet him. It appeared that the great debates of the 1780s between Madison and Henry would be resumed. Henry died, however, before the General Assembly convened. Republicans vented their frustration by defeating a bill to honor Henry's memory. They condemned him for betraying his principles, those of 1776, by opposing the Republican party and the Virginia Resolutions of 1798. In doing so, they let politics override any sense of fairness. After all, Henry had often been on the opposite side to Madison and Jefferson, and it was not surprising that he refused to join their efforts in the 1790s. His actions were a part of the growing discontent in the Southside with the Republican state government.[21] Henry was a provincial, country politician who was inclined to counter any perceived threat to the liberty of his countrymen. Against outside interference, he had led his fellow farmers against the British, the Madisonian reformers of the 1780s, the Federalists, and now the Republicans. His conduct could best be described as more anti-Republican than Federalist. Indeed, he ended his life as he had lived it, fighting for what he believed were the rights and interests of the farmers of Southside Virginia. Anti-British, Anti-Federalist, and anti-Republican, he was consistent throughout.

The Republicans were relieved at Henry's death, but, given the response from the other states against the Kentucky and Virginia Resolutions of 1798, they felt the need to explain and to defend themselves. Madison had also entered the legislature hoping to correct any misconceptions about the resolutions, and, at the end of the term, his *Virginia Report* was published. Moderate and conciliatory in tone, it presented a better picture of what he (and probably Jefferson) had intended. Madison defined *interposition:* it was the right of a state government to declare its opinion on, and draw its people's attention to, questions of constitutionality. This right was based on a theory of checks and balances that involved both the division of power between the central government and the states and the separation of powers between the branches. Each government or branch of government could declare its opinion on the Constitution on matters that affected it. Still, Madison recognized that without a unifying force, there would be as many interpretations of the Constitution as there were governments or parts of government involved on any issue. Madison, as a coauthor of *The Federalist*, remained consistent. Within the constitutional system, there had to be a supreme law of the land, and, if a law was passed by Congress and signed by the president and a case dealing with its constitutionality arose—unless that law was later repealed or nullified by a constitutional amendment—the Supreme Court made the final decision. On the question of sovereignty, Madison stated that only the people of the states in convention—and not the state governments—were parties to the ratification of the Constitution.[22]

Madison presented an interpretation of the resolutions and the Constitution, but in denying the extreme Republican construction of both, he could not abolish that construction. Was there a real distinction between the sovereignty of the state governments and of the people of the states? Could states defy federal law? Those of the extreme wing had their own answers and later claimed to espouse the true, old Republican doctrine of 1798.

The episode of the Resolutions of 1798 revealed a combination of interests and principle, politics and law, as well as the differences between the moderate and extreme Republicans. The principal subjects involved were legal and constitutional, but the motivation was political. Madison and Jefferson hoped that the Kentucky and Virginia Resolutions of 1798 would win over public opinion for the 1800 election. It was a propaganda ploy for the moderate Republicans, but it was a statement of principle for the extreme wing. The latter set forth their view of federalism and the Constitution and believed—or, in time, convinced themselves—that this was the Republican party consensus. They not only wanted to defeat the Federalists in 1800, they wanted to weaken the federal government, and, if given the chance, they knew what they would do with those judges they considered to be both foreign and tyrannical, the Federalist federal judges who had upheld the Alien and Sedition Acts. With the election of 1800 they had their chance.

Federalist fortunes had risen in Virginia with the patriotism generated by the Quasi-War with France, and now fell at its conclusion. Federalist gains in Virginia's congressional delegation were reversed, and the Northern Neck returned to the Republicans. With the election of 1800, the predominance of the Republican party at the state level had finally been secured.

At the federal level, the Republicans had won both houses of Congress along with the presidency. Now, they were in control, but the Federalists could return. While they still had the opportunity, they must act. In that spirit, Edmund Pendleton, president of Virginia's court of appeals, warned in his essay, *The Danger Not Over*, that merely replacing the Federalists with a new administration was not enough. Jefferson called the election of 1800 his "revolution," and Pendleton and the extreme Republicans sought to make it just that. After reviewing the Federalist era, Pendleton declared that the federal Constitution was defective. It had failed to meet the standards of fundamental principles. It had neither secured liberty nor been representative of the interests of the people nor seen to their common good, but had allowed a tyranny to emerge. In only a few years, the national government had proven corrupt. In Country, republican ideological terms, the Republicans, the Country, had seized the Court, the center of power and corruption, and they must destroy it quickly, or it would soon be too late.[23]

Jefferson spoke of reforming Federalist abuses and of reducing the size of government, yet he also took a moderate course between the Federalists and the extreme wing of his own party. Not a single act establishing the Hamiltonian system was repealed. Anti-Federalists or extreme Republicans wondered what happened to an opposition party when it won power or to the Country if it captured the Court. Would there be corruption and would principles be compromised? The old alliance between the Republicans and the Anti-Federalists had served its purpose, and after 1800, the relationship between the two wings of the Republican party became strained. The old Anti-Federalists or extreme Republicans did not want just a reduction in the size of the federal government. They wanted, in effect, to destroy it and to return America to the 1780s. The refusal by the Jefferson administration to advance the revolution was seen as a betrayal. Increasingly, the extreme Republicans altered the history of their party and insisted upon the existence of a consensus in the 1790s that had never actually existed. The moderate party leadership had never sought the destruction of the national government.[24]

The division within the Republican party was exacerbated by a major event that occurred before the Jefferson administration took office. Between the election of 1800 and the end of Adams's term, the Federalist Congress passed the Judiciary Act of 1801, expanding the federal judiciary, and Adams busily filled the appointments through his last day in office—his midnight appointments. He also appointed Marshall to be the chief justice of the Supreme Court. Jefferson's revolution of 1800 was limited by a Federalist judiciary that apparently would be used to strike down Republican reforms. The Republicans were outraged; they claimed that this was a denial of the will of the people, who had voted the Federalists out of power, and decided to repeal the Judiciary Act of 1801. Even though judicial reform had been discussed before the 1800 election and the 1801 judicial act contained improvements in the judicial system, such as ending the circuit duty, the timing of that act—the Federalists having waited until after the election to pass it, thereby preventing it from becoming a campaign issue—was horrible, and as a result, judicial reform became a political issue in any case.[25] Federalists charged that the Republicans played politics with the judiciary, but they had already begun the process.

Once in power, the Republicans repealed the 1801 act and replaced it with the Judiciary Act of 1802. The two annual terms of the Supreme Court were reduced to one. The next term of the Court was purposely postponed to 1803, so that the old judicial system could get back into full operation. Otherwise, the act basically returned to the judicial system established by the 1789 act, including the circuit-riding duty.

America was divided into six circuits, to each of which one member of the Court was assigned. Each circuit court was made up of a justice and the judge of the district wherein the court was being held; and each state continued to be a district. Virginia and North Carolina made up the fifth circuit.[26]

It must be noted that if the 1801 act had not been repealed, the number of federal judges and courts, the relative time courts were in session, and the size of court dockets would have been increased. The federal judiciary would have been able to handle more litigation and to execute it more efficiently. That was the last thing desired by extreme Republicans. They considered impeaching all of the Federalist judges or dissolving the whole judicial system and beginning anew, which was just the kind of radical action the Federalists had expected from the Republicans. Unless the extreme Republicans were tempered by the party moderates, the judicial issue could lead to the destruction of one of the branches of the federal government.[27]

In Congress, two extreme Republicans from Virginia were ready to lead the charge against the Federalist judiciary: William Branch Giles in the Senate and John Randolph in the House. They claimed that the federal judges had never been independent of Congress but had been in alliance with the Federalist majority, and that they had been tools for carrying out Federalist policy, especially during the Quasi-War. Giles and Randolph were determined that the judiciary should not continue to be a Federalist branch. There should be political uniformity even if that meant that the judiciary would continue dependent on Congress. The will of the people could not be thwarted by a band of judges.[28]

In this context, Republicans were informed that Marshall and the Supreme Court were preparing to engage them in battle, that a mandamus was going to be issued to instruct Madison, the secretary of state, upon the duties of his office. Republicans believed such a court order against the executive branch would be an attempt by the Supreme Court to establish its superiority over the other branches. They watched *Marbury v. Madison* closely and braced for a contest. Although *Marbury* was later used as a precedent for judicial review, the Court backed down and did not issue the mandamus. Soon after its decision in 1803 in *Marbury v. Madison*, the Court upheld the repeal of the Judiciary Act of 1801 and by implication its replacement act of 1802 in *Stuart v. Laird*.[29]

The Marshall Court retreated for several reasons: in *Marbury*, there was little the Court could do but lose face if, as was likely, the Jefferson administration refused to comply with the court order. When ruling in *Marbury* and *Stuart v. Laird*, Federalist judges had to seriously consider the possibility of their being impeached. The Republicans had won the contest. But Marshall and the other Federalist justices could hardly advance their nationalist principles by countering the Republican branches of the federal government. Checking the Republicans at the state level was another matter. The Court could meet a number of legal and constitutional objectives by directing its attention toward the states. A major reason for establishing the national government, after all, had been to check the states. The federal judiciary should carry the supreme law of the land throughout the nation.

Although the Court had neither issued the mandamus nor declared the repeal of the Judiciary Act of 1801 unconstitutional, the extreme Republicans were nonetheless determined to produce a conflict. Their antagonism toward the Court resulted in the impeachment movement. Their first major target was Samuel Chase, known for his partisanship and for the political harangues he delivered from the bench. Even worse, in the opinion of Virginians, he had enforced the Sedition Act in the federal circuit court in Richmond. (A possible precedent was the impeachment and conviction of John Pickering, a Federalist federal judge, criticized for being partisan, who was publicly known to be insane. Jefferson had communicated information on Pickering's conduct to the House.) Jefferson, like other Republicans, detested Chase's partisan conduct on the bench. There is no evidence, however—as Federalists would declare—that the Jefferson administration was directly involved in the 1804 impeachment of Chase. Randolph was the leader of the movement. He was, however, best at stinging, abusive oratory and not at presenting a well-argued case. Although he persuaded a predominantly Republican House to impeach Chase, he was not necessarily going to be able to persuade a less predominantly Republican Senate that Chase was guilty of committing high crimes and misdemeanors. Randolph headed the House management of the impeachment trial, and Giles tried to persuade his fellow Republican Senators to vote in a partisan manner. He put forward the following interpretation of impeachment: in a republic, when an official had sufficiently estranged himself from the public confidence that a majority of their representatives wished him removed from office, then the only question was whether he had broken his trust with the people, not whether he had literally committed high crimes and misdemeanors. The event was a trial and not a political show, Giles's interpretation of impeachment did not prevail, and Chase was acquitted.[30]

The results of the Chase trial were discouraging for the extreme Republicans. For Randolph it was a personal defeat, and he held the Jefferson administration responsible. From the beginning, as Randolph saw it, Jefferson had not shown enough resolve in ending Federalist power. The Republicans had stormed the capital city and were ready to destroy "foreign" law and courts at their source, only to be betrayed. Randolph realized that there had been a costly delay after the victory of 1800. They should have moved quickly and made a full sweep of all the Federalists in the judiciary. Now, it was probably too late. Randolph and the House impeachment managers did present resolutions proposing constitutional amendments whereby the president could remove federal judges following a majority vote in Congress and states could recall their senators. They were unsuccessful.[31] Randolph's assault upon the Court had been repelled. The opposition would now have to fall back and to rely on what they did best: defense. They at least had the consolation of knowing that if they had failed to destroy the national government, the victory of the nationalists in 1788 had not led to their own demise. They would persist.

Calling themselves Old Republicans, and, in Virginia, drawing from the old Anti-Federalist geographic base, the Tidewater to the Southside, Randolph and Taylor led a group who assured themselves that all Republicans had sought the destruction of the national government, but that after winning the "revolution of 1800," that aim was compromised by the moderate leadership and majority of the Republican party. A theme in Anglo-American history was being played out: the Country defeated the Court, only to find a new Court on the rise. From the Old Republican perspective, power had corrupted the administration and the majority in Congress. This was the reason, they contended, that the national government remained intact, the Constitution was not amended, the legislation establishing the Hamiltonian system was not repealed, and the Federalists had not been driven out of their administrative and judicial offices.[32]

The Old Republicans, however, would maintain their stand in opposition to government. They would continue a role Henry had played in 1788. He had opened the first of his great speeches in the ratifying convention stating that, "I consider myself as the servant of the people of this commonwealth, as a sentinel over their rights, liberty, and happiness." He proclaimed it his duty to inform the people of tyranny and to rally them to the banner of liberty. This manifesto revealed the self-image of the leaders of the Anti-Federalists and the extreme or Old Republicans, who followed in Henry's tradition.[33]

The Old Republicans believed that they had to continuously stand watch over government on behalf of the people. John Taylor made this his life's work, trying the acts of government by a test of principle, in numerous pamphlets and books. Randolph formally began his opposition in Congress by declaring that all political majorities eventually became corrupt. He was proud to be a member of a bold, independent minority "whose every act bore the test of rigorous principle." By the Old Republicans' test, the Jefferson and Madison administrations were found to be seriously wanting in principle. The Old Republicans fulfilled their duty to criticize the "insidious moderation" of the administration, and maintained their traditional stance, year after year. They believed that, without their vigilant watch over the federal government on behalf of the people, liberty would be lost.[34] The Old Republicans maintained the ideas of agrarianism and of the Country, republican ideology; continued developing their interpretation of the 1798 interposition and the glorification of that stand against the federal government; and set the stage for the next constitutional crisis, in the courts. Spencer Roane and the Virginia Supreme Court of Appeals would lead Virginia back to an opposition stand while using the Old Republicans' bulwark of liberty: state interposition.

4

A Shield of Liberty

Pendleton's and Roane's

Court of Appeals

The Propriety of Judicial Review

Pointing to the Virginia constitution, "I . . . will say, to them [the legislators], here is the limit of your authority; and, hither, shall you go, but no further." With those words, in the majority opinion in *Commonwealth v. Caton* (1782), George Wythe established an early precedent for judicial review, as a judicial check on the legislature. In this case, the Virginia Supreme Court of Appeals declared unconstitutional a resolution of the House of Delegates pardoning three men who had been found guilty of treason. This judicial power should certainly have benefitted the Madisonian reformers, who could have carried suits through the judiciary challenging legislation such as acts that infringed upon the property rights of creditors. But, in this same case, Edmund Pendleton, the president of the court, voiced his concerns about judicial review. He was relieved that, as he saw it, Wythe was in error in assuming that the case before them dealt with legislation. It was only a resolution with which the senate had not concurred, and it had not become law. Pendleton dissented, saying that the action by the court was unnecessary. Further, he hoped that the courts would not need to establish this power.[1] It was Pendleton's vision of the judiciary, not Wythe's, that was to be realized in the years ahead. A decision on the constitutionality of a resolution of the House of Delegates was not a solid precedent for the review of legislation passed by both houses of the General Assembly. As the 1780s progressed, the courts did not go further in establishing judicial review.

Madison's party therefore could not look to the judiciary for aid in its reform efforts. Indeed, in 1788, in another precedent for judicial review, the reformers were disheartened by the court of appeals' resistance to the new state district court system. The state judiciary—which they sought to expand—actually stood in the way of their planned reform. The original legislation required the judges to ride circuit through the state without an increase in their salaries. The court of appeals emphasized this personal hardship in the "Remonstrance of the Judges," a formal petition of grievances to the state legislature, wherein they stated that increasing the duties of judges without increasing their salaries compromised the independence of the judiciary; and, in their opinion, this was not in accord with the state constitution.[2]

Unlike Wythe's assertion in *Caton*, Pendleton's statements in the "Remonstrance" made it clear that the judiciary was only trying to guard its own rights. As long as the legislature had not intended to deprive the judiciary of its independence, then the judges should try to acquiesce in the situation as much as possible. He hoped that the General Assembly would respond to the court's petition so that a crisis could be avoided. It did so by repealing the first act and passing new legislation that established a district court system made up of judges riding circuit using only General Court judges; reduced the number of judges in the chancery court; created a new court of appeals with its own judges; and abolished the admiralty court—which the ratification of the United States Constitution had made obsolete—and appointed those judges to the General Court, thus expanding its size. The legislature did not increase the salary of the judges in any of the courts. For circuit riders, however, there would be traveling expenses by the mile for each judge each year for an amount not to exceed twenty-five pounds.[3]

The legislation raised a new question: Was it constitutional for members of the court of appeals, who sat ex officio because they were members of other superior courts, to now be relieved of their seats on the high court? Believing—or hoping—that the legislature had not intended to diminish their independence, the old court of appeals met and acquiesced, its members resigning so that the new court could be formed.[4] There would be further modifications of the judiciary, and the court of appeals would bend to the legislature. The court was not to judge the legislature, who represented the will of the people, by comparing statutes to judicial rules of reason or a construction of the state constitution that was set down by the court. The "Remonstrance" was a humble precedent for judicial review. It was far from Wythe's original vision of the court's role, and was more in keeping with Pendleton's.

Pendleton's leadership was strengthened by the legislation of 1788. Since Wythe headed the court of chancery, which was being reduced in number, it was natural that he would choose to stay there when the court of appeals was made a separate court. That removed him from the court of appeals. Pendleton was again chosen to preside over the high court, which, to Wythe's chagrin, could hear appeals from the court of chancery. Wythe was infuriated by Pendleton's opinions reversing his decisions. Wythe, a resident of Williamsburg, was the professor of law and police at the College of William and Mary. He was learned, and his opinions were more abstract and in great contrast to Pendleton's commonsense approach in his opinions.[5] In his political thoughts Pendleton, of Caroline County, was like his protégé John Taylor. A patriarch of Virginia conservatives, Pendleton became one of the original Old Republicans. He attained a higher judicial rank than Wythe, and he was elected president of the commonwealth's most distinguished gathering on the law, the ratifying convention. While he worked with Taylor to rally local conservatives to the Republican opposition, Wythe joined Marshall in organizing the Federalists. While Pendleton presided over the state's highest court of common law and had publicly defended the rights of juries, Wythe had chosen to remain a judge in the court of chancery, a court in equity law, which did not proceed by common law rules including the right of trial by jury.

The rivalry of Pendleton and Wythe was shortly followed by one between Spencer Roane and St. George Tucker; Roane was allied ideologically with Pendleton, and Tucker with Wythe. On the court of appeals, Roane became a great admirer of Pendleton, and, similar to Pendleton, Roane preferred a career in the state rather than the federal judiciary. Pendleton had turned down George Washington's requests that he accept a federal judicial appointment, and Roane could have tried to secure one from Jefferson but did not. (It was unlikely that Jefferson had considered appointing Roane chief justice, even if John Adams had not filled the position, but it was just as unlikely that Roane would have accepted the position if it had been offered to him.) Pendleton and Roane did not see their role in the state judiciary as inferior to that of federal judges. They felt that, if anything, their positions were superior, because they were the highest judges of the common law in their country. They did not want to be involved with a law foreign to the sovereign peoples of the states, with a federal and interstate law, or with international, commercial law.[6] Their legal experience and perspectives contrasted with those of Wythe and of his successor at the College of William and Mary, St. George Tucker.

While Roane grew up in Pendleton country, Essex County, Tucker enjoyed the town life of Williamsburg and did not wish to leave it even for the new state capital. Like Wythe, Tucker became friends with Marshall, and he did not feel committed to the cause of the state judiciary per se. He later accepted an appointment as the federal district court judge in Virginia. He shared Wythe's prejudices and appeared next in line to assume his mantle of leadership. He published his own edition of *Blackstone's Commentaries*. And he was appointed to a position on the court of appeals in 1803, after Pendleton's death. With Tucker on that court along with Roane, it was practically inevitable that the two would develop an antagonistic relationship. In their confrontations, Tucker represented professional law, the law of judges and of rationalism, and Roane represented the law of juries, of country lawyers, and of the common law.

Their differences were obvious before either was on the court of appeals, however. Unlike *Caton* and the "Remonstrance of the Judges"—the latter of dubious value, since the issue had not been brought before the court in a judicial manner—the 1793 decision in the General Court case of *Kamper v. Hawkins* provided a solid precedent for judicial review. The law in question was a part of the 1788 acts establishing the district courts. The power of injunction exercised by the chancery court in relation to judicial proceedings was given to the common law judges of the district courts. Yet, these district court judges were not also made chancery judges. The question was not whether the same individual could hold both common-law and equity-law judicial offices but whether a person appointed a common law judge could be given equity jurisdiction. The General Court, meeting in general session, held in *Kamper v. Hawkins* that the legislature had erred in the way it mixed the two jurisdictions in the district courts and declared that that portion of the legislation was unconstitutional. Roane thought the legislature had the power to give the two jurisdictions to the same judges, but that it needed to do so by creating two separate judicial appointments, one common law and the other equity. Though he joined the court's majority, he expressed doubts, similar to Pendleton's in *Caton*, about whether the judiciary should check the will of the legislature. In contrast, Tucker delivered the longest and most assertive opinion, which dealt mostly with the principle of judicial review rather than with the act in question.[7]

In his opinion, Tucker quoted from *The Federalist* as he explained that judicial review arose from the normal and proper functions of a judiciary. Legislatures enacted law, and courts interpreted and applied law and often had to deal with ambiguities involving two or more laws. It was inevitable that a conflict would arise between a law and a constitution. The court's objective was to interpret and to apply a law in conformity with a constitution, but when this could not be done, then the law must be declared void. Judicial review was the logical result of the development of a constitutional law superior to legislation. Tucker also advocated the court taking an active role in reviewing acts of the legislature. He stated that the judiciary should be "a barrier against the possible usurpations, or abuse of power in the other departments." He partly dissented from the court in that he wanted it to go further. He thought that the court should not just instruct the legislature that it had erred in the way it mixed the common-law and equity jurisdictions. The court should declare in general that this mixture of the two jurisdictions by the legislature was unconstitutional. Tucker's opinion in *Kamper* was in the spirit of Wythe's original assertion in *Caton*.[8]

At the same time the court was establishing the principle of judicial review, it had to grapple with the ambivalence of the state's constitution. There was a document called the "constitution," but it had been passed by the legislature in 1776 by majority vote. It was not a constitution in the sense of a grant of powers by the sovereign people to a government, nor one that could be amended only by again appealing to the people. Jefferson and Madison had earlier hoped that a convention would be called to draft a state constitution that would be put to the people for ratification. Of course, in terms of a federal constitution, Virginians in 1788 had met as a people in just such a convention, in an organic sovereign capacity—along with the people of the other states—and had helped to bring the United States Constitution to life. This ratifying convention—against all the warnings of the Anti-Federalists—had helped to create a supreme law for the nation (not that the Anti-Federalists recognized that this had occurred) that would be enforced and carried to all parts of the nation, and that thus would be carried into Virginia. Yet, ironically, Virginians had failed to do the same thing at the state level.[9]

There were, however, other kinds of constitutions. A fiction was accepted in the "Remonstrance of the Judges" and in *Kamper v. Hawkins*: the constitution of 1776 had been created by the people. A historical argument was advanced. The state constitution was made up of the acts and resolutions of the legislature in 1776 that had been accepted as the constitution over a period of time by the legislature, the courts, and the people. There had been no popular ratification, but the people had acquiesced. By *Kamper v. Hawkins*, state judges such as Tucker were trying to establish a state organic law, in Virginia's constitution of 1776, based on the sovereignty of the people, just as if they had met in convention.[10]

The historical basis for constitutionality was borrowed from the English. Laws became part of the constitution if they were accepted as such for a long enough time. But the court's position, as advanced by Tucker, was based upon written law and, specifically, upon those laws passed in 1776 called the constitution. The historical argument, however, could be carried a step farther. Any laws and customs that were accepted as being fundamental over a long enough period became part of the constitution. As practiced in England, this was the idea of the unwritten constitution. It was closer to what Roane envisioned as being Virginia's constitution. The fundamental principles of government could not be established by acts of a legislature or courts. Roane's opinion, like Pendleton's dissent from Wythe in *Caton*, was more expressive of the direction of the court than Tucker's.[11]

Kamper v. Hawkins, like the "Remonstrance," had been an assertion of judicial rights, but after the decision, there was no development of a written constitutional law separate from legislation that would be used by the courts, through judicial review, to check the state legislature. Instead, the judges would resist threats to their independence from another direction: the Marshall Court. In *Kamper v. Hawkins*, Tucker was interested in the establishment of a written constitutional law, the role of the judiciary in interpreting that law, and the judicial review of legislation. Roane would use state law and courts as a shield against the federal government. Tucker was limited to the review of laws by a comparison to a written constitution. Roane would find a source of power for the state judiciary in the tradition of the unwritten law.

It is interesting to compare both Roane's and Tucker's ideas concerning judicial review with those of Marshall, Roane's federal adversary. Like Tucker, Marshall drew upon *The Federalist* and the need for striking down laws that were at variance with the Constitution. Like Tucker, his opinion in *Marbury v. Madison* emphasized not just the supremacy of constitutional over statutory law but the fundamental character of a written constitution: it was not a tradition of vague principles but a definite law to which statutes could be compared. But, like Roane—and Pendleton—the Marshall Court would not make a practice of striking down acts of Congress. Only through cooperation with the Republican branches could they maintain the status of the judiciary and of national law and authority. Marshall would instead use the written Constitution and go through judicial review to strike down state legislation. And Roane would answer with the rights and principles of the ancient and unwritten constitution. The Supreme Court passing judgment upon the actions of a state would be countered by Roane. Marshall and Tucker may well have had their suspicions, in the 1790s, about Roane and where his principles might lead him. The two shared a note of alarm at the prospect of Roane's elevation to the court of appeals in 1794.[12]

Tucker Versus Roane

After Tucker also joined the court of appeals in 1803, a significant difference in how he and Roane viewed the law emerged in *Baring v. Reeder* (1806). They disagreed over how to use English common law. Tucker declared that English law before the Revolution applied as authority in America, and Roane, with the majority on the court, countered that Virginia's courts were bound neither by the law of England, before or after 1776, nor by those of sister states. Tucker asserted that there was a uniformity of law in some areas, where all common law courts agreed. Roane warned that there was always complexity and disagreement in the law, and he thought that such uniformity in theory would have little base in reality. Tucker, like Wythe, was viewing law in a more abstract and universal way, while Roane, like Pendleton, had a more commonsense approach and was more realistic—as well as provincial—in accepting diversity and the distinctiveness of Virginia law. The majority of the court agreed with Roane in this case. Roane would not find himself in the majority much longer, however.[13]

Tucker's and Roane's associates were three older men who had been judges since the Revolution, and these two were therefore the natural rivals for leadership in the state judiciary. After Pendleton's death, no one immediately replaced him as the leader of the court. After 1803, Peter Lyons presided over the court for only three years before becoming ill, and William Fleming was the acting president, then the president after 1809, of a court divided by the rivalry of Tucker and Roane. With Lyons ill and Paul Carrington retiring, there were only three active judges on the court after 1807. Taking the risk of having the court docket back up, the legislature decided not to replace either Carrington or Lyons and, instead, reduced the court to three judges—which left Fleming, Roane, and Tucker. A friendship developed between Fleming and Tucker that excluded Roane, which was the occasion for a crisis in the court.[14]

Tucker was more than willing to do the work of preparing opinions, and Fleming was inclined to allow him to do so, before conferences between the judges. This undermined the purpose of conferences and made Tucker a de facto president of the court—or, at least, that was how Roane viewed the matter. After 1807, for the next four years, Roane dissented more than at any other time during his tenure. Junior to Tucker in age but senior to him on the court, Roane was not disposed to assume a place second (or third) to him. The situation led Roane to suggest some significant reforms in the procedure of the court. In the fall term of 1808, Roane presented to the court a set of rule changes to end seriatim opinions. If the three judges had to meet and to confer with each other before a majority opinion was drafted, then Tucker's dominance of the court could possibly be ended. It could well be that the dynamic Roane believed he could better the thorough and methodical Tucker in verbal exchanges during conferences, but the odds were still against him, because, as long as Fleming remained, Roane could find himself in the minority. That was exactly what happened when Fleming and Tucker voted against his proposed rule changes. The following term, Roane resubmitted his reforms in a resolution before the court, but again, they were not accepted by Fleming and Tucker.[15]

Roane, undaunted, openly confronted Tucker and began a three-year feud. During a conference in 1809 while Tucker was reading an opinion suggesting, as Roane saw it, how they, or at least Fleming, should view the case, Roane, angered, went over to where Tucker was sitting, snatched the opinion out of his hands, threw it on the floor, and told him that he could not bear to listen to another one of his "long, tedious, and ridiculous" opinions. The next day, there was a similar occurrence. Tucker, affronted, refused to meet with Roane except in open court sessions, and would meet in conference only with Fleming. Tucker asked Fleming to write an account of the episodes. Fleming did and agreed with Tucker that Roane's conduct was entirely improper. Roane's moment of anger appeared to have placed him in an even worse situation than before. His next step was to carry the feud to open court. If he could not achieve a full discussion of the questions before them in conference, he would do it during the public courtroom proceedings. Tucker again appealed to Fleming, and again, the president of the court sided with Tucker. Fleming held that judges openly conferring upon a decision in the courtroom slowed the business of the court. He admitted, however, that a judge could propose a question for the bar or court, or could present his own views on a case before the court. This was enough for Roane. Although he worked with a friend, Creed Taylor, a judge of the General Court, who tried to mediate a peace in the dispute, Roane refused to desert his principles. Through Judge Taylor, Roane proposed that, in the best interest of the court and in order for them to fulfill their judicial duties, Tucker should give way and resume a full conference among the judges. Tucker remained adamant in refusing to deal with Roane.[16]

Tucker saw the dispute as only a personal rivalry that had been caused solely by Roane. It is understandable that, being the recipient of continuous insults and verbal abuse, Tucker referred to his experience as "the purgatory of my life." He believed he was being treated harshly by a man he had never harmed. Roane went beyond the bounds of decorum and revealed his temper and his inclination to get into disputes. Both of them refused to compromise, however, and Tucker exacerbated the situation by avoiding judicial conferences. He also failed to see that there was more involved in the dispute than personal differences. There was an emotional, an ideological, and even a cultural dimension to this rivalry between the country boy from Essex County and the college professor. Tucker shared with others his own confidence that he was absolutely right and was not at all at fault in the affair. Roane, less confident, gave an account of himself to others, including Fleming, and even Tucker. He explained that he firmly believed that Tucker had been slowly, methodically developing his power. Roane had risen in a mad rage against what he perceived to be a threat. He believed that he was acting in defense of his rights, and the lengths to which he was prepared to go and his persistence proved too much for his adversary to bear. Influenced as well by another crisis in his life, Tucker would soon leave the court.[17]

The reduction of the court of appeals to three judges had caused a steady increase in undecided cases on the dockets. In 1811, the legislature decided to return the court to five members and to lengthen its terms, without raising the judges' salaries. In a statement reminiscent of the 1788 "Remonstrance," Tucker declared that the act was unconstitutional, because it compromised the independence of the judges by adding duties without adding salary. Roane was not disturbed by the legislature's action, and, in this instance, he was joined by Fleming. The majority of the court therefore did not hold that the act was unconstitutional, and there was no new remonstrance. Fleming and Roane remained on the court, while Tucker protested the legislature's action in his letter of resignation. Tucker had wanted to leave his purgatory, and had not wanted to move from Williamsburg (which he felt the longer term in Richmond would require). He tried to exit on a note of principle, but the context of his resignation—the dispute with Roane—was generally known, and his move was seen as a retreat.[18]

The legislature then appointed Francis T. Brooke, from Essex County, and William H. Cabell, a former governor, to the court of appeals. The appointment of John Coalter, Tucker's son-in-law, might have appeared to have been an attempt to balance the court, but he was not inclined to continue the feud. In fact, there were fewer dissents than before, and Roane did not get into further disputes with the new judges.[19] He was partially successful in obtaining open conferences in which to discuss the questions of law and to come to some agreement on a majority decision before the judges wrote their opinions. And issues arose that allowed him to assume a leadership role.

In 1813, the Supreme Court would hand the state judiciary a challenge, and Roane would be ready to meet it. Tucker would have been unable to head the resistance. Roane's actions would represent a jurisprudence that was far from Tucker's image of the law and the courts' proper role. The Supreme Court's appellate jurisdiction and judicial review of state law was just the kind of rational law that Professors Wythe and Tucker had advocated. Within a year after his resignation, Tucker accepted an appointment as the federal district court judge in Virginia. While he sat on the federal circuit court developing his friendship with Marshall, and while Fleming, old and ill, remained away from the court of appeals, Roane—though officially never more than the acting president—finally filled the void that had been created by Pendleton's death in 1803. Virginia had another judicial leader.

Roane achieved notoriety through his opposition to Marshall. It should be noted that their antagonism was intense because they were actually similar in many ways, from believing that law was mixed with interests, politics, and power to envisioning a great role for the law in America: one saw it as a positive, unifying force that tied the nation together, and the other saw it as a protective and defensive or negative force that resisted centralization.

The antagonism between these two Virginians would appear to be—unlike the Pendleton-Wythe or the Roane-Tucker rivalries—more a division in terms of federal-state relations. But, the internal division within the state was also present from the commencement of their duel. Marshall had never been and could not be seen as just the federal foreigner. He was a Virginian tied up in the society, the politics, and the economics of the state. He was the commonwealth's leading Federalist and its most prominent professional jurist. His duties in the federal judiciary placed him between the circuit court in Raleigh and the Supreme Court in Washington with terms of the circuit court in Richmond. As a planter, he had his own interests to look after in the state, as he did in the Fairfax litigation. The Fairfax cases literally ranged throughout his career as a politician, lawyer, and judge and provided the occasion for the beginning of his antagonism with Roane. In broad strokes, this litigation well exemplified the battle between two kinds of law. It pitted Marshall, as the high Federalist, against Roane, as Anti-Federalist or Old Republican, with Marshall on the inside courting wealth and power and Roane on the outside defending the rights of juries and local interests.

5

The Fairfax Litigation

A Model in

Anti-Constitutional Law

The cause of the Fairfax litigation was the ambiguity of the legal status of the land that had been owned by Thomas Fairfax, sixth Baron Fairfax of Cameron. He had been the proprietor of about a third of the populated area of Virginia—which included the Northern Neck and much of the northern Valley. This had been practically a proprietary colony within a royal colony. Virginians believed that this feudal remnant had ended with the Revolution. Yet, a federal treaty, the ratification of the Constitution, and the establishment of a federal judiciary would assure that, years after independence was won, this proprietary domain could be reestablished through the Fairfax litigation.

During the War of Independence, because Lord Fairfax remained neutral, and was old and without children, the state allowed him to possess dual citizenship and did not declare him an alien enemy. When he died in 1781, without direct heirs in Virginia, the General Assembly assumed that his land passed to the state, did not pass laws for a general confiscation, and, during the 1780s, put up for sale the land that he had not developed or sold—what he called the waste and ungranted land—which involved about half of the original proprietary domain. Matters were complicated, however, because Lord Fairfax had willed his American property to a British subject, Denny Martin, his nephew, on the condition that he change his name to Fairfax, which he had done. The treaty of 1783 guaranteed British property against confiscation. This was of little concern to most Virginians as long as the state did not recognize the validity of the treaty. The ratification of the Constitution changed this, making the treaty the law of the land, and the establishment of a federal judiciary provided courts wherein British subjects could seek justice. Henry's party had made the Fairfax claims an issue in the Virginia ratifying convention. John Marshall, a lawyer for the Fairfax family, had assured the convention that the federal judiciary would never be used to support such claims against the interests of Virginians.[1]

When Denny Martin Fairfax attempted to collect his inheritance, his claim included the waste and ungranted land that had been sold by the state. The test case for the waste and ungranted land involved a tract in Shenandoah County that had been purchased from the state by David Hunter, who opened the litigation at both the state and federal levels. (Hunter, from a leading family in the northern Valley, was a land speculator.) The question was whether the sale of the disputed land by the state was legal. Hunter lost in 1794 in the state district court at Winchester as well as in the federal circuit court. He continued in possession of the disputed land while he appealed the cases, which had entered both dockets as *Hunter v. Fairfax's Devisee*. The loss had been particularly disappointing at the state level, where St. George Tucker had refused to sanction the position held by Henry's party, that the Fairfax land had been properly confiscated. However, he went on to spell out the common law procedure—the inquest of office found—modified by Virginia statute, that the government should have followed, and could still instigate. Juries should be called at the state district court level to determine whether a claimant could inherit the land.[2]

In 1794, another part of the litigation came into play. Could the plantations of Lord Fairfax, the land he had developed for his own personal use, which had not been confiscated and sold by the state, pass to a British heir? It was realized that this question could be intertwined with the issue over the waste and ungranted land. The state could bring actions against the titles of all the land developed as the Fairfax plantations in order to bargain for a clear title to the disputed waste and ungranted land that it had been selling. Linking the two issues was the easiest alternative for the state to pursue, because it would have been an arduous task to escheat each tract that had been sold by the state. It was a simpler matter to move against the plantations. Also, the latter could be accomplished—unlike the former—before the appeal of *Hunter v. Fairfax's Devisee* was heard in the Supreme Court. This appeal provided the state with plenty of motivation. The Court could determine both that the sales of the waste and ungranted land were illegal and that the treaty barred future actions being taken against any of the Fairfax titles. Further, it could be expected that Britain would add articles protecting former British property in the treaty that was being negotiated by John Jay. Fairfax could challenge Virginia through the Supreme Court, but the state could threaten him by escheating his plantations. Juries were called in district courts, and they found against Englishmen inheriting the Virginia estates. Fairfax challenged the procedure in the state district court at Dumfries, lost, and appealed the case to the court of appeals, in *Fairfax v. Commonwealth*. With each side capable of damaging the other, by 1796, the situation was ripe for a compromise.[3]

The development of an out-of-court settlement was also desirable because of yet another dimension to the issue. The possibility of losing his plantations to the state had encouraged Fairfax to sell them. If they were purchased by Americans, preferably Virginians, then the problem of Englishmen inheriting land in Virginia would be solved. The idea of purchasing the Fairfax plantations appealed to Henry Lee—war hero, politician, and avid land speculator—who, as governor of the state, directed the escheat proceedings against the Fairfax plantations. After Denny Martin Fairfax had decided to rid himself of his problems in America, the next step came easily enough. It came as no surprise that the lawyers who handled his affairs in Virginia, John Marshall and his brother, James, would have the first chance to purchase the plantations. To raise money, Lee and the Marshalls joined together to form a syndicate (which also included Rawleigh Colston, an in-law of the Marshalls, and John Ambler, a relative of John Marshall's wife, Polly). James Marshall was assisted in making European contacts, by Robert Morris, his father-in-law, and he went abroad to secure loans. In addition to trying to secure money for the transaction, John Marshall also wanted to make sure that, if needed, there was a route to the Supreme Court. In the event that the Eleventh

Amendment would prevent Fairfax from carrying his suit against Virginia into the Supreme Court, Marshall, as a purchaser of the Fairfax plantations, challenged the escheat proceedings in a case similar to *Fairfax v. Commonwealth*. After a loss in a state district court, the case was appealed to the court of appeals as *Marshall v. Commonwealth*.[4]

Denny Martin Fairfax offered to deed to Virginia the waste and ungranted land in return for a clear title to his plantations, so that he could sell them to Americans. The legislature accepted his offer. John Marshall managed an act through the General Assembly that became known as the Compromise of 1796. All of the principal parties gained something in the settlement: Fairfax swapped the vicissitudes of holding former proprietary land in postrevolutionary Virginia for 20,000 pounds sterling; the Marshall syndicate received some of the choicest plantations in northern Virginia; the state received a clear title to the waste and ungranted land, which made legitimate its sales of that land; and David Hunter and others who had purchased that land from the state received clear titles. This compromise appeared to end the litigation. The appeal of *Hunter v. Fairfax's Devisee* before the Supreme Court was dismissed. In *Fairfax v. Commonwealth*, since the point at issue—the titles to the Fairfax plantations—had already been settled, the court of appeals ruled (in 1798) for the Fairfax-Marshall side. And *Marshall v. Commonwealth* was not brought to trial.[5] But some questions remained. On the one hand, nothing was said about rents. Could the Marshall syndicate collect rents as the proprietor had done, and could back rents be collected? On the land the proprietor had sold, he had collected a permanent annual amount called a quitrent. Could Fairfax still claim these rents? On the other hand, would the state repeal the compromise legislation? It should also be noted that not all of the litigation was dropped following the compromise.

The Marshalls, having gained much through brilliant maneuvering, now faced the long task of paying for their plantations and making them turn a profit, and the Marshalls intended to collect any and all rents they could lay claim to. They sought to purchase from Fairfax all the rights to quitrents that had been collected by the lord proprietor. Although this attempt was not public knowledge, some of the citizens of the Northern Neck suspected as much. Not only were these landlords prominent Federalists in what was—by the end of the century—a Republican state, but James Marshall was not a master of public relations. While his brother, the chief justice, attended to his Supreme

Court and circuit-riding duties, James Marshall managed the family affairs in the Northern Neck. He was one of John Adams's "Midnight Appointments" whose office was terminated by the in-coming Republicans. His haughty manner appeared, to his neighbors, more appropriate to a British monarchy than to a republic, and it was believed that he wished to play "Lord Marshall" and to assume the privileges and expect the feudal dues owed to a proprietor. When he took up residence in Winchester and informed the citizens of the town that he would revive the old annual quitrents formerly collected by the proprietor, they refused to pay. The Marshalls went to court, at the state district level in *Marshall v. Conrad*, and lost.[6]

In the appeal of that case, the majority of the court of appeals determined that the disputed payment could be collected, because it was not technically a quitrent. The Marshalls had won, but two aspects of that decision tempered their victory. One was a dissenting opinion by Roane, which foreshadowed the direction in which the court was headed. In that opinion he recalled that John Marshall had once told the ratifying convention that the proprietary rents would never again be collected; now, Marshall and his brother were the ones collecting them. Nonetheless, there should not have been any Fairfax plantations to buy. Criticizing the legislature for agreeing to the Compromise of 1796, Roane declared that the juries that had threatened the Fairfax titles should have been allowed to complete their work. Instead, the titles to land that would have gone to the state were being used by the Marshalls to extend their claims to rents. Had the Revolution been fought so that, years later, lords could still collect their feudal dues? On the point at issue, Roane stated that the rent being collected in Winchester had always been known to be a quitrent; was similar to other fixed, permanent, annual dues called quitrents that were collected by a king or noble; and should therefore be considered a quitrent by the court.[7]

The other aspect of the court of appeals decision that tempered the Marshalls' victory was that Roane's dissent encouraged their tenants to continue their resistance. This resistance expanded beyond Winchester, and the Marshalls were forced to take all tenants to court or to give up the rent. They faced years of continuous litigation, and would encounter, at the state district court level, juries of their disloyal subjects. They realized that their situation was desperate. They wanted their claims to be founded on more than the Compromise of 1796, because that act made no mention of rents. They wanted to arrange a suit that would allow them to base their claims upon the proprietor's title secured by the treaty of 1783 and the Constitution.[8] But any new case would come after the passage of the Compromise of 1796. This was the context for an otherwise mysterious continuation of a suit that had apparently ended in 1796.

The case of *Hunter v. Fairfax's Devisee* had never been struck from the docket (of the court of appeals) and was continued through hearings, decisions, and appeals to *Martin v. Hunter's Lessee* in 1816, not by David Hunter (who had no substantial interests in the matter after 1806, when he sold the land that was in theory the subject of the controversy) or by the state—since the status of the waste and ungranted land was no longer in dispute—but by the Fairfax-Marshall side. The case had the advantages of, first, being one in which the litigants had already agreed upon the facts, which meant that the Marshalls would not have to suffer the issue being put before a jury; and, second, of predating 1796. They hoped that the judges of the court of appeals would not go beyond the state district court record to include the compromise, but the Marshalls watched as the majority that had ruled for them in *Marshall v. Conrad* disappeared. Peter Lyons and Paul Carrington retired (and were not replaced by the legislature) and Tucker—who, at least, had decided for them earlier, although not affirming the point of law they desired—withdrew from the case due to a conflict of interest. (Tucker's son, Henry, had married a niece of David Hunter.) That left Fleming and Roane.[9]

In *Hunter v. Fairfax's Devisee*, the court of appeals ruled against the Fairfax-Marshall side, refusing to bar the Compromise of 1796 and entering it upon the record. Fleming simply revised Tucker's original opinion, adding the conditions of the compromise. The state had not properly confiscated the disputed land, and had had to go through common law proceedings to do so, but the Compromise of 1796 changed this. The waste and ungranted land had been deeded to Virginia in exchange for the state's allowing Fairfax to sell his plantations to the Marshall syndicate. After the decision in this case, after the opinions of both Tucker and Fleming, the Marshalls' basis for their titles was, first, that Virginia had not confiscated Fairfax land, but could escheat it; and, second, that the state agreed in legislation to honor their title. But, this legislation could be repealed, and the escheat proceedings could be reconvened with local juries drawn from the neighbors, relatives, and friends of the tenants of "Lord Marshall." (Since the court of appeals in *Fairfax v. Commonwealth* had based its decision solely upon the Compromise of 1796, the bar to legal actions against the Fairfax titles could be removed by a repeal of that act.)[10]

The Marshalls also had to suffer another attack from the bench by Roane. In his opinion, he declared that the Fairfax-Marshall side had agreed earlier, to give up one half of the proprietary domain to get the other half, and now, they sought to throw out the agreement to gain the whole. They got the Fairfax plantations. Now they wanted all the proprietary rents as well. Roane again blasted the compromise and contended that the state had never needed any leverage against Denny Martin Fairfax. There had been no need to strike a bargain. Why escheat the waste and ungranted land if it had already been confiscated? Roane agreed with Tucker's earlier opinion that the state could go through a common law escheat procedure. They disagreed over whether the state had the option of administering a general confiscation. Roane took this opportunity to place the view of Henry and his party in the 1780s on the record of Virginia's highest court. The state had preferred a general confiscation to specifically escheating each individual tract of land. This was within the power of the sovereign state of Virginia, and was not affected by either the treaty of 1783 or the Constitution. It should be noted that Roane looked to the common law to support his position. He believed that under the broadest construction, the treaty of 1783 applied only to confiscation that was occasioned exclusively by the war. But, after 1776, the sovereign state of Virginia, through the common law, could move against the property of any alien.[11]

Roane declared that if the Compromise of 1796 had not been enacted, the court of appeals in *Fairfax v. Commonwealth* would have upheld the verdicts of the juries against the Fairfax titles. He had envisioned nothing short of another confrontation of juries of Virginians, backed by their courts, acting against a foreign threat. The state had been concerned about possible actions by the Supreme Court, but that did not worry Roane. The Marshalls had duped the legislature into thinking that a compromise was necessary. As a result, all that the state had accomplished in 1796 was to receive land it had already rightfully possessed in return for giving up land it was in the process of rightfully gaining. Roane did not want to see any such further injustice inflicted upon Virginians.[12]

From the Marshalls' perspective, it was obvious that the court of appeals was becoming hostile to their interest. They had failed to sidestep the compromise, and their only recourse was an appeal to the Supreme Court. It should not be supposed that John Marshall thus enthusiastically made the final move in a long-thought-out plan to have the Supreme Court and the court of appeals join in battle. Neither as a land-dispute litigant nor as the chief justice could he have expected a quick and conclusive victory. He and his brother were apprehensive and concerned because, if they were not careful, they could find themselves on the winning side as makers of a constitutional-law precedent and on the losing side as landholders in Virginia. What was most important was not the Marshall Court's decision but how well it would fare back home.

The Supreme Court made an unsurprising decision in favor of the Fairfax-Marshall side in *Fairfax's Devisee v. Hunter's Lessee* (1813). Due to his personal involvement, Marshall did not participate officially. Joseph Story gave the majority opinion. He ignored the Compromise of 1796, part of the record of the appeal from the court of appeals, though to comply with section 25 of the Judiciary Act of 1789 the Court was supposed to use the record from the lower court. Story also went beyond the record to include the Jay Treaty. He determined that Virginia had not properly confiscated the Fairfax land before 1783, could not legally do so after 1783, and could not legally escheat any of it due to the Jay Treaty. (Story included the Jay Treaty, because it confirmed the articles in the treaty of 1783 that protected British claimants from actions taken against them because of their alien status, and because it applied to any kind of escheat action, unlike the treaty of 1783, which, it could be argued, was restricted to unlawful confiscations.) This gave the Fairfax-Marshall side the right to all the plantations and the waste and ungranted land. The Marshalls finally received a solid judicial basis for their rights and claims to lands and rents under federal treaties.[13]

On the surface, this decision was ample proof that the Anti-Federalists, back in 1788, had been correct. The Supreme Court would have allowed the reestablishment of the Fairfax domain. As Henry had warned, Virginians could not trust federal judges to safeguard their interests against foreigners. Of course, those of the Anti-Federalist persuasion had the consolation of knowing that most of Story's opinion made for little more than poor federal-state relations. In the law, it was irrelevant to the extent that it gave to the Fairfax-Marshall side a right to land that had already been given up and deeded to the state. Regardless of the Court's decision, the Compromise of 1796 had been agreed to by all parties, and the legislation had not been reviewed and declared unconstitutional, and therefore was still in effect. It would have been more judicious on Story's part to have founded the Fairfax-Marshall title originally in the treaties and the Constitution, and then to mark out how and to what extent their compromise with Virginia had affected their title. Instead, by ignoring what was part of the record of the appeal and awarding land that had long been deeded away, Story's opinion appeared improper, anachronistic, and high-handed. If there was any doubt about it being high-handed, the conclusion of his opinion was a lecture to Roane on the value of due process of law as a protection for individual rights. The Supreme Court had reversed Virginia's highest court in *Fairfax's Devisee v. Hunter's Lessee* and returned the case to the court of appeals to be carried out. It was now the turn of Roane and the Virginia Supreme Court of Appeals to respond.[14]

The court of appeals—which, after Tucker's departure, consisted of Francis Brooke, William Cabell, and John Coalter along with Fleming and Roane—questioned a number of points in Story's opinion. A large part of the litigation concerned only state common law (not touching upon the Constitution, treaty, or federal statute), and no valid federal jurisdiction could be claimed regarding it. Story had illegally discarded the compromise legislation from the record of the appeal. And his opinion was faulty in that the treaty that related to the issues in the 1780s and early 1790s was the treaty of 1783, not the Jay Treaty. (Marshall later realized that Story's use of the Jay Treaty instead of the treaty of 1783 in this case had been a mistake.) There was the problem, too, of how the Virginia court could possibly comply with the ruling. Was it to grant land to Fairfax that had been deeded by him to the state? The decision and Story's opinion were taken as little more than a challenge, and the Virginia judges intended to respond. They went beyond the technical points and questioned the process itself that the Supreme Court expected them to exercise.[15]

The Virginia Supreme Court of Appeals called before them the bar of Virginia, to consider a question of great magnitude: as the highest state court, having made a final decision concerning state law in *Hunter v. Fairfax's Devisee*, would the court accept a reversal of that decision by the Supreme Court through an appeal—*Fairfax's Devisee v. Hunter's Lessee*—brought under section 25 of the Judiciary Act of 1789? The constitutionality of the section—and the appellate jurisdiction it authorized—was the main point at issue in *Hunter v. Martin, Devisee of Fairfax* (1814). A basic problem emerged in the hearing concerning section 25. Section 25 interconnected the federal and state governments in a way that violated dual sovereignty and went against the spirit of the Constitution by allowing the Supreme Court to act as the final court of appeals for each state, even on state law, and to send reversals back through the state courts to be carried out. But the two systems of government were supposed to be separate. After the judges of the court of appeals had formed their opinions, they agreed that if either party in a suit considered the Constitution, treaty, or federal statute to be involved, then the case should be entered in the federal judiciary at the commencement of the litigation. There should be no appeal from the state's highest court to the Supreme Court. The First Congress had erred in establishing this procedure. The court of appeals engaged in the judicial review of section 25 of the Judiciary Act of 1789 and declared it unconstitutional. Neither the Supreme Court's jurisdiction to hear *Fairfax's Devisee v. Hunter's Lessee* nor its reversal of the decision in *Hunter v. Fairfax's Devisee* was recognized.[16] The court of appeals had, in effect, denied that the Supreme Court alone determined the law of the land throughout the United States.

Roane, in his opinion, questioned whether federal judges should oversee the state judiciaries. Was there any doubt as to the ability of state judges or their devotion to justice or their impartiality in the law? Why had the Constitution obliged all state judges to swear an oath to uphold it unless it was expected that state courts would have concurrent jurisdiction with the federal courts on constitutional matters? The Supremacy Clause in Article Six meant that state judges as well as federal judges were to consider the Constitution, treaty, and federal statute made in pursuance thereof to be superior to state constitutions and laws. There was one supreme Constitution, but there were two separate sets of governments with two separate judiciaries, and neither of them had appellate jurisdiction over the other. This would prevent a uniformity in the law, but it would be only an inconvenience compared to the threat to liberty and states' rights caused by a federal appellate jurisdiction.[17]

The Supreme Court responded, in *Martin v. Hunter's Lessee* (1816), by upholding both its decision in *Fairfax's Devisee v. Hunter's Lessee* and the constitutionality of section 25. With Marshall again absent but behind the scenes, Story wrote the majority opinion. Marshall concurred with every word of it. The problems that had been raised concerning section 25 were dismissed. The Court did not act directly upon the states. When an appellant brought a case before the Court and there was a reversal, either a state supreme court would be requested to see to having it executed or the Court would see to the execution itself. There would not be an attempt to compel the state judiciary to act. Story also defended section 25 by using a historical argument. Since it had been acquiesced in by Congress, the Supreme Court, and the state judiciaries for twenty-five years without a challenge, it should be accepted as a proper means to establish appellate jurisdiction. The Court dismissed the distinction between a final appeal and a removal of a case from a state court at the commencement of the litigation. Both were applications of appellate power. It did not matter when an appeal was made to the federal judiciary: at the beginning, middle, or end of the litigation.[18]

Story, mainly responding to Roane, defended appellate jurisdiction by citing the Supremacy Clause in the Constitution and by stressing the need for uniformity. There could be no supreme law of the land if the Constitution, treaty, and federal statute were interpreted independently by every state supreme court. Also, he attacked concurrent jurisdiction on federal law by answering Roane's rhetorical questions about state judges. Yes, those who drafted the Constitution did expect that local prejudice and interests would bias the decisions of state judges in a manner detrimental to the good of the nation. State courts could not be entrusted with carrying out the supreme law of the land.[19]

Having declared that there must be one ultimate appellate court, the Supreme Court did not return *Martin v. Hunter's Lessee* to the court of appeals. Like *Marbury v. Madison,* this was a wise move, because the Court knew it could not have enforced a reversal. As matters stood, however, two courts had concurrently asserted their opinions on constitutional questions. No final decision had been made, and no single rule of law had been established. This litigation revealed the problem that the Supreme Court had in checking the states through its appellate jurisdiction. In the *Martin v. Hunter's Lessee* case, the Court upheld section 25 and set a constitutional law precedent for nationalism, but failed to secure Virginia's compliance with its decision. The Court affirmed the original judgment of the state district court at Winchester in favor of the Fairfax claims, but nothing came of this, and, therefore, this part of the litigation ended without the Supreme Court's ruling affecting the actions of the state.[20]

Regrettably for the Marshalls, their personal involvement in this litigation continued unabated. Since both the Supreme Court and the court of appeals had declared that their decisions were final, much depended on which decision the state courts followed. Their choosing the state's highest court meant that the Supreme Court's opinion was null and void for all practical purposes. In the suits involving the former Fairfax lands, the claims based on a federal treaty were not recognized, which kept open the status of the rents (because this was not mentioned in the Compromise of 1796). The Marshalls' dilemma was not over a question of law but in the force of the law. There was little to be gained in appealing another case to the Supreme Court as long as the state judiciary refused to be bound by the Court's ruling. They were beset by the immense problems of dealing with an obstinate popular resistance against which the power of the law and courts on their side appeared to be ineffective.[21]

While John Marshall continued his quest to win his point of law in litigation in Virginia, he championed a uniform law of the land as chief justice in such cases as *McCulloch v. Maryland* and *Cohens v. Virginia* and as an advocate of nationalism trying to win public opinion. At all levels, he encountered Roane. Indeed, *Hunter v. Martin, Devisee of Fairfax* was the beginning of the revival of a states' rights movement in Virginia, and, in response, *Martin v. Hunter's Lessee* began the era of the Marshall Court's defense of nationalism. Along with the battle between the courts, there was a battle between the judges, and the antagonism between Marshall and Roane would go beyond the courtroom to a duel in the press.

Their debate continued from the antagonism in the Fairfax litigation. There was the provincial and Old Republican position expressed by Roane, that Virginians would determine by their own juries and judges the legal questions most pressing to them, and that their interests must be safeguarded against all those construed as foreign. The opposite view was expressed in the *Martin* case and expounded upon by Marshall, that there must be a single judicial system and a uniformity of the law, which was necessary for the nation and would be the best means to assure an equal and impartial protection to all, Virginian or foreign. Neither side bowed to the other. *Martin v. Hunter's Lessee* set a nationalist precedent. *Hunter v. Martin, Devisee of Fairfax* stood in effect as Virginia's refusal to submit to the Supreme Court's appellate authority.

6

Against the "Era of Good Feelings" Round of Reform

The Threat at the Federal Level

Martin v. Hunter's Lessee in 1816 ushered in an era that witnessed most of the Marshall Court's great nationalist opinions. The opinions coincided with the nationalist mood at the close of the War of 1812, the end of the first party system, and a postwar boom—the Era of Good Feelings. The talk was of roads, canals, banks, and public education, and there was a demand for state as well as federal internal improvements. In Virginia, attention also returned to legal and constitutional reform. There would again be a call for a state constitutional convention. And a spirit of democracy rose west of the Blue Ridge that threatened the gentry-dominated local governments. The old order had again been challenged. A new round of reform had begun.

In *McCulloch v. Maryland* (1819), Marshall sanctified the Hamiltonian broad construction of the Constitution in favor of the Bank of the United States and replied to the states' rights arguments that the court of appeals had advanced, an opportunity denied to him in the Fairfax cases. Roane, leader of the court of appeals, responded, writing as "Hampden," in the *Richmond Enquirer*, by condemning the *McCul-*

loch opinion, which, he contended, would enable Congress to legislate in all matters, the very power that had been asserted by Parliament.[1]

Roane called on Virginians to protect their independence and liberty. He was afraid that prosperous times, after the war, would lull them into complacency. The Country, republican ideological rhetoric was advanced against the banking and government-expansion policies of the Era of Good Feelings. Then came the panic of 1819. If there had been any hopes that Virginia tobacco planters would escape from indebtedness, or that a new prosperity would keep Virginians in their state and indifferent to the lure of better times in the Cotton South, these hopes ended. Virginians had to face serious economic problems and a decline in the influence of the Old Dominion. The great age was over. There were alternatives, however, to giving up and leaving Virginia. One could romanticize the past and the life of a country gentleman while blaming banks for one's misfortune. The Country-republican ideology gave all the right rationales for others having caused Virginia's apparent demise. With the panic of 1819 and bad times ahead, Virginians were ready to answer Roane's call and to rally to the opposition banner. Thomas Ritchie put his *Richmond Enquirer*, the state's leading paper, to the task; the legislature debated resolutions against *McCulloch;* and John Marshall sighed to Story that the "Spirit of Virginia" was again rising. Marshall noted that Roane's essays were not having a great effect on the towns but were having a considerable influence on the country. Roane called for another interposition by the state legislature, as in 1798, and another popular revolution, as in 1800. Those who joined him looked back to *Hunter v. Martin, Devisee of Fairfax* as the first act of their renewed opposition.[2]

Marshall realized what could result from a revived states' rights movement led by Virginia. The development of the American nation was not secure enough to weather such a revival uncontested. The Supreme Court had to defend the national government against an attempt to replay the 1798–1800 scenario—or worse, an attempt to reverse the decision of 1788. Marshall saw the states' rights movement as a revival of Anti-Federalism. The issues of the 1780s were again being debated. Was America going to be a nation or a league of sovereign states? Marshall—believing that the thread that held America together, the federal supreme law of the land, was being threatened and that it needed to be defended—took up this cause in the papers, writing as a "Friend of the Union" and "A Friend of the Constitution."[3]

While the judges debated, while economic problems followed the panic of 1819, there were the Missouri crisis and the Missouri Compromise of 1820, which were attacked in resolutions passed by the legislature. Given the importance of slavery issues from the 1830s to the Civil War, it must be noted that those issues were not the cause of Virginia's renewed opposition to nationalism and the federal government. Virginia's traditional, conservative ideological and constitutional views were already established before 1820. The Old Republicans had from the first denounced giving in to the forces of change—or, as they charged—to corruption and tyranny; Roane had renewed state interposition in the Fairfax cases; and, in the bad times following the panic of 1819, Virginians were rallying to the cause—all before the issue of placing conditions upon Missouri's entrance into the union arose in Congress. The politicizing of slavery to curb the expansion of the slave-labor plantation economy into new territories was one of a number of ways a growing national government could hurt Virginians' interests. Other issues included the use of the federal government to raise the prices farmers paid because of protective tariffs to build industry in the Northeast, and the use of public money to subsidize western development through internal improvement projects. All of this was coming at the same time Virginians were realizing that their state, declining in population and wealth, was going to have less influence on directing the federal government. This reminded them of the 1780s, when many were concerned that establishing a new federal government would allow outside creditors to take Virginians to trial. What had changed since the 1780s was that there were even fewer Virginians who believed that a growing national government could aid their interests. The Marshall Court opinions, the panic of 1819, and the Missouri crisis all added to the sense that, once again, Virginians needed to protect themselves against threats from the outside. And, as Roane warned them of what could come from a superior federal law, the judicial controversy continued in the same context with *Cohens v. Virginia* (1821).[4]

The *Cohens* case dealt with a conflict between state and federal law. The Cohen brothers were arrested in Virginia and were found guilty and fined by the state for selling lottery tickets—illegal in Virginia—for a Washington, D.C., lottery authorized by Congress. The case was appealed through section 25 of the Judiciary Act of 1789 to the Supreme Court. The state argued that this was not one of the few situations prescribed by the Constitution in which a state could be a party before the Supreme Court and that a state could not be sued. Resolutions were passed in the legislature denying the Court's jurisdiction. The Court declared that the commonwealth was not being sued, nor was the case being brought before it because a state was a party, but that the Court had jurisdiction because a question of federal law was involved. This case provided the Marshall Court with an opportunity to defend nationalism and to take a direct shot at states' rights Virginia. The Court decided in favor of the Old Dominion, however, on the specific point at issue, by ruling that the Cohens' selling of lottery tickets had been illegal. Once again, the constitutionality of section 25 was upheld by the Court, but there was no practical effect and significance to the claim of appellate jurisdiction over the Virginia judiciary. The major significance of *Cohens* was in setting a nationalist precedent. The Supreme Court's actions were denounced within the state.[5]

Roane again responded, writing under the pseudonym "Algernon Sidney." Taylor produced another of his treatises, *Construction Construed and Constitutions Vindicated*, on the heresies of the Supreme Court. Jefferson joined in publicly criticizing the Marshall Court. And resolutions for limiting the Supreme Court's jurisdiction on state law were discussed in the House of Delegates. Again, as with the English opposing Stuart kings, or with the American colonists during the Revolution, Virginians could look to their government for a forum and a means of opposition, for protection against tyranny. As during the Revolution, and in 1790 and 1798, their state legislature passed resolutions. And their judges, led by Roane, had made it clear that the judiciary would also play a major role in the movement to counter the Marshall Court's nationalism. The General Assembly, repeating its 1798 action, interposed itself between its people and the federal government. Resolutions were passed declaring that there was no federal jurisdiction over cases determined by the state judiciary. The state would not recognize the legality of an appeal from a state court to the Supreme Court as authorized by section 25 of the Judiciary Act of 1789. *Hunter v. Martin, Devisee of Fairfax* had been confirmed by the legislature.[6]

By the 1820s, Roane, Ritchie, Taylor, and the Old Republicans, having rallied Virginians to the opposition banner, had to expand their concern beyond the Marshall Court. The panic of 1819 had revived criticism of national banking; the Missouri crisis and Compromise had added the potential for a volatile sectional issue; and the fear mounted that northerners and westerners would form an alliance for tariffs and federally funded internal improvements. Also, Monroe was completing the Virginia Dynasty. Who was going to be the next president, and would his policies be nationalist and hostile to their principles? The Old Republicans had to contemplate an opposition to the entire national government, as in the 1790s.

A majority in the state legislature in 1821 had confirmed the principles of the Old Republicans. Basically there was an alliance in the 1820s that was similar to the one in the 1790s between Anti-Federalists and Republicans. In the 1820s, Republican party moderates who had endorsed the banking and internal improvement projects of the Era of Good Feelings and who remained receptive to Court-style policies—if implemented by the state—appealed to extreme or Old Republican types through using the Country, republican rhetoric. They could on the need to oppose the federal government. But other Virginians would question whether it was to their benefit to continuously oppose the national government and federally funded internal improvements and whether the state needed constitutional reform. A new reform party emerged in the 1820s that saw itself following in the tradition of Madison and Jefferson's party of the 1780s and 1790s.

The major leader of the new reform party was John Hampden Pleasants, editor of the Lynchburg *Virginian*. His faction included his father, James, a former United States senator and governor of Virginia, 1822–25; James Barbour, United States senator and a former governor; Judge John Coalter of the court of appeals, the student and son-in-law of St. George Tucker; Chapman Johnson, lawyer and politician from the Valley; Archibald Stuart, politician and General Court judge from the Valley; and Richard Toler, who would succeed Pleasants as editor of the Lynchburg *Virginian*. The reformers wanted to challenge the Old Republican ideas and the majority of the Republican party—that worked through the party's legislative caucus. They sought to begin the new era of reform and change in Virginia. They concentrated their efforts on state legal and constitutional reform, including the calling of a constitutional convention, state and federal internal improvements, and the defeat of states' rights presidential candidates in the elections of 1824 and 1828. For the latter goal, they placed their hopes on John Quincy Adams, and built the foundations for the Whig party in the state.

The new reform party drew its greatest support in the state from the Northern Neck, the northern Valley, and northwest (or present-day West) Virginia, which wanted state constitutional revision, internal improvements, and more banks. The northern Valley and northwest (now West) Virginia, complaining of a lack of influence, wanted a reapportionment of the seats in the legislature. As long as all white males could not vote and property in slaves was counted in apportionment, the plantation gentry east of the Blue Ridge would remain predominant in the General Assembly. On this issue they would try to win over the southern Valley and the southwest of the state—called "Little Tennessee."[7]

The reform party sought to repeat what Madison and Jefferson had done by 1800, and to return to the days of the Virginia Dynasty and a close connection between the state and the federal government. They contended that there was more to gain through supporting the federal government than through opposing it. Their attack on the continuous opposition was reminiscent of Marshall's attack on the Republicans in the 1790s. They also asserted that the opposition to the federal government was a way to blame others for the Old Dominion's lingering agricultural depression and decline in importance within America. Attacking the federal government was popular, just as opposing British creditors had been in the 1780s. The reform party, however, would also advance Country, republican ideological themes in an attempt to win over areas from the agrarian or Country persuasion in the southern Piedmont and the Southside. They hoped to do to Roane, Ritchie, and the Old Republicans what Madison, Jefferson, and Henry Lee had done to Henry in 1790. They would form a new majority coalition like the Republican and Anti-Federalist alliance of the 1790s. In doing so, however, they repeated Madison and Jefferson in another way. To gain votes, they compromised the spirit of reform.[8]

From Petersburg to Lynchburg through the Valley and over to Fredericksburg, newspapers sounded the new opposition to the *Richmond Enquirer*. These newspapers shared their essays, and in 1824, Pleasants established an opposition paper in the capital city. Against the Court party that ruled Richmond and the state, the name Whig was invoked and the sanctity of the Constitution. Pleasants moved from the Lynchburg *Virginian* to be the editor of the Richmond *Constitutional Whig*. To the extent Pleasants and his newspaper cohorts played upon Country, republican themes, they could hope to succeed. And indeed, they had a story, which circulated through the North: Virginia was being controlled by a secret, all-powerful club, the Richmond junto. In advancing this idea, they had a great political and ideological heritage to play upon. The images and fears were there ready to be invoked. Far from Richmond, farmers would listen to the charges of a distant, corrupt power that wished to deprive them of their land and rights.[9]

According to the Country, republican ideology, central power concentrated, and those who wielded the power grew corrupt and sought to destroy the rights of citizens and to rob them of their property. But who were they? In a republic, the men ruling at the top would not want their Court activities to be known. They, therefore, had formed a secret organization, the Richmond junto. According to the Country, republican ideology also, the membership would consist of bankers and professional politicians, lawyers, and judges. Certainly, Republican party leaders in Richmond had endorsed state banks and state internal improvements. State banks and branches were established in Richmond, Norfolk, Alexandria, Petersburg, Fredericksburg, Winchester, and Lynchburg, and the legislature increased its commissions to raise funds and projects to improve the navigable waters of the state. But, did this constitute a Court party or a cabal? It is highly doubtful that any such organization existed. But, the new reform party could use the opposition rhetoric to court the Country.[10]

During the 1824 presidential campaign, Pleasants would also lead a corresponding committee that circulated and promoted a slate of presidential electors who supported John Quincy Adams for president and who opposed William Crawford. Crawford, a states' rights advocate, was supported by Virginia's Republican party leadership and legislative caucus, and was also supported by the Old Republicans. Pleasants and the future Whig party tried to build their coalition around John Quincy Adams. In the elections in Virginia, however, Crawford easily defeated Adams, although much of the western portions of the state did not go to Crawford. Not only did many counties in the northern Valley and northwest Virginia vote for Adams, several counties in the southwest did not go to Crawford either, but voted for Andrew Jackson. It was not clear to the Pleasants faction what their voting for Jackson meant. Perhaps the attempts to pull all the western areas away from the Southside were working.[11]

News soon arrived from Washington that Henry Clay had thrown his support in Congress to Adams; Adams appointed Clay to be his secretary of state, and Jackson and his supporters charged that Adams and Clay had made a corrupt bargain: Clay would make Adams president if Adams would make Clay his heir apparent. What was the ideological reaction in the Old Dominion? The call went out to rise again and to oppose corruption, and the Crawford and Jackson supporters answered the call. The traditional agrarian or Country regions of Virginia had mostly voted for Crawford or Jackson, and around the presidential issue, they formed an alliance against Adams. The Adams supporters' hopes of cutting into these regions of the state were frustrated by the antagonism between Adams and Jackson.

The Pleasants faction was having difficulty. The criticism of the corrupt bargain did not end, and a number of their objectives remained unpopular, especially the call for federal internal improvements. They supported the Adams administration, and, from Adams's inaugural address on, it was clear that he was a nationalist like his father. Also, something else was amiss. The Pleasants faction was opposing the state government while supporting the federal government. Ideologically, the long-accepted tradition of opposition was that of the local and provincial against the central and national (or imperial). And further criticism of the Richmond junto did nothing to diminish the effect of the corrupt bargain. Many concluded that there was more to fear from a corrupt Adams-Clay administration in Washington than from a political club in Richmond.

The future Whig party tried the same strategy again in 1828. Ironically, given their goal, the story of the 1790s was replayed in the 1820s, but with the Whigs playing the role of the Federalists. After a successful, popular president—Washington, then Monroe—came a president who was very unpopular with most Virginians, an Adams. Both the father and the son were nationalists. Each was confronted by a popular leader: Jefferson, then Jackson. Again, Virginians rallied around the opposition standard, and in 1828, they were again triumphant.[12]

In the end, no new alliance or coalition was formed. The attempt to create an east-west antagonism in the Old Dominion had failed. No consensus developed west of the Blue Ridge. The Valley split: while the northern Valley voted for Adams, the southern Valley voted against him. The same sort of split also occurred on votes for a state constitutional convention. Although the western regions were underrepresented in the legislature, the southwest part of the state joined the southern Valley in opposing the northern Valley and northwest Virginia. One reason for this was economic. Talk of federal internal improvements to link the Potomac and Ohio rivers was appealing to northwest Virginia and the northern Valley. But, such projects would provide little gain for the southern Valley and the southwest region.[13]

The basic north-south geographic division within Virginia remained. The northern Valley and northwest Virginia voted consistently nationalist and for a state constitutional convention. The Northern Neck and the cities, the swing area in the state, were part of the Republican opposition to the national government while forming the center of the Republican party within the state, but they still favored revising the Virginia constitution. The areas to the south were the heartland of the opposition to the national government and resisted calling a state constitutional convention.[14]

From the convention and legislative votes, and from election returns cited throughout this work, the following is clear (despite the changing alignments and the shifts in centers of power): rural areas from the Tidewater through the Southside, southern Piedmont, southern Valley, and southwest generally voted against legal, judicial, and constitutional reform, and measures that would increase the power of government and centralization; the towns and cities, the central Piedmont to the Northern Neck, northern Valley, and northwest Virginia generally voted in favor of those measures and reforms.

The rise of a reform party, from the northern Valley and northwest Virginia, that favored federal internal improvements and opposed the use of slaves for political apportionment, actually helped connect the interests of the Tidewater to the James River valley and Southside areas. To drop the use of measuring property in slaves for apportioning representation would have weakened the gentry. Like the issue of allowing creditors access to courts in the 1780s, apportionment reform was striking at the political and economic security of a dominant class. Indeed, the southern Virginia coalition appeared similar to Henry's in the 1780s. By the late 1820s, the Whigs complained not about the unequal power of the west against the east, but about that of the north against the south. The influence of the tobacco planters on Virginia politics appeared as strong as ever. Indeed, state internal improvements in roads and waterways, and the building of the canal up the James and the Roanoke–Dismal Swamp canal had made the Southside tobacco easier to market.[15] The southern Virginia alliance was like that in the 1790s between Republicans and Anti-Federalists. It joined moderates such as Ritchie with ideologues such as John Randolph. A compromise was achieved: some internal improvements were begun to the benefit of the tobacco gentry that worked through state and local governments—Court benefits contained and decentralized by the Country.

The Southside put John Randolph in the Senate, put Littleton Waller Tazewell in the Senate, and made Giles governor. Giles was a leader, following in the tradition of Henry, who sought the support of Southsiders, the gentry, and the justices of the peace who were still in strength in the House of Delegates. He opposed the national government, and, within the state, worked to preserve the power of the local elite, in Virginia's agrarian culture, at the county courthouse.

Giles, Roane, and the Old Republicans had effectively countered the new round of reform, and the reform momentum was lost with the economic problems following the panic of 1819 and the sectional issues that first arose with the Missouri crisis. The great opportunity for change and reform in Virginia decreased even further with the strategy of the Pleasants faction, as it sought to become the new majority party. After all, Madison's reform party had built a winning coalition in the 1790s through alliances and compromises. As the Pleasants faction drew upon the Country, republican ideology and began an opposition, and tried to win in the Southside to the southwest portion of the state, they tempered their nationalism and the urgency of their demands for reform. They did keep their attack focused on the state government, but their support of the Adams-Clay administration contradicted the traditional opposition thought and undermined their position in the state. And, in reaction to the forces of reform, from the Marshall Court to the efforts of the Whig faction, those of the Virginia school of politics rose to counter the threat to their principles and interests. It was their duty to defend the Old Dominion and to advocate and affirm their dogma, the Virginia Doctrine. The legacy of Henry, the Virginia Resolutions of 1798 and the *Virginia Report*, the judicial roles and opinions of Pendleton and Roane, the essays and treatises of Roane and John Taylor, and

Giles's and John Randolph's speeches were all passed down to the next generation of Virginians.

The developing conservatism proved stronger than the reform movement. Many resisted any kind of change, from aid to western Virginia to legal and constitutional reform. But, there was more than just an opposition to nationalism, the Marshall Court, the Adams administration, and national internal improvements; a defense also arose within the state—of Virginia's institutions, county courts, constitution, law, and society.

The Threat at the State Level

There were two major ways to reform Virginia's legal and constitutional system. First, there were attempts, through statute and the courts, to modify the state common law to make it more receptive to commercial development. Second, there was the call for a state constitutional convention.

The reform party's efforts at calling a state constitutional convention would be more successful than the Adams presidential campaigns. But, that success was tempered by the fact that Virginians of the north and west and future Whigs were not the only ones who advocated change in the state. If only to placate the west, there was growing support within the Republican party for more state banks and state internal improvements. Critics noted, however, that the party leadership focused most support on internal improvement projects on the James River system and in the Southside. Ritchie led moderate Republicans to accept the calling of a state constitutional convention for similar reasons: to prevent the Pleasants faction from winning all of the western parts of the state through exploiting that issue. This allowed Tidewater and Southside politicians to maintain leadership, gave them a way to keep the southern Valley and the southwest of the state on their side, and assured provincial and localist conservatives that they could prevent reform. Given the system of apportionment, conservatives would have the power in a state convention to win or to force a satisfactory compromise. Joined with the federal-level issues, however, the pressure for change and reform within the state gave them cause for anxiety. They could only hope that, from their juries and judges to the politicians, the good farmers of their country would take their stand to preserve Virginia's ancient constitution.

Two legal developments in particular, however, could have challenged the conservative order. One was the use of legal actions to thwart the power of the juries. Another was the potential for legal change inherent in the state's chartering of corporations for internal improvements. The law profession, particularly in the towns, could have influenced the state judges to accept a change in the law that would aid creditors and businessmen and promote economic progress. Virgina's law could become more professional and scientific, moving away from the law of country lawyers and juries, while the state was economically transformed.

Legal historians such as Morton Horwitz have argued that lawyers and business clients in other parts of America worked with the state judges to break down the rule of local courts, the power of juries, and the use of the law as a protector of the rights of farmers against those of merchants and capitalists. This kind of movement could have developed in the Old Dominion as well. Lawyers did argue for curtailing the power of the juries in cases before the state courts, and the court of appeals was given the opportunity to direct the law toward a stronger role for professional judges and a diminished role for the juries.[16]

A series of cases was brought before the court of appeals that raised the question of judges instructing juries. On the whole, the cases involved plaintiffs who had requested county or state district or superior court judges to instruct juries that the evidence they had presented was sufficient to prove their case. Generally the lower court judges had refused to do so. A judge instructing a jury was seen as an invasion of the province of the jury, which, by the common law, determined the facts of a case. Plaintiffs appealed to the court of appeals. They hoped that by removing a case to the state's high court, the decision would be in favor of judges using discretion over juries. But the court of appeals refused to rule in their favor. Lawyers, such as Daniel Call, presented arguments that there should be exceptional areas where a judge could be allowed to instruct a jury, such as when there is written testimony because the judge was responsible for determining the correct construction of written documents. The court refused to sanction any exceptions to the common law practice. Pendleton spoke of the juries' traditional rights, and, if anything, Roane advanced those rights.[17]

In *Whitacre v. M'Ilhaney*, (1814) the question was whether presenting the evidence before a jury made it possible for a judge to implicitly overstep his bounds. Roane stated, in the opinion of the court, that if a judge led a jury to believe that evidence had been given that would prove the matter in dispute, then the judge had gone beyond law to fact. The judge must decide only on the legal relevancy of evidence and cannot in any way persuade the jury of its weight and effect. In this particular case, the defendant had appealed, claiming that the state district court judges had, in effect, instructed the jury on a verdict. Although the judges had not actually explicitly instructed the jury, Roane and the court of appeals nonetheless ruled that implicit actions of judges were enough to compromise the jury's right to determine all questions of fact. (The case was returned to the district court to be retried.) It was clear that the judges had a duty not to overstep their power and make any assumption of fact as proved. Indeed, unlike in England and some of the states, judges in Virginia were not allowed to "sum up the evidence" at the end of a trial.[18]

Furthermore, it had become the practice in the common law in Virginia to accept that most of the time there would be no clear distinction between the law and the facts. Juries would therefore have to apply the facts of a particular case to the law, and in many cases, the jury either would have to distinguish the facts from the law, reserving the determination of the latter for the judge, or, as often happened, would itself determine the law as it related to the facts. It had generally been the practice for judges not to instruct juries upon the law. The further practice was now firmly established that judges should refrain from instructing juries even when requested to do so by the counsel of the litigants. The court of appeals upheld the Virginia common law rights of the jury. If requested to do so, a judge was only to answer a question concerning a specific point of law. In his *Commentaries*, Henry St. George Tucker contrasted Virginia's practice on judges not being allowed to invade the privileges of the jury with that of England and other states. For the most part, the business of common law trials would remain in the hands of the juries.[19]

Nor were appeals a way to move beyond the juries. Appeals remained few, and the court of appeals ruled that questions of fact should not be retried by a high court. The local jury was more knowledgeable hearing the whole of the evidence presented. Drawing upon the record of the lower court trial, the judges could clearly see the questions of law, but not of fact. Roane's opinion stated that even with the record before them, appellate judges were in the dark compared to the trial judges and jury. Any question of fact must be returned to a local, trial-court jury. There were yet other devices that could be used to thwart juries, such as judges allowing new trials because the jury had determined against the evidence. But, these devices did not become tools for the judges to wield against the juries. Despite any intentions by plaintiffs's lawyers to weaken the jury, the judges were not cooperative. Most motions for new trials were overruled. Indeed, as Henry Tucker noted in his *Commentaries*, Virginia's judges contrasted with those elsewhere in not tending to "lend too easy an ear" to new trials. Also, a defendant was as likely to ask for a new trial as a plaintiff, and judges were more likely to grant new trials to losing defendants than to losing plaintiffs. (See table 4.) Indeed, the defendant could use the motion for a new trial, just as he could the motion for an appeal. The development of alternatives allowed defendants to lengthen and to slow the legal process more than it brought speed and efficiency to the process and assisted plaintiffs.[20]

County courts and juries also assumed the role of protecting local interests in another area vital for the reform party, especially in the north and west of the state—that of internal improvements. There was more rhetoric about improvements than real economic transformation. But, a vast array of laws was passed by the legislature, establishing corporations for internal-improvement projects to improve river navigation and to build canals. Although most of the canal companies failed or, if they survived, never completed their canals, perhaps, in this area, the law was changing to transform Virginia economically. The legislature, however, did not break with the traditional pattern of having development proceed through county courts using common law procedure—the process of ad quod damnum. County courts had, since the colonial period, authorized the clearing of streams and the building of mills and millponds, and during the 1780s, the state legislature added canal building to their jurisdiction. The legislature had not attempted to move away from the common law in this regard, however, or toward a process that transcended county boundaries.[21]

All of these endeavors, from mills to canal companies, were estab-

TABLE 4 Special motions in jury trials, 1785–1825
(Campbell, Caroline, Cumberland, Frederick, Wythe, and York
county courts; the Fredericksburg City Hustings Court; and the state
district and superior courts at Prince Edward County)

Demurrer to the evidence	1%
Special verdict	1%
New trial	8%
No special motion made	90%
New-trial motions	
Requested by plaintiffs	50%
Requested by defendants	50%
Request granted	36%
Request overruled	64%
New-trial motions: results for plaintiffs and defendants	
Request by plaintiff	
granted	13%
overruled	87%
Request by defendant	
granted	59%
overruled	41%

Sources: Campbell County Court, OB, 4–5: 356–69; Caroline County Court, OB, 1804–5: 346–79; Cumberland County Court, OB, 1792–97: 313–30, 1824–26: 147–203; PED, 1:3 158, 2:1–50, 1805: 14–66; Frederick County Court, OB, 25:404–92; 36:145–240; Fredericksburg City Hustings Court, OB, H:1–152, 264–321; Prince Edward County Superior Court, District Court at Prince Edward County OB, 1804–31: 533–38; Wythe County Court, OB, 1795–96: 1–15; 1805–8: 81–98, 1815–20: 20–31, 1822–26: 183–206; York County Court, OB, 5:150–72, 6:693–714, 8:72–78, 9:21–37, 11:1–23.

Note: taken from jury trials in debt and "case" actions.

lished as quasi-public operations, owned privately but established for the public benefit and usually regulated by the county or state government. For the public benefit, the legislature incorporated internal-improvement companies and authorized them to commence eminent domain procedures through local courts. Whether the land was for mills or canals, there was no lack of local control. Not only was most legal action at the county level, but juries were called to determine the value of the land and whether it could be taken.[22]

Legal historians such as Horwitz and R. Kent Newmyer have argued that, during the early Republic, courts in New York and New England were giving millers more freedom to flood riparian owners. If this is so, state courts in Virginia did not do the same. Millers were held strictly accountable to the local jury, which determined whether a milldam could be built and what damages the miller paid for flooding other people's property. The state courts did not encourage business enterprise by neglecting or compromising the value of property or local jury control in determining the value of the land, even if the legislature had determined that this development would put the land to more constructive or profitable use. The promise of future benefits to the economy was not grounds to loosen the constraints of the law in Virginia. Property rights and local economic control had been the guiding principles of the state legislature and courts. A local, jury-oriented common law prevailed. Indeed, when the court of appeals struck down a jury finding, it was only on a question of law, that the traditional rules of ad quod damnum had not been followed. By that process, a local jury was to determine that a milldam would not cut off a public road, that navigation would not be impaired, that the passage of fish would not be prevented, that no one's house, orchard, or gardens would be destroyed, and that a stagnant pond would not result (which would be injurious to the community). When, for example, a jury had looked at damages to come from the extension of a dam, but had failed to reassess whether the change in the millpond would disturb the fishing, or the health of the area, that was, for Roane, grounds for quashing the inquisition. Otherwise, Roane was against discounting on technicalities the substance of a jury's finding.[23]

As the pace of internal improvements appeared to quicken during the Era of Good Feelings, an increasing number of Virginia's statutes on the subject urged county courts not to slow the process of improvement projects, but to give precedence to ad quod damnum procedures, and expressed an interest in adjusting the law to meet the needs of economic progress. If legislation such as the 1819 act establishing the Slate River Company had succeeded, then eminent domain in Virginia would have been modified by compromising the rights of property owners affected by a process of eminent domain. The act authorized opening navigation of the Slate River, part of the upper James River system, although this could have seriously endangered the interests of five mills on the river.[24]

The legislature authorized the Slate River Company to order the owners of the five mills on the river to build and to maintain, at their own expense, locks at their milldams for boats. If the millers failed to do so, the Slate River Company could destroy the milldams for being nuisances in a public waterway. Ashbury and Thomas B. Crenshaw, owners of one of the mills on the Slate River, brought a suit against the company.[25]

Crenshaw and Crenshaw v. Slate River Company raised the question of whether the legislature could authorize a company to lessen or to destroy the value of property without fair compensation. Attorneys for the Crenshaws argued, first, that it would be a great expense for the millers to build locks and to maintain them and that the change in the water level of the river could make their property worthless, and, second, that the state had the power to take or to destroy property only through eminent domain, with fair compensation. Attorneys for the Slate River Company argued that rivers were public waterways under the jurisdiction of the state, and no previous orders of a county court authorizing the building of mills on a river could bind the state legislature concerning the navigation of that river. No county could grant a right to build a mill that could not be later compromised or terminated by the legislature. Because the legislature had chartered the Slate River Company, the mills authorized by the county were no longer legally protected, and the millers did not need to be compensated for the destruction of their dams.[26]

If it had been the intent of the legislature to favor a state chartered internal-improvement company over the rights of mill owners, whose mills had been authorized by county courts, the appeal of *Crenshaw and Crenshaw v. Slate River Company* to the court of appeals presented an opportunity for Virginia's judges to join their New York and New England judicial brethren—at least according to the Horwitz-Newmyer thesis. The thesis, that lawyers and business clients worked with state judges to break down the rule of local courts, the power of juries, and the use of the law to protect agrarian interests against capitalists and economic development, is not confirmed by Virginia. The court of appeals—with opinions given by Judges Cabell, Coalter, Dabney Carr, and John W. Green—ruled against the Slate River Company. There was no question that the legislature had full authority to take land for public use, including dams previously authorized by county courts, but only through common law procedure—through eminent domain, with fair compensation paid. The argument that the rights and power of the state took precedence over those of the county was dismissed. Counties had the power to authorize the building of dams, and the state had the power to authorize the destroying of dams. But both were bound by the same fundamental rules pertaining to eminent domain.[27]

The decision meant several things. First, a canal and navigation improvement company would have to buy improved milldam property even if they could show that the milldams thwarted navigation of a public waterway and undermined the company's purpose as set out in its corporate charter granted by the legislature. This made canal building an even more expensive undertaking.

Second, with this decision, the court of appeals did something it rarely ever did: it informed the legislature that it had erred in passing the act. Although, unlike *Kamper v. Hawkins,* the *Slate River Company* case did not involve the judiciary's control over its own sphere, nonetheless this judicial review case was similar to earlier ones in that, following in the tradition of Pendleton and Roane, the court stated that it did not wish to act as an active check on the legislature. The court understood that the legislature, no doubt trying to do what was in the public's best interest, did not intend to disregard the rules governing eminent domain, but had made a mistake. It is interesting that only half of the judges giving seriatim opinions referred to Virginia's constitution. All of the judges agreed, however, that a common law principle had been violated. The court was correcting the legislature on the common law principle that citizens had the right to be compensated for property taken through eminent domain action by the state. This common-law property right was a fundamental principle that had passed the test of time, that was part of the "unwritten constitution," which no government could properly take away. The court recognized the legislature's sovereign power to modify the common law, but could not accept an act by the legislature that compromised a fundamental principle. This Virginia precedent for judicial review involved the violation not so much of a written constitution as of a fundamental principle, a property right.

While the suit was pending, the legislature did not respond with further legislation similar to the Slate River Company act. An indication of the legislature's pulling back from its Slate River Company act was the act incorporating the Northanna and Southanna river companies. Locks or slopes on dams were the responsibility of the navigation or canal company, not the miller. The companies were not authorized to destroy the dams as public nuisances. During the period of this study, there was no further attempt by the legislature to bypass Virginia's traditional eminent domain procedures as it had in the act incorporating the Slate River Company.[28]

A third outcome of the *Slate River Company* case was that, although politicians, and judges in their political capacity, supported internal improvements at least rhetorically—in order to appease the north and west of the state—the legal system in Virginia would remain as it was. If judges in the northeast states and in the federal judiciary were leading the way in a movement to alter the common law on eminent domain, Virginia judges were not going to follow. In the *Slate River Company* case, the court of appeals showed that it would favor the power of county courts and juries and the old common-law due process over attempts by heralds of improvement to use the law as a tool, a means to transform the Virginia economy. Internal improvements would not be the exceptional area where the law would change in order to change society.

Fourth, the case confirmed that, despite the spirit of change and reform during the Era of Good Feelings, the political economy of Virginia was not going through a substantial change. It might appear that the state was pursuing a new course, not necessarily moving from mercantilism to capitalism, but at least adding a state mercantilist structure to the county-level structure. Again, however, not only were Virginia's political leaders confronted with the dilemma of espousing agrarian principles while trying to engage in progressive measures, they did not wish to threaten their support at the local level. The internal-improvement corporations were not actually a departure from the old decentralized governing of the state. Just as the legislature only pointed in general directions and left the execution of its legislation to county governments, the corporations for internal improvements were authorized to proceed in the same way, through the county courts. Indeed, rather than the law transforming the economy, it made economic progress more difficult, if anything. One of the economic problems Virginia faced—which also included state-chartered corporations trying to raise capital by selling stocks to a heavily indebted agrarian population—was that the state's decentralized court system allowed locals to thwart state projects of improvement. The reformers had failed to change this. Although the legislature would note that the local juries and judges were slowing state development, little was done to remedy this situation.

There were a number of reasons why the law was not being transformed in Virginia. One was the makeup of the Virginia Supreme Court of Appeals. Pendleton, a founder of the Old Republicans, had used his opinion in *McCall v. Turner* like a manifesto, to proclaim the defense of juries and the use of the state's courts to protect its citizens. Roane did the same. The principles of the former leader of the court continued with the latter. The situation could have been different if the state's highest court had been led by Wythe or St. George Tucker.[29]

Another reason that the law remained the same was that Virginia was predominantly agricultural. Roane explained the connection between an agrarian society and the common law. The history of the common law in England had showed a slow development as precedents were established through centuries in an agricultural society. But, law—even the common law—could change relatively quickly, not only being modified by statute but being altered by court opinions if courts were responding to a fast-changing society. Roane held that changes occurred in the common law in England as it became predominantly commercial and was fast becoming industrial. Virginia's society was different from England's. Virginia needed less government: one that was republican, that did not move beyond fundamental principles, and was decentralized—in the law, one that worked through local courts. Its common law system was stable and not prone to change. This same comparison of the development of the common law in Virginia with that in England could increasingly be made with that in the northern states. The courts of a rural, agricultural society were going to be much slower in changing their law than those of a society where the economy was rapidly changing.[30]

Another and related reason was that, in the Old Dominion, with slow commercial and industrial development, the legal culture could not stand separate from and independent of the agrarian interests. Professional lawyers in Richmond could not exclusively take businessmen for clients. They also represented the gentry and argued for their interest. And they could not very well restrict themselves to just the most progressive and prosperous, diversified planters and wheat farmers of the central Piedmont and Northern Neck. Professional lawyers needed clients, and the latter, in Virginia, would include a good many tobacco planters of the James River valley and Southside. The interests of such clients and legal reform were not always compatible. So, earlier, Marshall defended debtors, and John Wickham was known to argue against the extension of the authority of judges over juries. After the former became a judge, the latter became Richmond's leading lawyer. Such men did not take up the agrarian or Country causes as a matter of principle. They needed the business.[31]

Only a few were growing wealthy at the bar in the commonwealth. This was already becoming a concern among lawyers before the panic of 1819. After that, several years of an agricultural depression followed, and the legal profession suffered along with everyone else in a predominantly agrarian economy. Because of the number of courts and lawyers and the depressed economy, the basic pattern of Virginia's law practices had not been greatly altered by the 1820s. When a lawyer still needed a farm to provide for a family, there was going to be little chance of the profession sharply breaking from its agrarian past. Farms provided food, a place where the family could live while the lawyer rode the circuit, security, a place to retire to, and an inheritance.[32]

Also, despite the efforts in legal education by Wythe and St. George Tucker at William and Mary and the founding of small, private law schools by Creed Taylor and Henry Tucker, most still read law as an apprentice under a practicing lawyer, then learned the common law in the county courthouses on a state circuit. Aspirations to becoming a country gentleman had not declined, however, and few lawyers and judges wished to desert the heritage that gave social prestige in the Old Dominion. Either the plantation was not given up upon pursuing a legal career, or, if one did gain wealth through a law practice, a plantation was acquired. Land was also the best investment in an agricultural society. In addition to social pressure or economic motivation, however, the ideal of the country gentleman had become romanticized. William Wirt's biography of Henry exemplified this tendency. Yet, lawyers like Wirt and Francis Walker Gilmer, who were advocates of legal education, tried to be critical of the country lawyer.[33]

Gilmer greatly admired Henry, but believed there were negative aspects to using him as a model. What would be the effect of continuing to try to copy him, the natural political speaker and lawyer? Henry was talented and had a natural wisdom. Most uneducated men, however, were only going to be able to lead and persuade those less educated than themselves. With a shallow knowledge of the principles of law and government, with no knowledge of history, with some confused, unorganized information drawn from a hasty perusal of a few law books, the young men would try to rely on their natural talents and common sense in order to become great lawyers and orators and then go into politics, like Henry. They would take the floor, and quickly "the bloom perishes without the fruit ensuing." They were "self-deluded boys." Virginia was a country of would-be Patrick Henrys.[34]

But, could the advocates of legal education expect Virginians to change? Wirt and Gilmer, for example, were critical of their fellows in the profession, who had pride but were lazy and ignorant, and who were satisfied with never being more than country lawyers or had notions of great success in the state as lawyers and political orators but had no discipline, no sacrifice. Yet while they looked down on those country lawyers going to the county courthouse on hog paths in the wilds of opossum country, they also knew well the pleasures of that country life. Wirt missed his early county practice, one reason his biography of Henry was so sympathetic. Wirt envied his friend Judge William H. Cabell for riding the circuit on the James above the fall line. He visited him as often as he could to enjoy that life on the farm, which he saw as one of innocence and happiness. As for Gilmer, Wirt's protégé, he often visited his brother, Peachy, a country lawyer in Henry county and longed to join him in his pursuit of the principles of the law and of deer hunting. Although he was succeeding at the bar in Richmond, he admired the independence that came with a good farm. He planned to buy property and to become a gentleman.[35]

If the legal profession was not ready to rid itself of its country-lawyer heritage, neither was the General Assembly. Little had been done to change the focus of power as well as law in Virginia from the county courthouse. Madison and Jefferson had always known, no complete redirection could be given the Old Dominion without first ending the power of the county courts. Once again, in the 1820s, the reformers criticized the local elites and demanded an end to their power or an end to the self-perpetuating status of the justices of the peace. With reform being advanced in the name of democracy in the 1820s, reformers called for an end to the appointive power of the legislature and the county courts. The governor, the executive and judicial officials of the state, and county judges should be chosen by popular election.[36]

Like Henry in 1788, the defenders of the old and the true in the 1820s had to oppose those of the new enlightened ideas. They were ready to be old-fashioned if, as they saw it, that was necessary to preserve liberty. Once again, the enemy sought to use written constitutions, new laws, and a new judicial system to carry out their reforms and to bring about a progressive government that would change with the interests of others besides the gentry. Old Republicans had long defended the sanctity of the ancient, unwritten constitution against the federal Constitution of 1787, and they were still doing so in the 1820s. But, they were now also defending those same principles in Virginia's constitution of 1776 against the demands for a new state constitution (or major revision of the old one). They could hardly bring themselves to uphold the sacred character of mere parchment. As is the nature of opposition, they mostly attacked the reformers' intents and painted a dark picture of what would result from letting reformers run amok with the government of the commonwealth. What they chose to defend in the state constitution was very revealing. Great importance was given to the justices of the peace and the county court system, which was not the creation of the 1776 document, which was a product of no written constitution at all but had slowly developed in English and colonial history.[37]

The two principal leaders of the opposition to reform were Giles and Benjamin Watkins Leigh, a Richmond attorney and later a reporter for the court of appeals, who wrote the most well-read pamphlet against revising the state constitution. During the 1820s, Giles, the recognized leader of the Old Republicans or the Virginia school of politics, a representative of the Southside, led the fight in the legislature against constitutional reform just as Henry had done in the 1780s. Leigh and Giles evaluated the government of the commonwealth by how well it measured up to fundamental principles and concluded that the government had been a success. Like Henry in 1788, Leigh and Giles stated that in the 1820s Virginians were happy, their liberty was secure, and they needed no change to preserve their rights. There was also a grave possibility, however, that the change being called for would be for the worse, and it would be better to conserve the present system.[38]

Opposing the new-fashioned preference for novelty, they noted the obvious: new was not necessarily better. The commonwealth had followed the other states by experimenting in banking, and the results, Leigh stated, were endless problems that were difficult to eradicate. Once a step was taken, it was hard to move back. Henry had warned Virginians of losing their liberty in attempts to gain wealth and to build an empire. Giles stated that, beginning with the Era of Good Feelings, a malignant star had shone above the United States. There was a love of novelty and splendor. Appealing to Virginians in terms of their leadership role in the early Republic, Giles called on them to maintain their political virtues and principles and to resist the exchange of all that was good, stable and solid, valuable and useful, old and venerable, for "brilliant, delightful glitter." He stated that, in order to preserve Virginia as the mightiest temple to liberty, wherein they enjoyed more political blessings than anywhere else, they had to look to first principles and to secure their state constitution in its most ancient and fundamental character.[39]

Leigh and Giles declared that the county court system was the most fundamental aspect of Virginia; its existence predated the Revolution, and it had been left intact by the state constitution of 1776. It was the state's oldest institution and had proven itself through the test of time. Judicially and administratively, the county court system was the foundation of government in the commonwealth. Giles stated that the justices of the peace tied the government together by sitting in the House of Delegates, making laws, and administering those laws in the counties. Furthermore, because there were few temptations for the judges, justice in the counties was impartial and fair. He asserted that the county court system had been more important in the maintaining of liberty than any other part of the state constitution and offered greater security than the federal Constitution, even with its Bill of Rights.[40]

Giles and Leigh defended justice at the county level, close to home. They wanted the judicial system to remain decentralized, with courts in each county and drawing jurors from that county. They noted that this could be criticized for not being the most rational system, but it had worked through the ages. They defended the tradition of judges not being elected. This system of justice was not democratic, but it was better than having political judges chosen by the populace.[41]

Of course, the protection of the Virginia system of justice advocated by Giles and Leigh meant preserving the power of local interests. After all, the gentry who gathered at the county courthouse would stand to lose a great deal if constitutional reform ended the local system of government. Giles and Leigh were unapologetic in their defense of the traditional system. Giles praised the practice of drawing local administrators and judges from the gentry. Country gentlemen were not the wealthiest few in the state, nor the poor populace as a whole, but in between, of the middling kind. These leaders of their communities would not threaten others' liberty, rights, or property. They would not grow corrupt and tyrannical. Giles contended that there was no better government than one dominated by the gentry. There was much more to fear from the tyranny of a powerful wealthy few or of a propertyless many, both of whom would aim at plundering society for their own benefit. Democracy in itself offered no security for liberty and property rights. Strong government, corrupt patronage, and tyranny must be opposed, whether it came from a monarchy or a democracy.[42]

In the 1820s as in the 1780s—whether from Henry and the Anti-Federalists or from Giles and the Old Republicans—the opposition to new, enlightened reform and the preference for conserving the old brought criticism that perhaps the gentry was not being republican and did not have the best interests of all, or even a majority, of the people at heart. Did they truly prefer the world before 1776? Just like Henry in 1788, Leigh's and Giles's answer was yes, that some of the most important principles and institutions had been established before 1776. The principle that government and law were to protect citizens in their life, liberty, and property; the common law tradition and trial by jury; the county court system; and the geographic representation of freeholders in the assembly all predated 1776. Leigh also defended the traditional sluggishness of geographic reapportionment. The long-established counties should have a greater representation in the House of Delegates than those on the frontier, because each of the former was a unique community, with its own history and characteristics as well as its local interests—indeed, a small country unto itself.[43]

They concluded that the state constitution was like the English constitution in that, in its fundamental form, it was unwritten and based on ancient principles. The unwritten constitution of Virginia was partly borrowed from England, but it had developed in its own way, and had been completed by the republican independence from the British monarchy in 1776. Constitutions were more than something written on parchment. A constitution must be found, Leigh stated, "in the hearts of the people; mixed up with their habits, deeply impressed on their minds, endeared by use, and sustained by veneration."[44]

7

Virginia's Plea for a Separate Realm

By the 1820s, there had been major legal changes in Virginia. They could be summed up as the adding of tiers above the counties that were different from, but for the most part not superior to, the local governments. The local governments were able to look after their interests and protect themselves. The state and federal governments and judiciaries were strong, but the result of their development was increased pluralism and complexity rather than centralization and uniformity in the law. Pendleton and Roane had led the judiciary in the preservation of the state- and local-oriented legal tradition, which was well established in precedents such as *McCall v. Turner*, *Whitacre v. M'Ilhaney*, and *Hunter v. Martin, Devisee of Fairfax*. That tradition was supported by the legislature and had become part of the ideological and rhetorical stand Virginians took by the 1820s.

The law in Virginia reflected the society: agrarian and conservative. It could do little to change the society. As the Old Dominion had developed, so had the judicial system and the law profession, but the latter was limited in what it could achieve, because, to a large extent, it was the result of or was compromised by Virginia's decentralized and rural government and society. The gentry elites remained powerful, particularly at the local level. Most government was still at the local level, and the state continued to be governed mostly through or in cooperation with the counties. In addition, the law for many Virginians was still primarily a matter of creditor-debtor concern—from the perspective of the debtor. Virginia's farmers could agree that law was a security for liberty, not a means of opening up the state's land and economy for progress.

This is not to say that the reformers had failed to make some changes. They had expanded the judiciary and the bar, and the law was more professional in the state courts, complete with court reports, and law schools were beginning, but from justices of the peace and country lawyers to the judges of the court of appeals, there was no great movement to change the law in order to change society. Indeed, by the Era of Good Feelings, a conservative reaction had developed in response to the talk of change, and it proved stronger than the reform movement. Further, the reformers' concentration of strength was simply too far to the north and west—particularly northwest Virginia—outside the area of political power in the state. And too often, reform in the state was advocated by nationalists—who were associated with Hamiltonianism, the Federalist Alien and Sedition Acts, the Marshall Court, the Adams presidencies, and the advocacy of tariffs and federal internal improvements. As a result, provincial conservatives could draw a connection between reform and nationalism. For them, conservation of the old order in the state and of states' rights went hand in hand.

Virginians' influence on the federal government was in decline, but, if their state was sovereign, and if their legal realm was distinct from the federal government, then they could control their own destiny, at least internally. In their own common law realm, they would move at their own pace, live by their own rules, and all in the name of those principles that they agreed were most dear. The provincial conservatives used Anti-Federalism, states' rights, and the law as a means of defense to keep the outside, federal government at a distance. They could only maintain their Virginia if their state's common law and sovereignty remained separate from the federal jurisdiction. For this reason, they had to make their plea for a separate realm.

In taking their stand, Virginians romanticized the past and looked to one event more than any other that symbolized their concerns and provided a model for action: Virginia's stand in 1798. The Virginia

Resolutions of 1798 and the interposition of the state against the Federalists' Alien and Sedition Acts had, in time, taken on mythical proportions. Indeed, this act was seen as grand if not greater than any other in Virginia's history. The major issue in 1798 was a legal one. The threat to freedom of speech in the Sedition Act was minor compared to the threat of the machinery that would be imposed to carry out the enforcement of these and any other acts. What so infuriated Virginians and got old Anti-Federalist leaders such as John Taylor talking about secession was not the arrests of Republican newspaper editors. It was the Federalists' contention that they had modified and improved upon a common law. Were they contending that there was a national common law, a law of the American people? The opposition insisted that there were as many common law systems in America as there were states. The Constitution had not authorized the federal government to assume the common law of England or the states. Citizens of a state shared a common law with one another, but with citizens of the other states, they shared only the Constitution, treaties, and federal statute. There was no national American realm of the law.[1]

To recognize an American common law would grant to the federal courts what the state courts already had, a long, well-evolved system of legal principles, procedures, and precedents. It would give them a civil and criminal jurisdiction that, through implication and a broad construction of the Constitution, would move greatly beyond the jurisdiction given them solely over matters relating to the Constitution, treaties, and federal statute. It would vastly accelerate the process of the federal courts breaking down the walls between the federal and state judiciaries. The common law was a rule of law, a law of the land, that was in force throughout the realm, and was superior to all local and particular laws in the realm. If this aspect of the common law was applied to the federal government, then not only would America be a single realm but federal law, the statutes of Congress, and the decisions of the federal courts, would all be superior to state law. This would not only undermine the independent status of the common law jurisdictions of each state's judiciary but would challenge state sovereignty. Indeed, the laws of the states, legislative as well as judicial, could be reviewed in the federal courts and would have to conform with federal law.

If the Federalists had had their way, Virginia Republicans were afraid that eventually there would have been just one federal common law and that the common law of Virginia and that of the other states would have disappeared. If America had a single common law realm, then nationalists could counter state sovereignty by going through the law to establish the idea—and source for the authorization of power—that there was a single, unified, American people and an indivisible sovereignty. The Federalists showed in the Sedition Act what could be expected from such a development. If the Federalists had succeeded, would the law then be a security or a threat? Many Virginia Republicans concluded that the Federalists were trying to use the common law against the people, which was like turning the militia upon them—an attempt to use, for the purpose of tyranny, the shield of liberty.

While the law was used as a protection at the local and state levels, Marshall replaced Madison among those Virginia reformers who had continued in their hope of using the law to make changes—even if that meant going through the federal government to impose a superior law upon the Old Dominion. Roane met Marshall in duels just like those of Madison and Henry in the 1780s.[2] The right of Virginians to rule Virginia versus the assertion of federal jurisdiction was the central issue in the debate between these two prominent Virginia jurists.

Marshall and Roane attacked each other for changing the rules of the game. Roane stated that a body of precedents was emerging—including *Martin v. Hunter's Lessee* and *McCulloch v. Maryland*—that could provide the Court with the exclusive power to interpret the Constitution and alter the Constitution with the force of amendments. Marshall defended the Court's actions as the logical result of a system with a supreme law of the land, and launched a counterattack, pointing to Virginia's own set of precedents that interpreted and changed the Constitution without it being amended, what Roane referred to as a "political bible" or "Magna Carta." They included *Hunter v. Martin, Devisee of Fairfax*, the Virginia Resolutions of 1798, and the *Virginia Report*.

The battle between the courts continued in the battle between the judges. Roane condemned section 25 of the Judiciary Act of 1789 and denied the Supreme Court's appellate jurisdiction over the state courts. Marshall, repeating the argument used by Story in *Martin* emphasized the need for uniformity in the law. Marshall—like Madison—believed that it was an essential part of the workings of the law that there be one final word. Concurrent jurisdiction was acceptable only if the superiority of the federal government over the states was recognized. The world of Henry and Roane lacked this logical precision. Coordinate concurrent jurisdictions within the federal structure were not repugnant to them. Indeed, legal pluralism and diversity were not only possible but desirable. From Roane's perspective, nothing had changed between 1750 and 1820, for example, that would make citizens of Massachusetts happy to live under Virginia law or vice versa or that would make citizens of both states happy to live under the same law.

Virginia's provincial conservatives had met threats both from the federal level and from within the state—and had countered each in much the same way, through decentralized court systems using local juries and through Roane's jurisprudence, which favored using the state courts and common law to protect Virginians against the federal government, but opposed using them to serve social and economic progress within the state. Those conservatives were not as successful at the federal level. Whereas they could only check federal jurisdiction but could not control it, inside Virginia they managed to contain the efforts of the reformers and to dominate the process that had been created. But, their means of reaction to change were similar in both areas. The means by which they supported localism within Virginia was mirrored by the means by which they supported provincialism toward the federal government. There was security in diversity, pluralism, and decentralization. A lack of uniformity was always better than a threat to liberty, which was often how they interpreted a perceived loss in state or local power.

Roane contended that tyranny was the result of uniformity and centralization and that Virginians had to defend themselves against outside interference from power beyond their state and local governments. Marshall's assurances that the law of the Supreme Court manifested the will of the nation mattered little to him. Roane—like Henry in 1788—did not believe Virginians' liberty should be entrusted to foreigners. Marshall denounced any attempt to place the whole at the mercy of one of its parts. The will and the law of the nation must be paramount to those of the individual states. Roane insisted that states were not parts of a unified sovereign nation but were members of a confederation.

For Marshall, the American people as a whole were sovereign, and federal law manifested their will. For Roane, the people of each of the states were sovereign, and their law was the state law for the people of Virginia and others for each of the other states, but there was no single common law for all of America. Marshall claimed that Roane could not see the whole for the parts. Roane's view of America paralleled what he had long believed about his state: if the Old Dominion was the sum of its counties, America was the sum of its states. For him, there could be no leap to a higher plane of sovereignty. This political and legal world was based upon local units, the people within communities and counties.

At the heart of the Marshall-Roane debate were opposite views of America. Roane still saw a league of sovereign states, while Marshall saw a growing nation. Roane claimed that the old confederation of the Articles had continued and that the Federalists and the Marshall Court had tried to subvert this system by destroying the sovereignty of the states. Marshall believed that Roane's objective was to return America to the 1780s. He reminded Roane of the defeat of the Anti-Federalists and of the replacement of the Articles of Confederation by the Constitution. He restated the goals of the Federalists of 1787–88, that the needs of the nation were great, that America was becoming an empire, and that it must have a government that could rule effectively and efficiently. Henry had told his fellow Virginians in 1788 that their mission was not to build an empire but to defend liberty. Roane reminded them of this purpose and declared that an independent and sovereign Virginia was sufficient to serve their needs. He believed that Marshall could build his new nation only upon the ruins of the states.

By the 1820s, of course, America had neither remained a league of sovereign states nor become a unified nation. Yet, the continuing debate inclined toward extreme stances that prevented any easy solutions. Questions of law had polarized the debate. The nationalist demand for a supremacy of the law had forced questions of sovereignty into an either-or situation: either the national government was sovereign or the state governments were, but not both.

The law had crossed the boundary lines between the branches of the federal government in establishing judicial review, and could cross over and blur the boundary lines between the national and state governments. It appeared that the law would extend into all areas and lead back to the Supreme Court, unless it was opposed. The matter did not lend itself well to moderation and compromise. There could be no lasting division of power or jurisdiction. As Roane explained to his fellow Virginians, the law was a power that both expanded its area and, like a whirlpool, drew all to its center. Either the state judiciaries were part of the overall federal legal system, or the will of the Supreme Court would be confronted and its authority denied at the state boundary.

Different conceptions remained of what kind of society and government and law there should be. The law could be a unifying force or it could be a force to maintain a decentralized society. The law in Virginia was seen as a protector of the liberty of farmers, landed property rights, and state and local interests because of the preference for trial by jury, a broad-based appellate structure, the personnel and traditions of the judges and the law profession, and the connection of law with federal-state politics. As seen in the Marshall-Roane debate, two conceptions of the law were opposed to each other. On the one hand, there was the law that led to centralization and uniformity; that was connected to towns, to the middle class, to professions and business; and that sought to reform and to economically transform society. By this view, law was a positive force that could consolidate Americans as one people and one nation. On the other hand, there was the law that was seen as a negative force. By this view, law could preserve an America that was a land of diversity, divided into state and local governments. It could preserve liberty by resisting the forces of unity, centralization, and homogeneity.

Madison, Marshall, and other reformers had tried to impose the law of an American nation upon Virginia and were willing to break down the barriers between the federal government and the state to accomplish their goal. Those in opposition to them believed it was more in keeping with a republic to limit the central government and to protect the interests of a common people, the Virginians. They viewed the law, not as a force to change society, but as one providing a forum in which to settle their disputes and as a protector of their rights and interests.

In Virginia in the 1820s, the provincial conservatives remained steadfast in resisting the reform of their society and government. Virginia served as a legal and political model, especially for those Southern states where power was centered at the county courthouse. And their states' rights movement against the expansion of the power of the federal government continued to be strong through the rest of the antebellum era. Although nationalism eventually triumphed over the Virginia Doctrine, the latter was reproduced throughout the South and left its legacy, as an undercurrent against nationalism and a federal supreme law of the land.

NOTES

BIBLIOGRAPHY

INDEX

NOTES

Abbreviations

AGA	*Acts of the General Assembly*
CA	Virginia Supreme Court of Appeals, VSLA
CCVA	United States Circuit Court, District of Virginia, VSLA
CW	*Constitutional Whig* (Richmond)
JHD	*Journal of the House of Delegates*
LC	Library of Congress, Washington, D.C.
OB	Order Books, VSLA
PED	OB, District Court at Prince Edward County, VSLA
PRG	Peachy Ridgeway Gilmer Papers, VHS
RE	*Richmond Enquirer*
RVJ	Registers of Virginia Justices and County Officers, 1775–1818, 1780–1811, 1777–1822, VSLA
TCP	Tucker-Coleman Papers, College of William and Mary, Williamsburg
UVA	University of Virginia Library, Charlottesville
VHS	Virginia Historical Society, Richmond
VSLA	Virginia State Library and Archives, Richmond

Introduction

1. *Martin v. Hunter's Lessee*, 1 Wheaton 304 (1816).
2. John Taylor, *New Views of the Constitution of the United States*.
3. Ibid.
4. Ibid.; John Randolph, speech on the tariff bill, in *Speeches . . . on the Tariff Bill*, 29–57.
5. Daniel P. Jordan, *Political Leadership in Jefferson's Virginia*.
6. Francis Walker Gilmer, *Sketches, Essays, and Translations*, 33–35.
7. William Wirt, Preface to *Sketches of the Life and Character of Patrick Henry*, 32–35, 55–62, 73, 86–88, 220–58, 281–92; Wirt to Dabney Carr, 9 Aug. 1817, in *Memoirs of the Life of William Wirt*, ed. John P. Kennedy, 2:22–25; Spencer Roane to Wirt, [n.d.], Henry Family Papers, VHS.
8. Wirt, *Sketches of Henry*, 258, 292.
9. George Webb, Preface to *The Office and Authority of a Justice of Peace*. Other manuals included: Richard Burn, *The Justice of the Peace and Parish Officer*; Michael Dalton, *The Country Justice*; and Giles Jacob, *Freeholder's Companion*. Jacob had an accompanying *Companion* volume on agriculture. See also William Hamilton Bryson, *Census of Law Books in Colonial Virginia*.

10. Richard Starke, *The Virginia Justice*; Preface to the 4th ed., William Waller Hening, *The Virginia Justice*.

11. Along with the manuals, other works that were available to colonial Virginians that emphasized the importance of juries in preserving liberty included: Henry Care, *English Liberties*; Edward Coke, *The First Part of the Institutes of the Laws of England; Or a Commentary upon Littleton*, particularly sections 365–68; Giles Dunmore, *Law of England concerning Juries*; Mathew Hale, *The History of the Common Law of England*. See also Bryson, *Census of Law Books*.

12. George Mason to Patrick Henry, 6 May 1783, in *The Papers of George Mason*, ed. Robert A. Rutland, 3:771–72.

13. A. G. Roeber, *Faithful Magistrates and Republican Lawyers*, 128–37.

14. Perez Zagorin, *The Court and the Country*; Isaac Kramnick, *Bolingbroke and His Circle*; Bernard Bailyn, *The Ideological Origins of the American Revolution*; Gordon S. Wood, *The Creation of the American Republic*; Lance Banning, *The Jeffersonian Persuasion*; John M. Murrin, "The Great Inversion, or Court versus Country."

15. Speeches of James Madison, in *The Debates in the Several State Conventions*, ed. Jonathan Elliot, 3:383, 399; speeches of George Nicholas, ibid. 3:246–47, 392–93; speeches of John Marshall, ibid. 3:232–35, 558–59; and see J. Thomas Wren, "The Ideology of Court and Country in the Virginia Ratifying Convention of 1788."

16. Speeches of John Page and William Branch Giles, *Annals of Congress*, 1st Cong., 3d sess., 2:1942–45; ibid., 2d Cong., 1st sess., 3:391–96, 399–400, 441–42, 546–47; and John Taylor, *A Definition of Parties* and *An Enquiry into the Principles and Tendency of Certain Public Measures*.

17. See John Taylor, *An Inquiry into the Principles and Policy of the Government of the United States*.

Chapter 1

1. See Roeber, *Faithful Magistrates and Republican Lawyers*, 160–202.

2. I analyzed votes on legal and constitutional issues, in the ratifying convention and in the legislature during the period of this study, using Earl G. Swem and John Williams, *A Register of the General Assembly of Virginia, 1776–1918*; *JHD*; and *Debates*. For a quantitative analysis of voting in the General Assembly that shows the development of parties led by Madison and Henry, see Gordon Denboer and Norman K. Risjord, "The Evolution of Political Parties in Virginia, 1782–1800." Madison, "Vices of the Political System of the United States," in *The Papers of James Madison*, ed. William T. Hutchinson, Robert A. Rutland, et al., 10:345–59; Madison to Edmund Randolph, 8 Apr. 1787, ibid., 9:368–71; Madison to George Washington, 16 Apr. 1787, ibid., 9:382–87; numbers 10 and 51 in *The Federalist*, ed. Jacob E. Cooke.

3. Speech of George Mason, in *Debates* 3:524–25; speech of Patrick Henry, ibid., 3:540; Swem and Williams, *Register of the General Assembly*; *JHD*; *Debates*; *RVJ*.

4. George Mason to George Mason, Jr., 1 June 1787, and George Mason, "Objections to the Constitution," in *Papers of Mason*, ed. Rutland, 3:890–93, 991–93.
5. Speech of Henry, in *Debates* 3:54. See also 3:21–23, 44–57, 128–29, 281.
6. Ibid., 3:21–23, 44–57, 128–29, 281.
7. Ibid.
8. Ibid., 3:47, 53, 45. See also 3:21–23, 44–57, 128–29, 281.
9. Ibid., 3:539, 545–49.
10. Madison to Washington, 4 and 13 June 1788, in *Papers of Madison*, ed. Hutchinson et al., 11:77, 134.
11. Speech of Mason, in *Debates* 3:524–25; speech of Henry, ibid., 3:540.
12. Speeches of Henry and Mason, ibid., 3:445–49, 523–26, 542–43, 551, 579–80.
13. Ibid.; speeches of Henry, ibid., 3:545–46, 578.
14. Ibid., 3:21–23, 44–57, 586–87; vote on ratification before amendments, and the ratification vote, ibid., 3:653–54, 654–55; James Monroe to Jefferson, 12 July 1788, in *The Writings of James Monroe*, ed. Stanislaus M. Hamilton, 1:184.
15. Recommended amendments, in *Debates* 3:657–61.
16. Madison to Jefferson, 8 Dec. 1788, in *Papers of Madison*, ed. Hutchinson et al., 11:381–85; a Madison campaign public letter, Jan. 1789, ibid., 11:428–29; Madison to Jefferson, 29 Mar. 1789, ibid., 12:37–40; speech of Madison, in *Annals of Congress*, 1st Cong., 1st sess., 1:431–40, 746–47.
17. William Maclay, *Journal of William Maclay*, ed. Edgar S. Maclay, 85–118; An act to establish the judicial courts of the U.S., generally known as the Judiciary Act of 1789, 24 Sept. 1789, in *The Statutes at Large of the United States*, ed. Richard Peters, 1:73–93 (hereafter cited as Peters, *Statutes*).
18. Vote on amendments to the Constitution, 6 Dec. 1793, Oct. session, 1793, *JHD*, 117–18; Taylor, *Enquiry*; Edmund Pendleton, "The Danger Not Over" (1801), in *The Letters and Papers of Edmund Pendleton*, ed. David John Mays, 2:695–99.
19. Speech of Page, *Annals of Congress*, 2d Cong., 1st sess., 3:391, 395. And also see the speeches of Page and Giles, ibid., 1st Cong., 3d sess., 2:1942–45; ibid., 2d Cong., 1st sess., 3:391–96, 399–400, 441–42, 546–47; and Taylor, *Definition of Parties* and *Enquiry*.
20. Votes on establishing a circuit court system on 13 Dec. 1785 and 18 Dec. 1786, Oct. session, 1785, and Oct. session, 1786, *JHD*, 89–90, 106–7; and vote on revising the Virginia constitution on 21 June 1784, May session, 1784, ibid., 86–87.
21. See acts pertaining to the county courts, 1792–95, in *The Statutes at Large of Virginia*, ed. Samuel Shepherd, 1:130, 136–45, 151, 158–59, 167–68, 173–93, 228–29, 342–43, 371–72 (hereafter cited as Shepherd, *Statutes*).
22. Charles S. Sydnor, *Gentlemen Freeholders*, and the sections on Virginia in his *The Development of Southern Sectionalism, 1819–1848*; Thomas Jefferson, *Notes on the State of Virginia*, chap. 14, on Virginia laws.
23. John Dawson to Madison, 10 Nov. 1787, in *Papers of Madison*, ed. Hutchin-

son et al., 10:247–48; Joseph Jones to Madison, 18 Dec. 1787, ibid., 10:329–30; An act establishing district courts, and for regulating the general court, 22 Dec. 1788, in *The Statutes at Large*, ed. William W. Hening, 12:730–61 (hereafter cited as Hening, *Statutes*); and, on an earlier district court act that did not go into effect, see Hening, *Statutes* 12:532–58, 644; "Remonstrance of the Judges," in *Case of the Judges of the Court of Appeals*, 4 Call 135 (1788).

24. District Court at Winchester, OB, 1:1–207; PED, 1:3–56.

25. On the debt cases, see chapter 2, below. In a comparison of sessions in 1785 and 1795, before and after the introduction of the district court reform for Richmond City Hustings Court and for the county courts of Frederick, in the Valley; Campbell, in the southwest Piedmont; York, in the Tidewater; and Spotsylvania, on the fall line south of the Rappahannock, there was no marked decrease in the volume of civil suits, and in Frederick County, there was a 33 percent increase (Richmond City Hustings Court, OB, 1:246–77 and 3:324–58; Frederick County Court, OB, 19:99–145 and 25:404–492; Campbell County Court, OB, 2:1–77 and 4–5:356–69; York County Court, OB, 5:150–72 and 6:693–714; Spotsylvania County Court, OB, 1782–86 and 1795–98). By the end of the period covered by this study, the county courts had still not become small-claims courts. For example, in a session in 1824 in Cumberland County, above the fall line south of the James, the county court dealt with over sixty cases for a value higher than one hundred dollars, and ten of these were for over a thousand dollars. Half of these were for a value higher than that in the suits of either of the 1824 sessions for the (later established) state superior court of adjoining Prince Edward County (Cumberland County Court, OB, 1788–92: 210–39; 1792–97: 313–69; and 1824–26: 147–203; Prince Edward County Superior Court and District Court at Prince Edward County OB, 1804–31: 602–21).

26. An act establishing district courts, and for regulating the general court, in Hening, *Statutes* 12:730–61.

27. Netti Schreiner-Yantis and Florence Speakman Love, *The 1787 Census of Virginia*; Campbell County Court, OB, 2:1–77, 4–5:356–69; Cumberland County Court, OB, 1788–92: 210–39; Frederick County Court, OB, 19:99–145, 25:404–92, 36:145–240; York County Court, OB, 5:150–72, 6:693–714; PED, 1:3–56, 102–158; CCVA, OB, 1:1–47. Jury trials in the county and state courts continued at a steady rate: there were as many jury trials in the Campbell and Frederick county courts in 1795 as there were in 1785, as many in the District Court at Prince Edward County in 1806 as there were in 1789, more in the county courts of Frederick and Wythe— in the southern Valley—by 1806 than there were in 1795; there were as many in 1815 as in 1795 in Wythe County court, and as many in 1825 as there were in 1815 in York County court. (Campbell County Court, OB, 2:1–77, 4–5:356–69; Frederick County Court, OB, 19:99–145, 25:404–92, 36:145–240; Wythe County Court, OB, 1:1–15, 1805–8: 81–98, 1815–20: 20–31; York County Court, OB, 5:150–72, 6:693–714, 9:21–37, 11:1–23; PED, 1:3–56, 4:14–66.)

28. Patrick Henry Account Book, VSLA.

29. PED, 1:1–274.

30. Ibid., 1:1–56; Prince Edward County Land Tax Books, 1789, VSLA.

31. PED, 1:1–56; RVJ; Swem and Williams, *Register of the General Assembly;* William Wirt to Dabney Carr, 23 Mar. 1811, *Memoirs of Wirt,* ed. Kennedy, 1:279–81.

32. PED, 1:1–56; Prince Edward County Land Tax Books, 1789, VSLA.

33. Jefferson to George Hammond, 29 May 1792, in *American State Papers,* ed. Walter Lowrie and Mathew Clark, 1:211.

34. For the development of the legal profession, particularly in Fredericksburg—at the fall line of the Rappahannock—and in the Northern Neck, see Roeber, *Faithful Magistrates and Republican Lawyers,* 203–29.

35. Fredericksburg City Hustings Court, OB, A:195–202; B:1–11; C:1–12, 131–34, 154–59, 244.

36. An act to organize and establish a superior court of law in each county of the commonwealth, 1 Feb. 1808, *AGA;* and also see an act, to amend an act, entitled an act, to organize and establish a superior court of law in each county of this commonwealth, and also an act supplemental thereto, 4 Feb. 1809, ibid.

37. An act, to amend an act . . . , 4 Feb. 1809, ibid.

38. Editorial on the Virginia court system, 3 Jan. 1826, *CW;* Notes on a conversation with Littleton Waller Tazewell, 6 Oct. 1828, Hugh Blair Grigsby Diary, VHS.

Chapter 2

1. Isaac Samuel Harrell, *Loyalism in Virginia;* Richard Sheridan, "The British Credit Crisis of 1772"; Emory G. Evans, "Planter Indebtedness"; T. H. Breen, *Tobacco Culture.*

2. John Hook to David Ross, 19 Aug. 1782, John Hook Papers, VSLA.

3. Conway Robinson, *The Practice in the Courts of Law and Equity in Virginia* 1:139–77, 207–18.

4. Henry St. George Tucker, *Commentaries on the Laws of Virginia,* 295–96.

5. I located sixty-two debtors using Earl G. Swem, *Virginia Historical Index;* and CCVA, OB, 1:1–231.

6. CCVA, OB, 1:1–231. On *Jones v. Walker,* see *Ware v. Hylton,* 3 Dallas 199 (1796); Charles F. Hobson, "The Recovery of British Debts."

7. Pendleton to Madison, 9 Dec. 1791, in *Letters and Papers of Pendleton,* ed. Mays, 2:582; Wirt, *Sketches of Henry,* 220–54. To reproduce Henry's argument, Wirt used the manuscript notes of David Robertson. Robertson had recorded the shorthand account of the Virginia ratifying convention and did the same for *Jones v. Walker.*

8. Wirt, *Sketches of Henry,* 249–54.

9. An act in addition to the act entitled an act to establish the judicial courts of the U.S., 2 Mar. 1793, in Peters, *Statutes* 1:333–35; Monroe to Jefferson, 1 May

1792, in *American State Papers* 1:234; Samuel Flagg Bemis, *Jay's Treaty*, 285; CCVA, OB, 1:1–141.

10. Three hundred and seven debtors made payments into the state loan office. (See Emory G. Evans, "Private Indebtedness.") *Ware v. Hylton*, 3 Dallas 199 (1796).

11. On the circuit court decision, see *Ware v. Hylton*, 3 Dallas 199 (1796).

12. Ibid.; CCVA, OB, 1:161–354.

13. *Ware v. Hylton*, 3 Dallas 199 (1796); *McCall v. Turner*, 1 Call 133 (1797).

14. *Ware v. Hylton*, 3 Dallas 199 (1796). Iredell's circuit court opinion is included in the Supreme Court report.

15. Ibid.; *Chisholm v. Georgia*, 2 Dallas 419 (1793).

16. *Ware v. Hylton*, 3 Dallas 199 (1796).

17. Ibid.

18. Jefferson to Hammond, 29 May 1792, in *American State Papers* 1:201–14; Jefferson to Madison, 4 June 1792, in *Papers of Madison*, ed. Hutchinson et al., 14:314–15; resolutions on British compliance with the treaty of 1783, 11 Dec. 1793, in Shepherd, *Statutes* 1:285.

19. Lewis Cecil Gray, *History of Agriculture in the Southern United States* 2:595–99.

20. Resolutions on the Jay Treaty, 15 Dec. 1795, in Shepherd, *Statutes* 1:434; speech of Madison, in *Annals of Congress*, 4th Cong., 1st sess., 5:976–87; and see the pages following, in *Annals of Congress*, 4th Cong., 1st sess., 5:987, as the Virginia Republicans took turns attacking the treaty.

21. Bemis, *Jay's Treaty*, 283–86, 356–58, 438–39.

22. Ibid., 438–41; John Bassett Moore, *International Adjudications*.

23. Answer of Hook, 20 Aug. 1801, in *Ross v. Hook*, John Hook Papers, VSLA. William W. Hening to Hook, 10 Feb. 1800, John Hook Papers, UVA.

24. William Cabell to Joseph Cabell, 2 Jan. 1810, Cabell Family Papers, UVA; CCVA, OB, 11:1–84; Francis Walker Gilmer to Peachy Ridgeway Gilmer, 14 Mar. and 14 June 1819, 22 Feb. 1821, 17 Feb. 1822, and 30 Mar. 1823, PRG. I looked at sessions in the order books of the county courts of York, Wythe, Cumberland, and Frederick and found a steady number of debt cases. Counting only debt-action cases—excluding debt cases in "case" and bond—for individual sessions, 31 percent of the cases in Frederick County in 1785 were of this type, 32 percent ten years later, and 41 percent in 1805; in Cumberland County 49 percent were debt-action cases in 1795 and 57 percent thirty years later; 11 percent were such cases in Wythe County in 1795, 52 percent ten years later, 50 percent in 1815, and 41 percent in 1825; 27 percent were such cases in York County in 1785, 36 percent in 1795, 40 percent in 1805, 58 percent in 1815, and 38 percent in 1825. (Frederick County Court, OB, 19:99–145, 25:404–92, 36:145–240; Cumberland County Court, OB, 1792–97: 313–30; 1824–26: 147–203; Wythe County Court, OB, 1795–96: 1–15; 1805–8: 81–98; 1815–20: 20–31; 1822–26: 183–206; York County Court, OB, 5:150–72, 6:693–714, 8:72–78, 9:21–37, 11:1–23.)

Chapter 3

1. Banning, *Jeffersonian Persuasion*.
2. Resolutions of 1790, 21 and 23 Dec. 1790, in Hening, *Statutes* 13:234-39; proceedings and votes, 2 Nov.-16 Dec. 1790, Oct. session, 1790, *JHD*, 36-37, 45, 81-82, 141-42.
3. Edmund Randolph to Madison, 10 Mar. 1790, in *Papers of Madison*, Hutchinson et al., 13:96-97; Henry Lee to Madison, 13 Mar. 1790, ibid., 13:102-3; Madison to Edmund Randolph, 21 Mar. 1790, ibid., 13:110; Joseph Jones to Madison, 25 Mar. 1790, ibid., 13:123-24; Edmund Randolph to Madison, 20 May 1790, ibid., 13:224-25; Philip Freneau to Madison, 25 July 1791, ibid., 14:57; Madison to Joseph Jones, ibid., 14:71-72; and see the editorial note, ibid., 14:56-57.
4. Swem and Williams, *Register of the General Assembly*; Resolutions of 1790, 21 and 23 Dec. 1790, in Hening, *Statutes* 13:234-39; proceedings and votes, 2 Nov.-16 Dec. 1790, Oct. session, 1790, *JHD*, 36-37, 45, 81-82, 141-42; vote on amendments to the Constitution, 6 Dec. 1793, Oct. session, 1793, ibid., 117-18; Madison, "Parties" and "A Candid State of Parties," *National Gazette* (Philadelphia), 23 Jan. and 26 Sept. 1792, in *Papers of Madison*, ed. Hutchinson et al., 14:197-98, 370-72; Taylor, *Definition of Parties*; Noble E. Cunningham, Jr., *The Jeffersonian Republicans*.
5. Swem and Williams, *Register of the General Assembly*; RVJ.
6. See acts pertaining to the county courts, 1792-95, in Shepherd, *Statutes* 1:130, 136-45, 151, 158-59, 167-68, 173-93, 228-29, 342-43, 371-72.
7. Speech of Madison, *Annals of Congress*, 1st Cong., 3d sess., 2:1894-1902, 1956-59; speeches of Page and Giles, ibid., 1st Cong., 3d sess., 2:1942-45; ibid., 2d Cong., 1st sess., 3:391-96, 399-400, 441-42, 546-47; Jefferson's opinion on the Bank presented to Washington, 15 Feb. 1791, in *The Papers of Thomas Jefferson*, ed. Julian P. Boyd et al., 19:275-80; vote on amendments to the Constitution, 6 Dec. 1793, Oct. session, 1793, *JHD*, 117-18; Taylor, *Enquiry*; *The Virginia Report of 1799-1800 . . . Together with the Virginia Resolutions . . . Including the Debate and Proceedings Thereon . . .* (hereafter cited as *Virginia Report, Resolutions, Debate*). On the differences between the Anti-Federalists and the Republicans in the 1790s, see my "Liberty, Order, and a Balanced Constitution," and chapter 3 in my "Juries and Judges versus the Law."
8. Swem and Williams, *Register of the General Assembly*; vote on amendments to the Constitution, 6 Dec. 1793, Oct. session, 1793, *JHD*, 117-18.
9. Edmund Randolph to Madison, 6 and 10 Mar. 1790, in *Papers of Madison*, ed. Hutchinson et al., 13:92-93, 96-97; Madison to Edmund Randolph, 21 Mar. 1790, ibid., 13:110; Henry Lee to Madison, 10 Sept. 1792, and John Dawson to Madison, 27 Nov. 1792, ibid., 14:363-64, 417-18; "Petitions" [1791]; Madison to Jefferson, 2 Sept. 1793, in *The Writings of James Madison*, ed. Gaillard Hunt, 6:190-97; An act for establishing a bank in the town of Alexandria, 23 Nov. 1792, and an act

for establishing a bank in the city of Richmond, 23 Dec. 1792, in Hening, *Statutes* 13:592–98, 599–607.

10. Proceedings and votes, 2 Nov.–16 Dec. 1790, Oct. session, 1790, *JHD*, 36–37, 45, 81–82, 141–42. On the state's two-party system and the parts played by John Marshall and George Wythe for the Federalists and by Madison, Monroe, and John Taylor for the Republicans, see Caroline County meeting, resolutions, 10 Sept. 1793, in *Letters and Papers of Pendleton*, ed. Mays, 2:608–13; Richmond meeting, address and resolutions, 17 Aug. 1793, and John Marshall as "Aristides" and "Gracchus," 11 Sept., 16 Oct., and 13 and 20 Nov. 1793, from *Virginia Gazette and General Advertiser*, in *The Papers of John Marshall*, ed. Charles T. Cullen, Herbert A. Johnson, and Charles F. Hobson, 2:196–200, 201–6, 221–28, 231–47. See also Philip Marsh, "James Monroe as 'Agricola' in the Genet Controversy, 1793."

11. Henry Lee to Alexander Hamilton, 6 May 1793, in *The Papers of Alexander Hamilton*, ed. Harold C. Syrett, 14:416–17; Lee to Hamilton, 15 June 1793, ibid., 14:549–50; Lee to [?], 17 Sept. 1793, Lee Family Papers, UVA.

12. Proceedings and votes, 2 Nov.–16 Dec. 1790, Oct. session, 1790, *JHD*, 36–37, 45, 81–82, 141–42; vote on establishing a bank in Alexandria, 20 Nov. 1792, Oct. session, 1792, ibid., 129–30; vote on the Virginia Resolutions of 1798, 21 Dec. 1798, Dec. session, 1798, ibid., 32–33.

13. Jefferson to John Taylor, 1 June 1798, in *The Writings of Thomas Jefferson*, ed. Andrew A. Lipscomb and Albert E. Bergh, 10:44–47.

14. Adrienne Koch, *Jefferson and Madison*, 174–211; Virginia Resolutions of 1798, Shepherd, *Statutes* 2:192–93; and see J. G. A. Pocock, ed., *Three British Revolutions*.

15. See in particular the speeches of John Taylor, Giles, Henry Lee, and G. K. Taylor, in *Virginia Report, Resolutions, Debate*, 24–38, 103–9, 111–48.

16. Ibid.

17. See speeches of John Taylor and Giles, in *Virginia Report, Resolutions, Debate*, 24–29, 111–21, 143–48, 211–17, 226; resolutions on the common law, 10 Jan. 1800, Dec. session, 1799, *JHD*, 77–83; St. George Tucker, *Examination of the Question, How Far the Common Law of England Is the Law of the Federal Government of the United States?*; Madison to Jefferson, 12 Jan. 1800, in *Writings of Madison*, Hunt, 6:345–47; Monroe to St. George Tucker, 12 July 1800, in *Writings of Monroe*, ed. Hamilton, 3:192–93.

18. *Virginia Report, Resolutions, Debate*, 24–29, 111–21.

19. Ibid., 149–50.

20. Vote on the Virginia Resolutions of 1798, 21 Dec. 1798, Dec. session, 1798, *JHD*, 32–33; Henry Lee, *An Address of the Fifty-Eight Federal Members of the Virginia Legislature*; Henry Lee, *Plain Truth*; *State Documents on Federal Relations*, ed. Herman V. Ames, 15–26.

21. Vote on the memorial to Henry, 13 Dec. 1799, Dec. session, 1799, *JHD*, 72; Swem and Williams, *Register of the General Assembly*, 50–54.

22. Madison, *Virginia Report*, in *Virginia Report, Resolutions, Debate*, 190–96, 230; Madison to Jefferson, 29 Dec. 1798, in *Writings of Madison*, ed. Hunt, 6:327–29.

23. Pendleton, *The Danger Not Over* (1801), in *Letters and Papers of Pendleton*, ed. Mays, 2:695–99.

24. Ibid.; correspondence of Jefferson, Feb.–July 1801, to Monroe, Giles, Page, Thomas Lomax, John Dickinson, Joel Barlow, Thomas Paine, Joseph Priestley, Nathaniel Niles, Benjamin Waring, Henry Knox, Samuel Adams, Elbridge Gerry, and Levi Lincoln, in *Writings of Jefferson*, ed. Lipscomb et al., 10:210–76; Jefferson, first inaugural address, 4 Mar. 1801, and first annual message to Congress, 8 Dec. 1801, in *Writings of Jefferson*, ed. Lipscomb et al., 3:317–23, and 327–40; Taylor to John Breckinridge, 22 Dec. 1801, in "Letters of John Taylor," ed. William E. Dodd, 2:284–88; Monroe to Jefferson, 6 Jan., 3 and 18 Mar., and 29 Apr. 1801, in *Writings of Monroe*, ed. Hamilton, 3:253–79; Message of Governor Monroe to the Virginia General Assembly on proposing amendments to the Constitution, 7 Dec. 1801, in *Writings of Monroe*, ed. Hamilton, 3:302–18.

25. An act to provide for the more convenient organization of the courts of the U.S., known as the Judiciary Act of 1801, 13 Feb. 1801, Peters, *Statutes* 2:89–100.

26. Ibid.; An act to repeal certain acts respecting the organization of the courts of the U.S., and for other purposes, 8 Mar. 1802, ibid., 2:132; An act to amend the judicial system of the U.S., known as the Judiciary Act of 1802, 29 Apr. 1802, ibid., 2:156–67.

27. Monroe to Jefferson, 3 Mar. 1801, in *Writings of Monroe*, ed. Hamilton, 3:261–64; Jefferson to John Dickinson, 19 Dec. 1801, and Jefferson to Benjamin Rush, 20 Dec. 1801, in *Writings of Jefferson*, ed. Lipscomb et al., 10:301–3, 303–4; Pendleton, *The Danger Not Over* (1801), and Pendleton, *Observations on the Repeal of the Judiciary Act of 1801* (1802), in *Letters and Papers of Pendleton*, ed. Mays, 2:695–99, and 703–6; Taylor to John Breckinridge, 22 Dec. 1801, "Letters of Taylor," ed. Dodd, 2:284–88.

28. Speeches of John Randolph and Giles, *Annals of Congress*, 7th Cong., 1st sess., 11:519–21, 579–602.

29. Speech of John Randolph, ibid., 11:650–65; *Marbury v. Madison*, 1 Cranch 137 (1803); Monroe to Jefferson, 14 Mar. and 25 Apr. 1802, in *Writings of Monroe*, ed. Hamilton, 3:338–39 and 341–44; *Stuart v. Laird*, 1 Cranch 309 (1803).

30. Jefferson to Joseph Nicholson, 13 May 1803, in *Writings of Jefferson*, ed. Lipscomb et al., 10:387–90; Dumas Malone, *Jefferson and His Time*, 4:458–74; *The Diary of John Quincy Adams*, ed. Allen Nevins, 26; *William Plumer's Memorandum of Proceedings in the United States Senate, 1803–1807*, ed. E. S. Brown, 100–103, 228–30, 239, 280–315; John Randolph's resolution for inquiring into the conduct of Justice Samuel Chase, 5 Jan. 1804, and speech, *Annals of Congress*, 8th Cong., 1st sess., 13:806, and 851–56; "Trial of Samuel Chase," *Annals of Congress*, 8th Cong., 2d sess., vol. 14.

31. *Annals of Congress*, 8th Cong., 2d sess., 14:1213–14; speech of John Randolph, ibid., 9th Cong., 1st sess., 15:499–502; *Plumer's Memorandum*, ed. Brown, 269–72, 310–11.

32. The Anti-Federalist, Old Republican base continued in votes on legal and constitutional reform: see vote on calling a constitutional convention, 9 Jan. 1804, Dec. session, 1803, *JHD*, 71–72; vote on an act to organize and establish a superior court of law in each county of this commonwealth, 21 Jan. 1808, Dec. session, 1807, *JHD*, 83; and vote on an act to amend an act, entitled an act, to amend an act, reducing into one act, the several acts concerning the Court of Appeals, 4 Jan. 1811, Dec. session, 1810, *JHD*, 53–54.

33. Speech of Henry, *Debates* 3:21–23.

34. Speech of Randolph, *Annals of Congress*, 8th Cong., 2d sess., 14:1107–8; John Taylor to Monroe, 22 Feb. 1808, 15 Jan. and 8 Nov. 1809, 10 Feb., 12 Mar., and 26 Oct. 1810, and 31 Jan. 1811, in "Letters of Taylor," ed. Dodd, 2:291–94, 298–306, 309–11, 315–19; John Randolph to Monroe, 16 Sept. 1806, *Writings of Monroe*, ed. Hamilton, 4:486–88; John Taylor, *Arator, Being a Series of Agricultural Essays, Practical and Political*; Taylor, *A Pamphlet Containing a Series of Letters*, Taylor, *Inquiry*.

Chapter 4

1. *Commonwealth v. Caton*, 4 Call 5 (1782).

2. "Remonstrance of the Judges," in *Case of the Judges of the Court of Appeals*, 4 Call 135 (1788).

3. An act establishing district courts, and for regulating the General Court, 22 Dec. 1788, Hening, *Statutes* 12:730–61; An act for amending the act entitled an act concerning the court of appeals, 22 Dec. 1788, ibid., 12:764–66; An act for amending the several acts of the General Assembly, concerning the high court of chancery, 22 Dec. 1788, ibid., 12:766–68; An act concerning the court of admiralty, and the judges thereof, 25 Dec. 1788, ibid., 12:769–70; An act concerning the General Court, 25 Dec. 1788, ibid., 12:770–71; An act allowing traveling expenses to the judges of the General Court, 23 Dec. 1788, ibid., 12:768–69.

4. "Remonstrance of the Judges," *Case of the Judges of the Court of Appeals*, 4 Call 135 (1788).

5. See E. Lee Shepard, "George Wythe."

6. Pendleton to Washington, 13 Oct. 1789, in *Letters and Papers of Pendleton*, ed. Mays, 2:558–59; and, on the lack of evidence for the claim that Jefferson intended to appoint Roane chief justice of the Supreme Court, see Clyde C. Gelbach, "Spencer Roane of Virginia, 1762–1822," 104–5.

7. *Kamper v. Hawkins*, 1 Brockenbrough and Holmes 20 (1793).

8. Ibid.

9. Ibid.; Jefferson, *Notes on the State of Virginia*, chap. 13, on Virginia's constitu-

tion; Madison's notes for a speech on the revision of Virginia's constitution, June 1784, *Papers of Madison*, ed. Hutchinson et al., 8:75–79.

10. "Remonstrance of the Judges," *Case of the Judges of the Court of Appeals*, 4 Call 135 (1788); *Kamper v. Hawkins*, 1 Brockenbrough and Holmes 20 (1793).

11. Ibid.

12. John Marshall to St. George Tucker, Dec. 1794, in *Papers of Marshall*, ed. Cullen, Johnson, and Hobson, 2:303.

13. *Baring v. Reeder*, 1 Hening and Munford 154 (1806). See also *Lightfoot v. Colgin*, 5 Munford 42 (1813).

14. Biographical sketch of the judges of the court of appeals, 4 Call (1827); An act to amend the act, entitled an act, to amend an act reducing into one act the several acts concerning the court of appeals, 9 Jan. 1811, *AGA*.

15. See the analysis of dissenting opinions by the judges of the court of appeals in Gelbach, "Spencer Roane," 45, 109; Roane's proposed reforms in the rules of the court, 2 Dec. 1808 and 7 Mar. 1809, CA, OB, 6:161, 169, 217; opinion of William Fleming, Virginia Court of Appeals Manuscripts, VHS; account by Fleming of the conduct of Roane, Fleming to St. George Tucker, 13 May 1809, TCP; Roane to Tucker, 30 May and 2 June 1809, TCP.

16. Account by Fleming of the conduct of Roane, in Fleming to Tucker, 13 May 1809, TCP. See also St. George Tucker to Fleming, 29 Apr. and 11 May 1809, ibid.; Fleming to Tucker, 30 Apr., 8, 10, and 13 May 1809, ibid.; Roane to Tucker, 30 May and 2 June 1809, ibid.; Roane to Fleming, quoted in Fleming to Tucker, 8 May 1809, ibid.; Creed Taylor to Fleming, 20 Apr. 1810, and Fleming to Tucker, 2 Apr. 1811, William Fleming Papers, VHS.

17. St. George Tucker to John Coalter, 22 Nov. 1811, Grinnan Family Papers, TCP. See also Roane to Fleming, quoted in Fleming to Tucker, 8 and 10 May 1809, ibid.; Roane to Tucker, 30 May and 2 June 1809, ibid.; Tucker to Fleming, 29 Apr. and 10 and 11 May 1809, ibid.

18. Coalter to St. George Tucker, 18 and 31 May 1811, TCP; An act to amend the act, entitled an act, to amend an act reducing into one act the several acts concerning the court of appeals, 9 Jan. 1811, *AGA*; St. George Tucker's letter of resignation, 2 Munford (1811); Henry Tucker to St. George Tucker, 27 Feb., 4 Apr., and 13 Dec. 1811, TCP.

19. Henry Tucker to St. George Tucker, 22 June 1811, TCP; Gelbach, "Spencer Roane," 109.

Chapter 5

1. *Debates* 3:528–29, 559; and see John Alfred Treon, "*Martin v. Hunter's Lessee*," 28–42, 57–71.

2. Northern Neck Grants and Surveys Index, VSLA; CA, OB, 7:75, 88; Swem

and Williams, *Register of the General Assembly;* Swem, *Virginia Historical Index;* Shenandoah County Land Tax Books, 1794–1806, VSLA; *Hunter v. Fairfax's Devisee,* 3 Dallas 305 (1796); *Hunter v. Fairfax* (1794), District Court at Winchester, OB, 1:192, VSLA; St. George Tucker's opinion, in his "Notes on Cases before the General Court, the Court of Appeals and the District Court of Virginia, 1786–1811," TCP (which appears in an edited form in the appendix of Treon, "Martin v. Hunter's Lessee," 258–63, see also 28–42).

3. Resolutions, 11–12 Dec. 1793, in Shepherd, *Statutes* 1:285; correspondence of Robert Brooke and Henry Lee, governor, 4 Jan., 4 May, 1 June, and 23 Oct. 1794, and other state papers on the escheat actions against the Fairfax plantations and *Fairfax v. Commonwealth,* in *Calendar of Virginia State Papers,* comp. William P. Palmer, Sherwin McRae, and Raleigh Colston, 7:4–5, 130–31, 158–59, 255, 296–97, 352–53, 394–95, 446, 469–70.

4. John Marshall to Charles Lee, Dec. 1795, in *Papers of Marshall,* ed. Cullen, Johnson, and Hobson, 2:329–30; John Marshall to Richard Henry Lee, 18 Jan. 1793, ibid., 2:138–39. See also the editorial notes, ibid., 2:140–49, 5:228–36.

5. An act concerning certain lands lying in the Northern Neck, 10 Dec. 1796, generally known as the Compromise of 1796, in Shepherd, *Statutes* 2:22–23; *Hunter v. Fairfax's Devisee,* 3 Dallas 305 (1796); *Fairfax v. Commonwealth,* CA, OB, 3:244–45, and 3:124, 150–52, VSLA.

6. John Marshall to Denny Martin Fairfax, 6 Sept. 1797, Wykeham-Martin Papers, VSLA; Henry Tucker to St. George Tucker, 3 Dec. 1805, TCP; *Marshall v. Conrad,* 5 Call 364 (1805).

7. *Marshall v. Conrad,* 5 Call 364 (1805).

8. Henry Tucker to St. George Tucker, 3 Dec. 1805, TCP; John Marshall to James Marshall, 13 Feb. 1806, John Marshall Papers, LC; John Marshall to James Marshall, 21 Nov. 1808, Ambler Family Papers, VHS.

9. Shenandoah County Land Tax Books, VSLA; CA, OB, 3:183, 4:326, 5:75, 427, 437; 6:258, VSLA; An act to amend an act for reducing into one act the several acts concerning the court of appeals, 11 Jan. 1807, Shepherd, *Statutes* 3:299; Henry Tucker to St. George Tucker, 4 and 27 Aug. and 2 and 30 Sept., 1806, TCP.

10. *Hunter v. Fairfax's Devisee,* 1 Munford 218 (1809); *Fairfax v. Commonwealth,* CA, OB, 3:244–45.

11. *Hunter v. Fairfax's Devisee,* 1 Munford 218 (1809); *Reed v. Reed,* 1 Munford 611 (Appendix).

12. *Hunter v. Fairfax's Devisee,* 1 Munford 218 (1809).

13. *Fairfax's Devisee v. Hunter's Lessee,* 7 Cranch 602 (1813).

14. Ibid.

15. John Marshall to James Marshall, 9 July 1822, Marshall Papers, LC; *Hunter v. Martin, Devisee of Fairfax,* 4 Munford 1 (1814).

16. *Hunter v. Martin, Devisee of Fairfax,* 4 Munford 1 (1814).

17. Ibid.

18. Story to Ticknor, 22 Jan. 1831, Story, *Life and Letters of Story*, ed. William W. Story, 2:48–49; *Martin v. Hunter's Lessee*, 1 Wheaton 304 (1816).
19. *Martin v. Hunter's Lessee*, 1 Wheaton 304 (1816).
20. Ibid.; Treon, "*Martin v. Hunter's Lessee*," 246.
21. John Marshall to James Marshall, 9 July 1822, John Marshall Papers, LC; John Marshall to James Marshall, Jr., 11 Jan. 1832, John Marshall Papers, VSLA; and, on questions settled by the Fairfax litigation, see *Williams v. Price*, 5 Munford 507 (1817); and Robinson, *Practice in the Courts*, 1:237–40.

Chapter 6

1. *McCulloch v. Maryland*, 4 Wheaton 316 (1819); Roane, writing as "Hampden," *RE*, 11, 15, 18, and 22 June 1819.
2. John Marshall to Story, 26 Mar., 1819, in Marshall, "Story-Marshall Correspondence," ed. Charles Warren. See also John Marshall to Story, 17 May, and 13 July 1819, ibid. Roane, writing as "Hampden," *RE*, 11, 15, 18, and 22 June 1819; John Marshall to Bushrod Washington, June 1819, John Marshall Papers, LC.
3. John Marshall to Story, 26 Mar., 17 May, and 13 July 1819, in Marshall, "Story-Marshall Correspondence," ed. Warren; John Marshall to Story, 15 June, 13 July, and 18 Sept. 1821, ibid.; Marshall, writing as "A Friend to the Union," in *Union* (Philadelphia), 24 and 28 Apr. 1819, and as "A Friend of the Constitution," in *Alexandria Gazette*, 30 June, and 1–3, 5, 6, 9, 14, 15 July 1819, both in *John Marshall's Defense of* McCulloch v. Maryland, ed. Gerald Gunther, 155–214; Story to Jeremiah Mason, 10 Jan. 1822, in *Life and Letters of Story*, ed. Story, 1:411.
4. On the report and resolutions on the Missouri crisis in the House of Delegates, see *Niles' Register* (Philadelphia), 22 Jan. and 5 Feb. 1820; see also resolutions on the Missouri Compromise, 1 Feb. 1820, in *State Documents*, ed. Ames, 201–2; Roane to Monroe, 16 Feb. 1820, in "Letters of Spencer Roane."
5. *Cohens v. Virginia*, 6 Wheaton 264 (1821); resolutions on the Supreme Court and *Cohens v. Virginia*, 19 Feb. 1821, in *State Documents*, ed. Ames, 103–4.
6. Roane, writing as "Algernon Sidney," *RE*, 25 and 29 May, and 1, 5, and 8 June 1821; John Taylor, *Construction Construed and Constitutions Vindicated*; Jefferson's open letter for circulation, included in Jefferson to Roane, 27 June 1821, in *Writings of Jefferson*, ed. Lipscomb et al., 15:326–29; resolutions on the Supreme Court and *Cohens v. Virginia*, 19 Feb. 1821, in *State Documents*, ed. Ames, 103–4.
7. Vote on a constitutional convention, 24 Jan. 1817, Nov. session, 1816, *JHD*, 169–70; issue of drawing up a revised code, debated in conjunction with a publication of statutes, vote, 10 Mar. 1819, Dec. session, 1818, ibid., 221; election returns in the Nov. 1824 and 1828 issues of *RE*; and Henry H. Simms, *The Rise of the Whigs in Virginia, 1824–1840*, 32–33.
8. Editorials, *Virginian* (Lynchburg), 22 Nov. 1822, 23 Jan., 15, 29 Apr., 12 Aug. 1823, 17 Aug. 1824; "A Virginian," ibid., 20 Nov. 1824; editorials, *CW*, 22 Nov. and

6 Dec. 1825; Peyton Harrison to Randolph Harrison, 5 Dec. 1825, Harrison Family Papers, VHS.

9. "To the People of Virginia," *Republican Farmer* (Staunton, Va.), 21 Mar. 1822; editorial, *Virginia Herald* (Fredericksburg), 18 Apr. 1822; editorials, *Intelligencer* (Petersburg, Va.), 26 July 1825 and 1 Sept. 1826; editorials, *Virginian* (Lynchburg), 22 Oct. and 20 Dec. 1822; "Citizen of the Potomac," *CW*, 6 Jan. 1826; editorial, *CW*, 16 Dec. 1825; A Virginian, *Letters on the Richmond Party*.

10. On support for state banking and internal improvements, see *RE*, 1 June, 6, 13 July, 10, 14, 24 Aug., 31 Sept., 6, 9, 16, 26 Nov., and 10, 14, 21 Dec. 1816; see also my "Richmond Junto."

11. Election returns in the Nov. 1824 issues of *RE*.

12. Benjamin Watkins Leigh to Henry Lee, 29 Nov. 1824 and 30 July 1826, and Benjamin Watkins Leigh to William Leigh, 3 Feb. 1828, Benjamin Watkins Leigh papers, VHS; John Randolph, *Substance of a Speech on Retrenchment and Reform;* Simms, *Rise of the Whigs*, 32–33; and 1828 election returns in *RE*.

13. 1828 election returns in *RE;* vote on a constitutional convention, 24 Jan. 1817, Nov. session, 1816, *JHD*, 169–70.

14. 1828 election returns, *RE; CW*, 27 Jan., 17 Feb., and 15 Dec. 1826; vote on a constitutional convention, 24 Jan. 1817, Nov. session, 1816, *JHD*, 169–70; issue of drawing up a revised code, debated in conjunction with a publication of statutes, vote, 10 Mar. 1819, Dec. session 1818, *JHD*, 221.

15. Editorial, *CW*, 20 Feb. 1828.

16. Morton J. Horwitz, *The Transformation of American Law, 1780–1860*.

17. See *Ross v. Gill*, 1 Washington 87 (1792); *Keel v. Herbert*, 1 Washington 203 (1793); *Wroe v. Washington*, 1 Washington 357 (1794); *Blincoe v. Berkeley*, 1 Call 412 (1798); *Bogle, Somerville & Co. v. Sullivant*, 1 Call 561 (1799); *Martin v. Stover*, 2 Call 514 (1801); *Baring v. Reeder*, 1 Hening and Munford 154 (1806); *Fisher v. Duncan*, 1 Hening and Munford 563 (1807); *Moore v. Chapman*, 3 Hening and Munford 260 (1808); *Crabtree v. Horton*, 4 Munford 59 (1813); *Whitacre v. M'Ilhaney*, 4 Munford 310 (1814); *Fowler v. Lee*, 4 Munford 373 (1815); *Hollingsworth v. Dunbar*, 5 Munford 199 (1816); *Brooke v. Young*, 3 Randolph 106 (1824); *Dabney v. Taliaferro*, 4 Randolph 256 (1826); *M'Rae v. Scott and Saunders*, 4 Randolph 463 (1826); *Kitty v. Fitzhugh*, 4 Randolph 600 (1827); *Pleasants v. Pendleton*, 6 Randolph 473 (1828).

18. *Whitacre v. M'Ilhaney*, 4 Munford 310 (1814); Henry St. George Tucker, *Commentaries*, 294.

19. On the jury's role in distinguishing between and determining both law and fact, see the cases cited in note 17, above, and Robinson, *Practice in the Courts* 1:338–44; Henry St. George Tucker, *Commentaries*, 294.

20. See *Ross v. Pines*, 3 Call 568 (1790); *Sayre v. Grymes*, 1 Hening and Munford 404 (1807); *M'Rae's Executors v. Wood's Executors*, 1 Hening and Munford 548 (1807); *Wingfield v. Crenshaw*, 3 Hening and Munford 245 (1808); *Shanks and M'Rae v. Fenwick*, 2 Munford 478 (1811); *Chaney v. Saunders*, 3 Munford 51 (1811); *Keys v.*

M'Fatridge, 6 Munford 18 (1817); *Bennett v. Hardaway, Administrator of Jones*, 6 Munford 125 (1818); Henry St. George Tucker, *Commentaries*, 299–300.

21. On the vast number of statutes authorizing state internal-improvement projects, see John Williams, *Index to Enrolled Bills of the General Assembly, 1776 to 1910*, and the bills in the *AGA*.

22. On Virginia's corporations and their quasi-public nature, see Roane's opinion, *Currie's Administrators v. The Mutual Assurance Society*, 4 Hening and Munford 315 (1809); Horwitz, *Transformation of American Law*, 112; and Bruce A. Campbell, "John Marshall, the Virginia Political Economy, and the Dartmouth College Decision."

23. Horwitz, *Transformation of American Law*; R. Kent Newmyer, *Supreme Court Justice Joseph Story*, 115–54; see also An act concerning milldams and other obstructions of water courses, Hening, *Statutes* 12:187–90; *Home v. Richards*, 2 Call 507 (1800); and *Mayo v. Turner*, 1 Munford 405 (1810); *Kownslar v. Ward*, Gilmer 127 (1820); Roane's opinions in *Coleman, Executor and Trustee of Rowlett v. Moody*, 4 Hening and Munford 1 (1809); and *Eppes v. Cralle*, 1 Munford 258 (1810); and Coulter's opinion in *Crenshaw and Crenshaw v. Slate River Company*, 6 Randolph 245 (1828).

24. See An act incorporating the Potomac Canal Company, 22 Feb. 1823, *AGA*, 59–67; and An act making more effectual provision to carry into effect, the act, entitled an act, to amend the act, entitled an act, for clearing and improving the navigation of James River, and for uniting the eastern and western waters, by the James and Kanawha rivers, and for other purposes, 24 Feb. 1823, ibid., 50–58; Act to improve the navigation of the Slate River, 29 Jan. 1819, ibid. 68–73.

25. Act to improve the navigation of the Slate River, 29 Jan. 1819, *AGA*, 68–73; *Crenshaw and Crenshaw v. Slate River Company*, 6 Randolph 245 (1828).

26. *Crenshaw and Crenshaw v. Slate River Company*, 6 Randolph 245 (1828).

27. Ibid.

28. An act incorporating a company for the purpose of improving the navigation of the Northanna River, 1 Mar. 1821, *AGA*, 71–79; An act for incorporating a company for the purpose of improving the navigation of the Pamunkey and Southanna rivers, 2 Mar. 1821, ibid., 79–87. I looked at all the bills in *AGA*, using its indices; and in Williams, *Index to Enrolled Bills*; and in *Supplement to the Revised Code of the Laws of Virginia*.

29. *McCall v. Turner*, 1 Call 133 (1797); Pendleton to Madison, 21 Apr. 1790, and Pendleton to Washington, 11 Sept. 1793, in *Letters and Papers of Pendleton*, Mays, 2:564–67, 613–15; Spencer Roane to William Roane, 10 Mar. 1815, Roane Family Papers, VSLA.

30. Roane's opinion in *Baring v. Reeder*, 1 Hening and Munford 154 (1806).

31. *Ware v. Hylton*, 3 Dallas 199 (1796); *Martin v. Stover*, 2 Call 514 (1801).

32. Wirt to Dabney Carr, 13 Feb. and 20 Mar. 1803, in *Memoirs of Wirt*, ed. Kennedy, 1:93–97; Francis Walker Gilmer to Peachy Ridgeway Gilmer, 14 Oct.

1813, 9 Feb. 1817, 22 Feb. 1818, 14 Mar. 1819, PRG; Peyton Harrison to Randolph Harrison, 11 May 1823, 1 Aug. 1824, 19 Jan. 1826, 12 May 1829, Harrison Family Papers, VHS; E. Lee Shepard, "Lawyers Look at Themselves."

33. Susan A. Riggs, "Creed Taylor;" J. Randolph Tucker, "Henry St. George Tucker."

34. Francis Walker Gilmer, *Sketches, Essays, and Translations*, 52. See also ibid., 33–35, 43–51; Wirt to Francis Walker Gilmer, 23 July and 29 Aug. 1815, in *Memoirs of Wirt*, ed. Kennedy, 1:342–43, 349–51; Francis Walker Gilmer to Peachy Ridgeway Gilmer, 7 Feb. and 22 May 1813, 9 Feb. 1817, PRG.

35. Wirt to Dabney Carr, 9 Sept. 1810, 8 Mar. and 11 Aug. 1811, in *Memoirs of Wirt*, ed. Kennedy, 1:258–60, 275–76, 286–89; Francis Walker Gilmer to Peachy Ridgeway Gilmer, 3 Mar. and [?] Oct. 1809, 27 [?] and 10 Apr. 1811, 22 May and 21 Dec. 1813, 25 May and 25 Oct. 1816, 9 Feb. 1817, 22 Feb. 1818, 25 Mar. 1819, PRG.

36. Editorials, *Republican Farmer* (Staunton, Va.), 21 Mar. and 18 Apr. 1822; *Virginian* (Lynchburg), 27 Sept. 1822, 13 Aug. 1824, and 15 Feb. 1825; *Intelligencer* (Petersburg, Va.), 26 July 1825; CW, 31 Dec. 1824, 3 Jan. and 24 Feb. 1826.

37. Benjamin Watkins Leigh, *Substitute . . . on the Subject of a Convention*, 4–13; William Branch Giles, *Speech . . . on the Bill, "Concerning a Convention,"* 22–24.

38. Giles, *Speech . . . on the Bill, "Concerning a Convention,"* 27; Leigh, *Substitute . . . on the Subject of a Convention*, 4–7.

39. Leigh, *Substitute . . . on the Subject of a Convention*, 6, 22; Giles, *Speech . . . on the Bill, "Concerning a Convention,"* 1–3, 27–28.

40. Giles, *Speech . . . on the Bill, "Concerning a Convention,"* 22–24; Leigh, *Substitute . . . on the Subject of a Convention*, 10–13.

41. Leigh, *Substitute . . . on the Subject of a Convention*, 10–14; Giles, *Speech . . . on the Bill, "Concerning a Convention,"* 22–26.

42. Giles, *Speech . . . on the Bill, "Concerning a Convention,"* 22–28.

43. Ibid.; Leigh, *Substitute . . . on the Subject of a Convention*, 10–21.

44. Leigh, *Substitute . . . on the Subject of a Convention*, 25. See also ibid., 10–21; Giles, *Speech . . . on the Bill, "Concerning a Convention,"* 27–28.

Chapter 7

1. Jefferson to John Taylor, 1 June 1798, in *Writings of Jefferson*, ed. Lipscomb et al., 10:44–47; resolutions on a federal common law, 10 Jan. 1800, Dec. session, 1799, *JHD*, 77–83; St. George Tucker, *Examination of the Question, How Far the Common Law of England Is the Law of the Federal Government of the United States?* Madison to Jefferson, 12 Jan. 1800, in *Writings of Madison*, ed. Hunt, 6:345–47.

2. For the discussion here and in the following paragraphs on the Marshall-Roane debate, see Roane, writing as "Hampden," in *RE*, 11, 15, 18, and 22 June 1819, Marshall, writing as "A Friend to the Union," in *Union* (Philadelphia), 24,

28 Apr. 1819, and as "A Friend of the Constitution," in *Alexandria Gazette*, 30 June and 1–3, 5, 6, 9, 14, 15 July 1819: both reprinted in *Marshall's Defense of McCulloch v. Maryland*, ed. Gunther, 155–214; Marshall's opinion in *Cohens v. Virginia*, 6 Wheaton 264 (1821); Roane, writing as "Algernon Sidney," in *RE*, 25, 29 May and 1, 5, 8 June 1821.

BIBLIOGRAPHY

Personal Papers

College of William and Mary Library, Williamsburg
   Tucker-Coleman Papers

Library of Congress, Washington, D.C.
   Thomas Jefferson Papers
   John Marshall Papers
   John Marshall Papers, compiled by Albert J. Beveridge (bound manuscripts)
   Wilson Cary Nicholas Papers
   Joseph Story Papers

University of Virginia Library, Charlottesville
   Cabell Family Papers
   John Hook Papers
   Lee Family Papers
   Wilson Cary Nicholas Papers

Virginia Historical Society, Richmond
   Ambler Family Papers
   Robert A. Brock Papers
   Byrd Family Papers
   Memo of Periods in the Life of William H. Cabell
   Henry Carrington Papers
   Henry Curtis Papers
   William Fleming Papers
   William Branch Giles Papers
   Peachy Ridgeway Gilmer Papers
   Gooch Family Papers
   Hugh Blair Grigsby Diary
   Grinnan Family Papers
   Harrison Family Papers
   Henry Family Papers
   Henry Lee Papers
   Benjamin Watkins Leigh Papers
   Carter Braxton Page Papers
   John Randolph Papers

Thomas Ritchie Papers
Stuart Family Papers
Virginia Court of Appeals manuscripts

Virginia State Library and Archives, Richmond
Patrick Henry Account Book
John Hook Papers
John Marshall Papers
Roane Family Papers
John Wickham Papers
Wykeham-Martin Papers (microfilm)

Government Records, Virginia State Library and Archives

District Court at Prince Edward County. Records at Large.

General Court Records: List of Judgements, Auditor of Public Accounts

Northern Neck Grants and Surveys Index

Order Books
Campbell County Court
Caroline County Court
Caroline County Superior Court
Cumberland County Court
District Court at Fredericksburg
District Court at Prince Edward County (PED)
District Court at Winchester
Frederick County Court
Fredericksburg City Hustings Court
Fredericksburg and Spotsylvania Superior Court
Prince Edward County Court
Prince Edward County Superior Court
Richmond City Hustings Court
Spotsylvania County Court
United States Circuit Court, District of Virginia
Virginia Supreme Court of Appeals
Wythe County Court
York County Court

Prince Edward County Land Tax Books

Registers of Virginia Justices and County Officers

Shenandoah County Land Tax Books

Published Court Reports

United States

Hayburn's Case, 2 Dallas 409 (1792).
Chisholm v. Georgia, 2 Dallas 419 (1793).
Hylton v. United States, 3 Dallas 171 (1796).
Ware v. Hylton, 3 Dallas 199 (1796).
Hunter v. Fairfax's Devisee, 3 Dallas 305 (1796).
Hollingsworth v. Virginia, 3 Dallas 378 (1798).
Marbury v. Madison, 1 Cranch 137 (1803).
Stuart v. Laird, 1 Cranch 309 (1803).
Fletcher v. Peck, 6 Cranch 87 (1810).
United States v. Hudson and Goodwin, 7 Cranch 32 (1812).
Fairfax's Devisee v. Hunter's Lessee, 7 Cranch 602 (1813).
Terrett v. Taylor, 9 Cranch 43 (1815).
Martin v. Hunter's Lessee, 1 Wheaton 304 (1816).
McCulloch v. Maryland, 4 Wheaton 316 (1819).
Dartmouth College v. Woodward, 4 Wheaton 518 (1819).
Cohens v. Virginia, 6 Wheaton 264 (1821).

Virginia

Commonwealth v. Caton, 4 Call 5 (1782).
Foushee v. Lea, 4 Call 279 (1785).
Hague v. Stratton, 4 Call 84 (1786).
Case of the Judges of the Court of Appeals, 4 Call 135 (1788).
Ross v. Pines, 3 Call 568 (1790).
Ross v. Gill, 1 Washington 87 (1792).
Hoomes v. Kuhn, 4 Call 274 (1792).
Keel v. Herbert, 1 Washington 203 (1793).
Kamper v. Hawkins, 1 Brockenbrough and Holmes 20 (1793).
Boswell v. Jones, 1 Washington 322 (1794).
Wroe v. Washington, 1 Washington 357 (1794).
Richards v. Hoome, 2 Washington 36 (1794).
Bernard v. Brewer, 2 Washington 76 (1795).
Wroe v. Harris, 2 Washington 126 (1795).
Lee v. Turberville, 2 Washington 162 (1795).
McCall v. Turner, 1 Call 133 (1797).
Barrett and Company v. Tazewell, 1 Call 219 (1798).
Blincoe v. Berkeley, 1 Call 412 (1798).
Noel v. Sale, 1 Call 495 (1799).
Bogle, Somerville & Co. v. Sullivant, 1 Call 561 (1799).
Home v. Richards, 2 Call 507 (1800).

Martin v. Stover, 2 Call 514 (1801).
M'Lean v. Cropper and Others, 3 Call 367 (1803).
Goosely v. Holmes, Administrator of Elliot, 3 Call 424 (1803).
Marshall v. Conrad, 5 Call 364 (1805).
Martin v. Beverley and Norman, 5 Call 444 (1805).
Fine v. Cockshut, 6 Call 16 (1806).
Baring v. Reeder, 1 Hening and Munford 154 (1806).
Robinson's Administrator v. Brock, 1 Hening and Munford 213 (1807).
Henderson v. Allens, 1 Hening and Munford 235 (1807).
Sayre v. Grymes, 1 Hening and Munford 404 (1807).
M'Rae's Executors v. Wood's Executors, 1 Hening and Munford 548 (1807).
Fisher v. Duncan, 1 Hening and Munford 563 (1807).
Gordon and Others v. Brown's Executor, 3 Hening and Munford 219 (1808).
Wingfield v. Crenshaw, 3 Hening and Munford 245 (1808).
Moore v. Chapman, 3 Hening and Munford 260 (1808).
Wilkinson v. Mayo, 3 Hening and Munford 565 (1809).
Coleman, Executor and Trustee of Rowlett v. Moody, 4 Hening and Munford 1 (1809).
Brooke's Administrators v. Shelly, 4 Hening and Munford 266 (1809).
Currie's Administrators v. the Mutual Assurance Society, 4 Hening and Munford 315 (1809).
Marks v. Morris, 4 Hening and Munford 463 (1809).
Hunter v. Fairfax's Devisee, 1 Munford 218 (1809).
Verdier v. Hume and Hume, 4 Hening and Munford 479 (1810).
Eppes v. Cralle, 1 Munford 258 (1810).
Mayo v. Turner, 1 Munford 405 (1810).
Clay v. Ransome, 1 Munford 454 (1810).
Tunnell and Wife v. Watson and Wife, 2 Munford 283 (1811).
Shanks and M'Rae v. Fenwick, 2 Munford 478 (1811).
Chaney v. Saunders, 3 Munford 51 (1811).
Geddy and Knox v. Butler and Wife, 3 Munford 345 (1812).
Blank's Administrator v. Foushee, 4 Munford 61 (1812).
Crabtree v. Horton, 4 Munford 59 (1813).
Lightfoot v. Colgin, 5 Munford 42 (1813).
Hunter v. Martin, Devisee of Fairfax, 4 Munford 1 (1814).
Whitacre v. M'Ilhaney, 4 Munford 310 (1814).
Fowler v. Lee, 4 Munford 373 (1815).
Chapman v. Armistead, 4 Munford 382 (1815).
Bohn v. Sheppard, 4 Munford 403 (1815).
Maddox v. Jackson, 4 Munford 462 (1815).
Dawson v. Moons, 4 Munford 535 (1815).
Ligon v. Ford, 5 Munford 15 (1816).
Hollingsworth v. Dunbar, 5 Munford 199 (1816).

Williams v. Price, 5 Munford 507 (1817).
Keys v. M'Fatridge, 6 Munford 18 (1817).
Bennett v. Hardaway, Administrator of Jones, 6 Munford 125 (1818).
Woodward v. Woodson's Heirs, 6 Munford 227 (1818).
Cropper v. Carlton and Wife, 6 Munford 277 (1819).
Dimmett v. Eskridge, 6 Munford 308 (1819).
Kownslar v. Ward, Gilmer 127 (1820).
Rixey v. Ward, 3 Randolph 52 (1824).
Brooke v. Young, 3 Randolph 106 (1824).
Humphrey's Administrator v. West's Administrator, 3 Randolph 516 (1825).
M'Michen v. Amos and Others, 4 Randolph 134 (1826).
Dabney v. Taliaferro, 4 Randolph 256 (1826).
M'Rae v. Scott and Saunders, 4 Randolph 463 (1826).
Kitty v. Fitzhugh, 4 Randolph 600 (1827).
Green v. Judith, 5 Randolph 1 (1827).
Caton and Veale v. Lenox, 5 Randolph 31 (1827).
Stribbling v. Bank of the Valley, 5 Randolph 132 (1827).
Pleasants v. Pendleton, 6 Randolph 473 (1828).
Crenshaw and Crenshaw v. Slate River Company, 6 Randolph 245 (1828).
Miscellaneous Material in the Court Reports
    Reed v. Reed, 1 Munford 611 (Appendix).
    Tucker's Letter of Resignation, 2 Munford (1811).
    Biographical Sketch of the Judges of the Court of Appeals, 4 Call (1827).

Newspapers

Constitutional Whig (Richmond, Va.).
Intelligencer (Petersburg, Va.).
Niles' Register (Philadelphia).
Republican Farmer (Staunton, Va.).
Richmond Enquirer.
Virginia Herald (Fredericksburg).
Virginian (Lynchburg).
Winchester Gazette, (Va.).

Other Published Primary Sources

Acts of the General Assembly. Richmond, Va. Printed for the government annually.
Adams, John Quincy. *The Diary of John Quincy Adams, 1794–1845*. Edited by Allen Nevins. New York: Longmans, Green, and Co., 1929.
American State Papers. Edited by Walter Lowrie and Mathew Clark. 38 vols. Washington: Gales & Seaton, 1832–61.

Annals of the Congress of the United States. 42 vols. Washington: Gales & Seaton, 1834–56.
Brooke, Francis T. *Narrative of My Life for My Family.* Richmond: by the author, 1849.
Burn, Richard. *The Justice of the Peace, and Parish Officer.* 3 vols. 1754; rpt. ed., London: A. Millar, 1764.
Calendar of Virginia State Papers and Other Manuscripts. Compiled by William P. Palmer, Sherwin McRae, and Raleigh Colston. 11 vols. Richmond, 1875–93.
Care, Henry. *English Liberties: Or, The Free-Born Subject's Inheritance.* London: G. Larkin, 1680.
Coke, Edward. *The First Part of the Institutes of the Laws of England; Or, a Commentary upon Littleton.* Edited by Thomas Day. 1628 [1st American ed.]; Philadelphia: Johnson and Warner and Samuel R. Fisher, Jr., 1812.
Dalton, Michael. *The Country Justice: Containing the Practice of the Justices of the Peace.* London: Society of Stationers, 1619; rpt. ed., London: Professional Books Limited, 1973.
The Debates in the Several State Conventions on the Adoption of the Federal Constitution. Edited by Jonathan Elliot. 5 vols. Washington: Congressional publication, 1830–36; rpt. ed., Philadelphia: J. B. Lippincott Co., 1941.
Dunmore, Giles. *Law of England Concerning Juries.* London: George Dawes, 1682.
The Federalist. Edited by Jacob E. Cooke. Middletown, Conn.: Wesleyan Univ. Press, 1961.
Ford, Paul Leicester, ed. *Essays on the Constitution of the United States.* New York: Historical Printing Club, 1892.
Giles, William Branch. *Speech . . . on the Bill, "Concerning a Convention."* Richmond, Va.: T. W. White, 1827.
———. *Speech on Clay's Speech upon the Tariff: Or the "American System" So Called; Or the Anglican System in Fact.* Richmond, Va.: T. W. White, 1827.
———, comp. *To The Public: Containing All the Publications . . . Relating to . . . Mr. Jefferson's Letter to Governor Giles.* Richmond, Va.: T. W. White, 1828.
Gilmer, Francis Walker. *Sketches of American Orators.* 1816; in *Sketches, Essays, and Translations.* Baltimore: Fielding Lucas, 1828.
Grigsby, Hugh Blair. *Letters of a South-Carolinian.* Norfolk, Va.: C. Bonsal, 1827.
Hale, Mathew. *The History of the Common Law of England.* 2d ed. London: E. Nutt, 1716.
Hamilton, Alexander. *The Papers of Alexander Hamilton.* Edited by Harold C. Syrett. 26 vols. New York: Columbia Univ. Press, 1961–79.
Hening, William Waller. *The Virginia Justice: Comprising the Office and Authority of a Justice of the Peace.* 4 editions, Richmond, Va.: 1795, 1809, 1820, 1825.
Jacob, Giles. *Freeholder's Companion: Containing the Laws, Statutes, and Customs Relating to Freehold.* London: R. Nutt and R. Gosling, 1740.

Jefferson, Thomas. *Notes on the State of Virginia*. 1787; Chapel Hill: Univ. of North Carolina Press, 1954; New York: Norton Library, 1972.
——. *The Writings of Thomas Jefferson*. Edited by Andrew A. Lipscomb and Albert E. Bergh. 20 vols. Washington: Thomas Jefferson Memorial Association of the United States, 1903–4.
——. *The Papers of Thomas Jefferson*. Edited by Julian P. Boyd et al. Multi-volumed. Princeton, N.J.: Princeton Univ. Press, 1950– .
Journal of the House of Delegates of the State of Virginia. Richmond, Va. Printed for the government annually.
The Laws of Virginia: Being a Supplement to Hening's The Statutes at Large, 1700–1750. Edited by Waverly K. Winfree. Richmond: Virginia State Library, 1971.
Lee, Henry. *An Address of the Fifty-Eight Federal Members of the Virginia Legislature*. Augusta, Maine: Peter Edes, 1799.
——. *Plain Truth: Addressed To The People Of Virginia*. Richmond, Va.: n.p., 1799.
Lee, Richard Henry. *The Letters of Richard Henry Lee*. Edited by James Curtis Ballagh. 2 vols. New York: Macmillan Company, 1912–14.
Leigh, Benjamin Watkins. *The Letters of Algernon Sidney: In Defense of Civil Liberty and Against the Encroachments of Military Despotism*. 1818–19; rpt. ed., Richmond, Va.: T. W. White, 1830.
——. *Substitute Intended To Be Offered to the Next Meeting of the Citizens of Richmond On the Subject of a Convention*. Richmond, Va.: Shepard & Pollard, 1824.
Maclay, William. *Journal of William Maclay, United States Senator from Pennsylvania, 1789–1791*. Edited by Edgar S. Maclay. New York: D. Appleton and Company, 1890.
Madison, James. *The Writings of James Madison*. Edited by Gaillard Hunt. 9 vols. New York: G. P. Putnam's Sons, 1900–1910.
——. *The Papers of James Madison*. Edited by William T. Hutchinson, Robert A. Rutland, et al. Volumes 8–14. Chicago: Univ. of Chicago Press, 1962–76; Charlottesville: Univ. Press of Virginia, 1977– .
Marshall, John. *The Life of George Washington*. 5 vols. Philadelphia: C. P. Wayne, 1807.
——, and Story, Joseph. "Story-Marshall Correspondence," edited by Charles Warren. *William and Mary Quarterly* 2d ser. 21 (1941): 1–26.
——. *John Marshall's Defense of McCulloch v. Maryland*. Edited by Gerald Gunther. Stanford, Calif.: Stanford Univ. Press, 1969.
——. *The Papers of John Marshall*. Edited by Charles T. Cullen, Herbert A. Johnson, and Charles F. Hobson. Multi-volumed. Chapel Hill: Univ. of North Carolina Press, 1977– .
Mason, George. *The Papers of George Mason, 1725–1792*. Edited by Robert A. Rutland. 3 vols. Chapel Hill: Univ. of North Carolina Press, 1970.
Monroe, James. *The Writings of James Monroe*. Edited by Stanislaus M. Hamilton. 7 vols. 1898–1903; rpt. ed., New York: AMS Press, 1969.

Pendleton, Edmund. *The Letters and Papers of Edmund Pendleton, 1734–1803.* Edited by David John Mays. 2 vols. Charlottesville: Univ. Press of Virginia, 1967.
"Petitions" [from meetings of citizens in Alexandria, Norfolk, and Richmond, for the establishment of branches of the Bank of the United States, 1791]. *Virginia Magazine of History and Biography* 8 (1901): 287–95.
Plumer, William. *William Plumer's Memorandum of Proceedings in the United States Senate, 1803–1807.* Edited by E. S. Brown. New York: Macmillan Co., 1923.
Randolph, John. *Speeches on the Greek Question, on Internal Improvements; and on the Tariff Bill.* Washington, D.C.: Gales & Seaton, 1824.
———. *Substance of a Speech on Retrenchment and Reform.* Washington, D.C.: Green and Jarvis, 1828.
———. "Selected Speeches and Letters." Appendix in Russell Kirk, *John Randolph of Roanoke: A Study In American Politics.* 1951; rpt. ed., Indianapolis: Liberty Fund, 1978.
The Revised Code of the Laws of Virginia: Being a Collection of All Such Acts of the General Assembly, of a Public and Permanent Nature, As Are Now in Force. 2 vols. Richmond: 1819.
Ritchie, Thomas. "Unpublished Letters of Thomas Ritchie," ed. William E. Dodd. *John P. Branch Historical Papers of Randolph-Macon College* 3 (1911): 199–357.
Roane, Spencer. "Roane Correspondence," ed. William E. Dodd. *John P. Branch Historical Papers of Randolph-Macon College* 2 (1905): 123–42.
———. "Letters of Spencer Roane, 1788–1822." *New York Public Library Bulletin* 10 (1906): 167–80.
Robinson, Conway. *The Practice in the Courts of Law and Equity in Virginia.* Richmond, Va.: Samuel Shepherd and Co., 1832.
Schreiner-Yantis, Netti, and Love, Florence Speakman, comps. *The 1787 Census of Virginia.* Springfield, Va.: Geneological Books in Print, 1987.
Starke, Richard. *The Virginia Justice: The Office and Authority of a Justice of Peace Explained and Digested.* Williamsburg, Va.: Alexander Purdie and John Dixon, 1774.
State Documents on Federal Relations: The States and the United States. Edited by Herman V. Ames. 1900–1906; rpt. ed., New York: Da Capo Press, 1970.
The Statutes at Large; Being a Collection of All the Laws of Virginia, from the First Session of the Legislature, in the Year 1619. Edited by William W. Hening. 13 vols. 1819–23; rpt. ed., Charlottesville: Univ. Press of Virginia, 1969.
The Statutes at Large of the United States of America. First 8 vols. edited by Richard Peters. Boston: Little, Brown, and Company, 1846–54.
The Statutes at Large of Virginia, from October Session 1792, to December Session 1806. Edited by Samuel Shepherd. 3 vols. Richmond: 1835; rpt. ed., New York: AMS Press, 1970.
Storing, Herbert J., ed. *The Complete Anti-Federalist.* 7 vols. Chicago: Univ. of Chicago Press, 1981.

Story, Joseph. *Life and Letters of Joseph Story.* Edited by William W. Story. 2 vols. Boston: Charles C. Little and James Brown, 1851.

Supplement to the Revised Code of the Laws of Virginia: Being a Collection of all the Acts of the General Assembly, of a Public Nature, Passed since the Year 1819. Richmond, 1833.

Swem, Earl G., comp. *Virginia Historical Index.* 2 vols. Roanoke, Va.: Stone Printing and Manufacturing Company, 1934–36.

———, and Williams, John, comps. *A Register of the General Assembly of Virginia 1776–1918, and of the Constitutional Conventions.* Richmond: 1918.

Taylor, John. *A Definition of Parties: Or the Political Effects of the Paper System Considered.* Philadelphia: Francis Bailey, 1794.

———. *An Enquiry into the Principles and Tendency of Certain Public Measures.* Philadelphia: Thomas Dobson, 1794.

———. *An Argument Respecting the Constitutionality of the Carriage Tax.* Richmond, Va.: Augustine Davis, 1795.

———. *A Pamphlet Containing A Series Of Letters.* Richmond, Va.: E. C. Stanard, 1809.

———. *An Inquiry into the Principles and Policy of the Government of the United States.* 1814; rpt. ed., New Haven, Conn.: Yale Univ. Press, 1950.

———. *Arator, Being a Series of Agricultural Essays, Practical and Political.* Reprint edited by M. E. Bradford. 1818; rpt. ed., Indianapolis: Liberty Fund, 1977.

———. *Construction Construed and Constitutions Vindicated.* Richmond, Va.: Shepherd and Pollard, 1820.

———. *Tyranny Unmasked.* Reprint edited by F. Thornton Miller. 1822; rpt. ed., Indianapolis: Liberty Fund, 1992.

———. *New Views of the Constitution of the United States.* Washington, D.C.. Way & Gideon, 1823.

———. *Disunion Sentiment in Congress in 1794: A Confidential Memorandum Hitherto Unpublished.* Edited by Gaillard Hunt. Washington, D.C.: W. H. Lowdermilk and Company, 1905.

———. "Letters of John Taylor," ed. William E. Dodd. *John P. Branch Historical Papers of Randolph-Macon College* 2 (1908): 253–353.

Tucker, Henry St. George, *Commentaries on the Laws of Virginia: Comprising the Substance of a Course of Lectures Delivered to the Winchester Law School.* Winchester: Winchester Virginian, 1831.

Tucker, St. George. *Examination of the Question, How Far the Common Law of England Is the Law of the Federal Government of the United States?* Richmond, Va.: John Dixon, 1800.

———, ed. *Blackstone's Commentaries: With Notes of Reference to the Constitution and Laws of the United States and of the Commonwealth of Virginia.* Philadelphia: William Birch Young and Abraham, 1803; rpt. ed., New York: Augustus M. Kelley, 1969.

Tyler, Lyon G., ed. *Letters and Times of the Tylers*. Richmond, Va.: Whittest & Stepperson, 1884.
A Virginian. *Letters on the Richmond Party*. Richmond, Va.: The Hornet Office, 1823.
The Virginia Report of 1799–1800, Touching the Alien and Sedition Laws, Together with the Virginia Resolutions of December 21, 1798, Including the Debate and Proceedings Thereon in The House of Delegates of Virginia. . . . Richmond: J. W. Randolph, 1850; rpt. ed., New York: Da Capo Press, 1970.
Washington, George. *The Writings of George Washington*. Edited by John C. Fitzpatrick. 39 vols. Washington: United States Government Printing Office, 1931–44.
Webb, George. *The Office and Authority of a Justice of Peace*. Williamsburg, Va.: William Parks, 1736; rpt. ed., Homes Beach, Fla.: William W. Guant & Sons, 1969.
Williams, John, comp. *Index to Enrolled Bills of the General Assembly, 1776 to 1910*. Richmond, Va.: printed by the government, 1911.
Wirt, William. *The British Spy, or Letters, to a Member of the British Parliament*. Newburyport, Mass.: 1804.
———. *The Old Bachelor*. Richmond, Va.: Thomas Ritchie & Fielding Lucas, 1814.
———. *Sketches of the Life and Character of Patrick Henry*. 1817; rev. ed., Philadelphia: Thomas Cowerthwait & Co., 1841.
———. *Memoirs of the Life of William Wirt*. Edited by John P. Kennedy. 2 vols. 1849; rev. ed., Philadelphia: Blanchard and Lea, 1856.

Secondary Sources

Books

Abernethy, Thomas Perkins. *The South in the New Nation, 1789–1819*. Baton Rouge: Louisiana State Univ. Press, 1961.
Adams, Henry. *John Randolph*. Boston: Houghton Mifflin Company, 1882.
Ambler, Charles Henry. *Sectionalism In Virginia from 1776 to 1861*. 1910; rpt. ed., New York: Russell & Russell, 1964.
———. *Thomas Ritchie: A Study in Virginia Politics*. Richmond, Va.: Bell Book and Stationery Co., 1913.
Ammon, Harry. *The Genet Mission*. New York: W. W. Norton & Company, 1973.
Anderson, Dice R. *William Branch Giles: A Study in the Politics of Virginia and the Nation from 1790 to 1830*. 1914; rpt. ed., Gloucester, Mass.: Peter Smith, 1965.
Appleby, Joyce. *Capitalism and a New Social Order: The Republican Vision of the 1790s*. New York: New York Univ. Press, 1984.

Bailyn, Bernard. *The Ideological Origins of the American Revolution*. Cambridge, Mass.: Harvard Univ. Press, 1967.

Baker, J. H. *An Introduction to English Legal History*. London: Butterworth and Co., 1971.

Banner, James M. *To the Hartford Convention: The Federalists and the Origins of Party Politics in Massachusetts, 1789–1815*. New York: Alfred A. Knopf, 1969.

Banning, Lance. *The Jeffersonian Persuasion: Evolution of a Party Ideology*. Ithaca, N.Y.: Cornell Univ. Press, 1978.

Beard, Charles A. *Economic Origins of Jeffersonian Democracy*. New York: The Macmillan Company, 1915; rpt. ed., 1952.

Beeman, Richard R. *The Old Dominion and the New Nation, 1788–1801*. Lexington: Univ. Press of Kentucky, 1972.

——. *Patrick Henry: A Biography*. New York: McGraw-Hill, 1974.

——. *The Evolution of the Southern Backcountry: A Case Study of Lunenburg County, Virginia, 1746–1832*. Philadelphia: Univ. of Pennsylvania Press, 1984.

Bemis, Samuel Flagg. *Jay's Treaty: A Study in Commerce and Diplomacy*. 1923; rev. ed., New Haven, Conn.: Yale Univ. Press, 1962.

Beveridge, Albert J. *The Life of John Marshall*. 4 vols. Boston: Houghton Mifflin Company, 1916–19.

Billings, Warren M., John E. Selby, and Thad W. Tate. *Colonial Virginia: A History*. White Plains, N.Y.: KTO Press, 1986.

Bloomfield, Maxwell. *American Lawyers in a Changing Society, 1776–1876*. Cambridge, Mass.: Harvard Univ. Press, 1976.

Bodenhamer, David J., and James W. Ely, Jr., eds. *Ambivalent Legacy: A Legal History of the South*. Jackson: Univ. Press of Mississippi, 1984.

Brant, Irving. *James Madison, Father of the Constitution, 1787–1800*. New York. Bobbs Merrill Company, 1950.

Breen, T. H. *Tobacco Culture: The Mentality of the Great Tidewater Planters on the Eve of Revolution*. Princeton, N.J.: Princeton Univ. Press, 1985.

Brown, Imogene E. *American Aristides: A Biography of George Wythe*. London: Associated Univ. Presses, 1981.

Brugger, Robert J. *Beverly Tucker: Heart over Head in the Old South*. Baltimore: The Johns Hopkins Univ. Press, 1978.

Bryson, William Hamilton. *Census of Law Books in Colonial Virginia*. Charlottesville: Univ. Press of Virginia, 1978.

——. *A Bibliography of Virginia Legal History before 1900*. Charlottesville: Univ. Press of Virginia, 1979.

——, ed. *The Virginia Law Reporters before 1880*. Charlottesville: Univ. Press of Virginia, 1977.

Buel, Richard. *Securing the Revolution: Ideology in American Politics, 1789–1815*. Ithaca, N.Y.: Cornell Univ. Press, 1972.

Chambers, William Nesbit. *Political Parties in a New Nation: The American Experience, 1776–1809*. New York: Oxford Univ. Press, 1963.

Charles, Joseph. *The Origins of the American Party System: Three Essays*. Williamsburg, Va.: Institute of Early American History and Culture, 1956.

Clinton, Robert Lowry. *Marbury v. Madison and Judicial Review*. Lawrence: Univ. Press of Kansas, 1989.

Colbourn, Trevor H. *The Lamp of Experience: Whig History and the Intellectual Origins of the American Revolution*. New York: W. W. Norton & Company, 1965.

Cole, Arthur C. *The Whig Party in the South*. 1914; rpt. ed., Gloucester, Mass.: Peter Smith, 1962.

Corwin, Edward S. *John Marshall and the Constitution: A Chronicle of the Supreme Court*. New Haven, Conn.: Yale Univ. Press, 1919.

Cunningham, Noble E., Jr. *The Jeffersonian Republicans: The Formation of Party Organization, 1789–1801*. Chapel Hill: Univ. of North Carolina Press, 1957.

———. *The Jeffersonian Republicans in Power: Party Operations, 1801–1809*. Chapel Hill: Univ. of North Carolina Press, 1963.

———. *The United States in 1800: Henry Adams Revisited*. Charlottesville: Univ. Press of Virginia, 1988.

Dangerfield, George. *The Era of Good Feelings*. New York: Harper & Row, 1952.

———. *The Awakening of American Nationalism, 1815–1828*. New York: Harper & Row, 1965.

Dewey, Frank L. *Thomas Jefferson: Lawyer*. Charlottesville: Univ. Press of Virginia, 1986.

Dumbauld, Edward. *Thomas Jefferson and the Law*. Norman: Univ. of Oklahoma Press, 1978.

Ellis, Richard E. *The Jeffersonian Crisis: Courts and Politics in the Young Republic*. New York: Oxford Univ. Press, 1971.

Ferguson, Robert A. *Law and Letters in American Culture*. Cambridge, Mass.: Harvard Univ. Press, 1984.

Freyer, Tony A. *Forums of Order: The Federal Courts and Business in American History*. Greenwich, Conn.: JAI Press, 1979.

———. *Harmony and Dissonance: The Swift and Erie Cases in American Federalism*. New York: New York Univ. Press, 1981.

Friedman, Lawrence M. *A History of American Law*. New York: Simon and Schuster, 1973.

Gray, Lewis Cecil. *History of Agriculture in the Southern United States to 1860*. 2 vols. Washington, D.C.: Carnegie Institution of Washington, 1933.

Greene, Jack P. *The Quest For Power: The Lower Houses of Assembly in the Southern Royal Colonies, 1689–1776*. Chapel Hill: Univ. of North Carolina Press, 1963.

———. *Peripheries and Center: Constitutional Development in the Extended Polities of the British Empire and the United States, 1607–1788*. New York: W. W. Norton and Company, 1986.

Grigsby, Hugh Blair. *The History of the Virginia Federal Convention of 1788: With Some Account of the Eminent Virginians of That Era Who Were Members of the Body.* Edited by R. A. Brock. Richmond: Virginia Historical Society, 1890.

Hall, Kermit L. *The Magic Mirror: Law in American History.* New York: Oxford Univ. Press, 1989.

———, and James W. Ely, Jr., ed. *An Uncertain Tradition: Constitutionalism and the History of the South.* Athens: Univ. of Georgia Press, 1989.

Harrell, Isaac Samuel. *Loyalism in Virginia: Chapters in the Economic History of the Revolution.* Durham, N.C.: Duke Univ. Press, 1926.

Hart, Freeman H. *The Valley of Virginia In The American Revolution, 1763–1789.* Chapel Hill: Univ. of North Carolina Press, 1942.

Haskins, George Lee, and Herbert A. Johnson. *Foundations of Power: John Marshall, 1801–15.* New York: Macmillan Publishing Co., 1981.

Hill, C. William, Jr. *The Political Theory of John Taylor of Caroline.* Cranbury, N.J.: Associated Univ. Presses, 1977.

Hogue, Arthur R. *Origins of the Common Law.* Bloomington: Indiana Univ. Press, 1966.

Horwitz, Morton J. *The Transformation of American Law, 1780–1860.* Cambridge, Mass.: Harvard Univ. Press, 1977.

Isaac, Rhys. *The Transformation of Virginia, 1740–1790.* Chapel Hill: Univ. of North Carolina Press, 1982.

Jordan, Daniel P. *Political Leadership in Jefferson's Virginia.* Charlottesville: Univ. Press of Virginia, 1983.

Koch, Adrienne. *Jefferson and Madison: The Great Collaboration.* New York: Alfred A. Knopf, 1950; rpt. ed., Oxford and New York: Oxford Univ. Press, 1977.

Kramnick, Isaac. *Bolingbroke and His Circle: The Politics of Nostalgia in the Age of Walpole.* Cambridge, Mass.: Harvard Univ. Press, 1968.

Kulikoff, Allan. *Tobacco and Slaves: The Development of Southern Cultures in the Chesapeake, 1680–1800.* Chapel Hill: Univ. of North Carolina Press, 1986.

Kutler, Stanley I. *Privilege and Creative Destruction: The Charles River Bridge Case.* Philadelphia: J. B. Lippincott Company, 1971.

Lutz, Donald S. *The Origins of American Constitutionalism.* Baton Rouge: Louisiana State Univ. Press, 1988.

McCoy, Drew R. *The Elusive Republic: Political Economy In Jeffersonian America.* Chapel Hill: Univ. of North Carolina Press, 1980.

———. *The Last of the Fathers: James Madison and the Republican Legacy.* Cambridge: Cambridge Univ. Press, 1989.

McDonald, Forrest. *We The People: The Economic Origins of the Constitution.* Chicago: Univ. of Chicago Press, 1958.

———. *E. Pluribus Unum: The Formation of the American Republic, 1776–1790.* Boston: Houghton Mifflin Company, 1965.

———. *The Presidency of George Washington.* Lawrence: Univ. Press of Kansas, 1974.
———. *The Presidency of Thomas Jefferson.* Lawrence: Univ. Press of Kansas, 1976.
———. *Alexander Hamilton: A Biography.* New York: W. W. Norton and Company, 1979.
———. *Novus Ordo Seclorum: The Intellectual Origins of the Constitution.* Lawrence: Univ. Press of Kansas, 1985.
Main, Jackson Turner. *The Antifederalists: Critics of the Constitution, 1781–1788.* Chapel Hill: Univ. of North Carolina Press, 1961.
———. *Political Parties Before The Constitution.* Chapel Hill: Univ. of North Carolina Press, 1973.
Malone, Dumas. *Jefferson and His Time.* 6 vols. Boston: Little, Brown, and Company, 1948–81.
May, Henry F. *The Enlightenment in America.* Oxford: Oxford Univ. Press, 1976.
Mays, David John. *Edmund Pendleton.* Cambridge, Mass.: Harvard Univ. Press, 1952.
Meyers, Marvin. *The Jacksonian Persuasion: Politics and Belief.* Stanford, Calif.: Stanford Univ. Press, 1957.
Middlekauff, Robert. *The Glorious Cause: The American Revolution, 1763–1789.* New York: Oxford Univ. Press, 1982.
Miller, John C. *The Federalist Era, 1789–1801.* New York: Harper & Row, 1960.
Milsom, S. F. C. *Studies in the History of the Common Law.* London: Hambledon Press, 1985.
Moore, John Bassett. *International Adjudications.* 8 vols. New York: Oxford Univ. Press, 1929–36.
Morgan, Edmund S. *The Birth of the Republic, 1763–89.* Chicago: Univ. of Chicago Press, 1956; rev. ed., 1977.
Morgan, Robert J. *James Madison on the Constitution and the Bill of Rights.* Westport, Conn.: Greenwood Press, 1988.
Morris, Thomas R. *The Virginia Supreme Court: An Institutional and Political Analysis.* Charlottesville: Univ. Press of Virginia, 1975.
Nelson, Margaret V. *A Study of Judicial Review in Virginia, 1789–1928.* New York: Columbia Univ. Press, 1947.
Nelson, William E. *Americanization of the Common Law: The Impact of Legal Change on Massachusetts Society, 1760–1830.* Cambridge, Mass.: Harvard Univ. Press, 1975.
Newmyer, R. Kent. *Supreme Court Justice Joseph Story: Statesman of the Old Republic.* Chapel Hill: Univ. of North Carolina Press, 1985.
Palmer, Robert R. *The Age of the Democratic Revolution: A Political History of Europe and America, 1760–1800.* Princeton, N.J.: Princeton Univ. Press, 1959.
Pancake, John S. *Thomas Jefferson and Alexander Hamilton.* Woodbury, N.Y.: Barron's Educational Series, 1974.

Peterson, Merrill D. *Thomas Jefferson and the New Nation: A Biography*. New York: Oxford Univ. Press, 1970.
Peterson, Norma Lois. *Littleton Waller Tazewell*. Charlottesville: Univ. Press of Virginia, 1983.
Pocock, J. G. A., ed. *Three British Revolutions: 1641, 1688, 1776*. Princeton, N.J.: Princeton Univ. Press, 1980.
Remini, Robert V. *Andrew Jackson*. 3 vols. New York: Harper & Row, 1977–84.
Risjord, Norman K. *The Old Republicans: Southern Conservatism in the Age of Jefferson*. New York: Columbia Univ. Press, 1965.
———. *Chesapeake Politics, 1781–1800*. New York: Columbia Univ. Press, 1978.
Reid, John Philip. *The Concept of Liberty in the Age of the American Revolution*. Chicago: Univ. of Chicago Press, 1988.
Robbins, Caroline. *The Eighteenth-Century Commonwealthman: Studies in the Transmission, Development, and Circumstance of English Liberal Thought from the Restoration of Charles II until the War with the Thirteen Colonies*. Cambridge, Mass.: Harvard Univ. Press, 1959.
Roeber, A. G. *Faithful Magistrates and Republican Lawyers: Creators of Virginia Legal Culture, 1680–1810*. Chapel Hill: Univ. of North Carolina Press, 1981.
Royster, Charles. *Light-Horse Harry Lee and the Legacy of the American Revolution*. New York: Alfred A. Knopf, 1981.
Rutland, Robert A. *The Birth of the Bill of Rights, 1776–1791*. Chapel Hill: Univ. of North Carolina Press, 1955.
Shalhope, Robert E. *John Taylor of Caroline: Pastoral Republican*. Columbia: Univ. of South Carolina Press, 1980.
Siegel, Frederick F. *The Roots of Southern Distinctiveness: Tobacco and Society in Danville, Virginia, 1780–1865*. Chapel Hill: Univ. of North Carolina Press, 1987.
Simms, Henry H. *The Rise of the Whigs in Virginia, 1824–1840*. Richmond: William Byrd Press, 1929.
Smelser, Marshall. *The Democratic Republic, 1801–1815*. New York: Harper & Row, 1968.
Smith, James Morton. *Freedom's Fetters: The Alien and Sedition Laws and American Civil Liberties*. Ithaca, N.Y.: Cornell Univ. Press, 1956.
Stites, Francis N. *John Marshall: Defender of the Constitution*. Boston: Little, Brown, and Company, 1981.
Storing, Herbert J. *What the Anti-Federalists Were For*. Vol. 1 of *The Complete Anti-Federalist*. Chicago: Univ. of Chicago Press, 1981.
Sydnor, Charles S. *The Development of Southern Sectionalism, 1819–1848*. Baton Rouge: Louisiana State Univ. Press, 1948.
———. *Gentlemen Freeholders: Political Practices in Washington's Virginia*. Chapel Hill: Univ. of North Carolina Press, 1952.
Tachau, Mary K. Bonsteel. *Federal Courts in the Early Republic: Kentucky, 1789–1816*. Princeton, N.J.: Princeton Univ. Press, 1978.

Trout, W. E. *A History of Navigation on the Upper James*. Lexington: Virginia Canals and Navigation Society, 1985.

Warren, Charles. *The Supreme Court in United States History*. 3 vols. Boston: Little, Brown, and Company, 1922.

White, G. Edward. *The American Judicial Tradition: Profiles of Leading American Judges*. Oxford: Oxford Univ. Press, 1976.

———. *The Marshall Court and Cultural Change, 1815–35*. Vols. 3–4 of *History of the Supreme Court of the United States*. New York: Macmillan Publishing Company, 1988.

Wiebe, Robert H. *The Opening of American Society: From the Adoption of the Constitution to the Eve of Disunion*. New York: Alfred A. Knopf, 1984.

Wood, Gordon S. *The Creation of the American Republic, 1776–1787*. Chapel Hill: Univ. of North Carolina Press, 1969.

Zagorin, Perez. *The Court and the Country: The Beginning of the English Revolution*. New York: Atheneum, 1970.

Zainaldin, Jamil. *Law in Antebellum Society: Legal Change and Economic Expansion*. New York: Alfred A. Knopf, 1983.

Articles and Theses

Adair, Douglass. "The Tenth Federalist Revisited" and "'That Politics May Be Reduced to a Science': David Hume, James Madison, and the Tenth Federalist." In *Fame and the Founding Fathers: Essays by Douglass Adair*, edited by Trevor Colbourn, 75–106. New York: W. W. Norton & Company, 1974.

Amar, Akhil Reed. "Marbury, Section 13, and the Original Jurisdiction of the Supreme Court." *University of Chicago Law Review* 56 (1989): 443–500.

Ammon, Harry. "The Formation of the Republican Party in Virginia, 1789–1796." *Journal of Southern History* 19 (1953): 283–310.

———. "The Richmond Junto, 1800–1824." *Virginia Magazine of History and Biography* 61 (1953): 395–418.

———. "The Jeffersonian Republicans in Virginia: An Interpretation." *Virginia Magazine of History and Biography* 71 (1963): 153–67.

———, and Koch, Adrienne. "The Virginia and Kentucky Resolutions: An Episode in Jefferson's and Madison's Defense of Civil Liberties." *William and Mary Quarterly*, 3d ser., 5 (1948): 145–76.

Appleby, Joyce. "Commercial Farming and the 'Agrarian Myth' in the Early Republic." *Journal of American History* 68 (1982): 833–49.

———. "Republicanism in Old and New Contexts." *William and Mary Quarterly*, 3d ser., 43 (1986): 20–34.

Banning, Lance. "Republican Ideology and the Triumph of the Constitution, 1789–1793." *William and Mary Quarterly*, 3d ser., 31 (1974): 167–88.

———. "Jeffersonian Ideology Revisited: Liberal And Classical Ideas In The New American Republic." *William and Mary Quarterly*, 3d ser., 43 (1986): 3–19.

Beach, Rex. "Spencer Roane and the Richmond Party." *William and Mary Quarterly*, 2d ser., 22 (1942): 1–17.
Beeman, Richard R., and Rhys Isaac. "Cultural Conflict and Social Change in the Revolutionary South: Lunenburg County, Virginia." *Journal of Southern History* 46 (1980): 525–50.
Brisbin, Richard A., Jr. "John Marshall and the Nature of Law in the Early Republic." *Virginia Magazine of History and Biography* 98 (1990): 57–80.
Bryson, W. Hamilton. "English Common Law in Virginia." *Journal of Legal History* 6 (1985): 249–56.
———. "Law Reporting and Legal Records in Virginia, 1607–1800." In John H. Baker, ed., *Judicial Records, Law Reports, and the Growth of Case Law*. Berlin: Duncker and Humblet, 1989.
Campbell, Bruce A. "John Marshall, the Virginia Political Economy, and the Dartmouth College Decision." *American Journal of Legal History* 19 (1975): 40–65.
Chafee, Zechariah, Jr. "Colonial Courts and the Common Law." In *Essays in the History of Early American Law*, ed. David H. Flaherty, 53–82. Chapel Hill: Univ. of North Carolina Press, 1969.
Cornell, Saul. "Aristocracy Assailed: The Ideology of Backcountry Anti-Federalism." *Journal of American History* 76 (1990): 1148–72.
Corwin, Edward S. "National Power and State Interposition, 1787–1861." *Michigan Law Review* 10 (1912): 535–51.
Cullen, Charles T. "St. George Tucker and Law in Virginia, 1772–1804." Ph.D. diss., University of Virginia, 1971.
———. "Completing the Revisal of the Laws in Post-Revolutionary Virginia." *Virginia Magazine of History and Biography* 82 (1974): 84–99.
———. "St. George Tucker." In *Legal Education in Virginia, 1779–1979: A Biographical Approach*, ed. W. Hamilton Bryson, 657–86. Charlottesville: Univ. Press of Virginia, 1982.
Cunningham, Noble E., Jr., "Who Were The Quids?" *Mississippi Valley Historical Review* 50 (1963): 252–63.
Dauer, Manning J., and Hans Hammond. "John Taylor: Democrat or Aristocrat?" *The Journal of Politics* 6 (1944): 381–403.
Denboer, Gordon, and Norman K. Risjord. "The Evolution of Political Parties in Virginia, 1782–1800." *Journal of American History* 60 (1974): 961–84.
Dodd, William E. "Chief Justice Marshall and Virginia, 1813–1821." *American Historical Review* 12 (1907): 776–87.
Dry, Murray P. "The Case Against Ratification: Anti-Federalist Constitutional Thought." In *The Framing and Ratification of the Constitution*, ed. Leonard W. Levy and Dennis J. Mahoney, 271–91. New York: Macmillan Publishing Company, 1987.
Ellis, Richard E. "The Persistence of Antifederalism after 1789." In *Beyond Confed-*

eration: Origins of the Constitution and American National Identity, ed. Richard Beeman, Stephen Botein, and Edward C. Carter, 295–314. Chapel Hill: Univ. of North Carolina Press, 1987.

Evans, Emory G. "Planter Indebtedness and the Coming of the Revolution in Virginia." *William and Mary Quarterly*, 3d ser., 19 (1962): 511–33.

———. "Private Indebtedness and the Revolution in Virginia, 1776–1796." *William and Mary Quarterly*, 3d ser., 28 (1971): 349–74.

Freyer, Tony A. "Reassessing the Impact of Eminent Domain in Early American Economic Development." *Wisconsin Law Review* 6 (1981): 1263–86.

———. "Law and the Antebellum Southern Economy: An Interpretation." In *Ambivalent Legacy: A Legal History of the South*, ed. David J. Bodenhamer and James W. Ely, Jr., 49–68. Jackson: Univ. Press of Mississippi, 1984.

Gelbach, Clyde C. "Spencer Roane of Virginia, 1762–1822: A Judicial Advocate of State Rights." Ph.D. diss., University of Pittsburgh, 1955.

Goebel, Julius, Jr. "The Common Law and the Constitution." In *Chief Justice John Marshall: A Reappraisal*, ed. W. Melville Jones, 101–23. Ithaca, N.Y.: Cornell Univ. Press, 1956.

Gunther, Gerald. "John Marshall, 'A Friend of the Constitution': In Defense and Elaboration of McCulloch v. Maryland." *Stanford Law Review* 21 (1969): 449–99.

Harrison, Fairfax. "The Proprietors of the Northern Neck: Chapters of Culpepper Genealogy." *Virginia Magazine of History and Biography* 34 (1926): 19–64.

Harrison, Joseph. "Oligarchs and Democrats: The Richmond Junto." *Virginia Magazine of History and Biography* 78 (1970): 184–98.

Haskins, George L. "Reception of the Common Law in Seventeenth-Century Massachusetts: A Case Study." In *Law and Authority in Colonial America*, ed. George Athan Billias, 17–31. Barre, Mass.: Barre Publishers, 1965.

Hobson, Charles F. "The Negative on State Laws: James Madison, the Constitution, and the Crisis of Republican Government." *William and Mary Quarterly*, 3d ser., 36 (1979): 215–35.

———. "The Recovery of British Debts in the Federal Circuit Court of Virginia, 1790 to 1797." *Virginia Magazine of History and Biography* 92 (1984): 176–200.

———. "The Tenth Amendment and the New Federalism of 1789." In *The Bill of Rights: A Lively Heritage*, ed. Jon Kukla, 153–63. Richmond: Virginia State Library and Archives, 1987.

Hoffer, Peter C. "Disorder and Deference: The Paradoxes of Criminal Justice in the Colonial Tidewater." In *Ambivalent Legacy: A Legal History of the South*, ed. David J. Bodenhamer and James W. Ely, Jr., 187–201. Jackson: Univ. Press of Mississippi, 1984.

Horn, James. "Cavalier Culture? The Social Development of Colonial Virginia." *William and Mary Quarterly*, 3d ser., 48 (1991): 238–45.

Hutson, James H. "Country, Court, and Constitution: Antifederalism and the Historians." *William and Mary Quarterly*, 3d ser. 38 (1981): 337–68.
Jacobs, Clyde E. "Prelude to Amendment: The States before the Court." *American Journal of Legal History* 12 (1968): 19–40.
Kenyon, Cecelia M. "Men of Little Faith: The Anti-Federalists on the Nature of Representative Government." *William and Mary Quarterly*, 3d ser., 12 (1955): 3–43.
Konig, David Thomas. "Country Justice: The Rural Roots of Constitutionalism in Colonial Virginia." In *An Uncertain Tradition: Constitutionalism and the History of the South*, ed. Kermit L. Hall and James W. Ely, Jr., 63–82. Athens: Univ. of Georgia Press, 1989.
Kuroda, Tadahisa. "The County Court System of Virginia from the Revolution to the Civil War." Ph.D. diss., Columbia University, 1969.
Liddle, William D. " 'A Patriot King, or None': Lord Bolingbroke and the American Renunciation of George III." *Journal of American History* 65 (1979): 951–70.
Luce, Willard Ray. "*Cohens v. Virginia* (1821) The Supreme Court And State Rights: A Reevaluation Of Influences And Impacts." Ph.D. diss., University of Virginia, 1978.
Lutz, Donald S. "The First American Constitutions." In *The Framing and Ratification of the Constitution*, ed. Leonard W. Levy and Dennis J. Mahoney, 69–81. New York: Macmillan Publishing Company, 1987.
Main, Jackson Turner. "The Distribution of Property in Post-Revolutionary Virginia." *Mississippi Valley Historical Review* 41 (1954): 241–58.
——. "The One Hundred." *William and Mary Quarterly*, 3d ser. 11 (1954): 354–84.
——. "Sections and Politics in Virginia, 1781–87." *William and Mary Quarterly*, 3d ser. 12 (1955): 96–112.
Malone, Kathryn Ruth. "The Virginia Doctrines, the Commonwealth and the Republic: The Role of Fundamental Principles in Virginia Politics, 1798–1833." Ph.D. diss., University of Pennsylvania, 1981.
——. "The Fate of Revolutionary Republicanism in Early National Virginia." *Journal of the Early Republic* 7 (1987): 27–51.
Marsh, Philip. "James Monroe as 'Agricola' in the Genet Controversy, 1793." *Virginia Magazine of History and Biography* 62 (1954): 472–76.
Mason, Alpheus Thomas. "The Federalist—a Split Personality." *American Historical Review* 57 (1952): 625–43.
Mays, David J. "William Fleming, 1736–1824." *Proceedings of The Virginia State Bar Association*, 1927.
Miller, F. Thornton. "Liberty, Order, and a Balanced Constitution: A Study of Virginia Ideologies, 1788–1794." M.A. thesis, University of Alabama, 1980.
——. "Juries and Judges versus the Law: Virginia from the Revolution to the

Confrontation between John Marshall and Spencer Roane." Ph.D. diss., University of Alabama, 1986.

———. "John Marshall versus Spencer Roane: A Reevaluation of *Martin* v. *Hunter's Lessee.*" *Virginia Magazine of History and Biography* 96 (1988): 297–314.

———. "The Richmond Junto: The Secret All-Powerful Club—or Myth." *Virginia Magazine of History and Biography* 99 (1991): 63–80.

Mitnick, John M. "From Neighbor-Witness to Judge of Proofs: The Transformation of the English Civil Juror." *American Journal of Legal History* 32 (1988): 201–35.

Murrin, John M. "The Great Inversion, or Court versus Country: A Comparison of the Revolution Settlements in England (1688–1721) and America (1776–1816)." In *Three British Revolutions: 1641, 1688, 1776,* ed. J. G. A. Pocock, 368–453. Princeton, N.J.: Princeton Univ. Press, 1980.

———. "The Legal Transformation: The Bench and Bar of Eighteenth-Century Massachusetts." In *America: Essays in Politics and Social Development,* ed. Stanley N. Katz and John M. Murrin, 3d ed., 540–72. New York: Alfred A. Knopf, 1983.

———. "A Roof without Walls: The Dilemma of American National Identity." In *Beyond Confederation: Origins of the Constitution and American National Identity,* ed. Richard Beeman, Stephen Botein, and Edward C. Carter, 333–48. Chapel Hill: Univ. of North Carolina Press, 1987.

———, and A. G. Roeber. "Trial by Jury: The Virginia Paradox." In *The Bill of Rights: A Lively Heritage,* ed. Jon Kukla, 109–29. Richmond: Virginia State Library and Archives, 1987.

Nelson, William E. "The Eighteenth-Century Background of John Marshall's Constitutional Jurisprudence." *Michigan Law Review* 76 (1978): 893–960.

———. "Reason and Compromise in the Establishment of the Federal Constitution, 1787–1801." *William and Mary Quarterly,* 3d ser., 44 (1987): 458–84.

Newmyer, R. Kent. "Harvard Law School, New England Legal Culture, and the Antebellum Origins of American Jurisprudence." *Journal of American History* 74 (1987): 814–35.

———. "John Marshall and the Southern Constitutional Tradition." In *An Uncertain Tradition: Constitutionalism and the History of the South,* ed. Kermit L. Hall and James W. Ely, Jr., 105–24. Athens: Univ. of Georgia Press, 1989.

Onuf, Peter S. "State Sovereignty and the Making of the Constitution." In *Conceptual Change and the Constitution,* ed. Terence Ball and J. G. A. Pocock, 35–54. Lawrence: Univ. Press of Kansas, 1988.

———. "Reflections on the Founding: Constitutional Historiography in Bicentennial Perspective." *William and Mary Quarterly* 46 (1989): 341–75.

Pocock, J. G. A. "Machiavelli, Harrington, and English Political Ideologies in the Eighteenth Century." *William and Mary Quarterly,* 3d ser., 22 (1965): 549–83.

———. "1776: The Revolution against Parliament." In *Three British Revolutions:*

1641, 1688, 1776, ed. J. G. A. Pocock, 265–88. Princeton, N.J.: Princeton Univ. Press, 1980.

Radabaugh, John. "Spencer Roane and the Genesis of Virginia Judicial Review." *American Journal of Legal History* 6 (1962): 63–70.

Rich, Myra. "Speculation of the Significance of Debt: Virginia, 1781–1789." *Virginia Magazine of History and Biography* 76 (1968): 301–17.

Riesman, Janet A. "Money, Credit, and Federalist Political Economy." In *Beyond Confederation: Origins of the Constitution and American National Identity*, ed. Richard Beeman, Stephen Botein, and Edward C. Carter, 128–61. Chapel Hill: Univ. of North Carolina Press, 1987.

Riggs, Susan A. "Creed Taylor." In *Legal Education in Virginia, 1779–1979: A Biographical Approach*, ed. W. Hamilton Bryson, 589–95. Charlottesville: Univ. Press of Virginia, 1982.

Risjord, Norman K. "The Virginia Federalists." *Journal of Southern History* 33 (1967): 486–517.

———. "Virginians and the Constitution: A Multivariant Analysis." *William and Mary Quarterly*, 3d ser., 31 (1974): 613–32.

Scheiber, Harry N. "The Road to *Munn*: Eminent Domain and the Concept of Public Purpose in the State Courts." In *Perspectives in American History*: vol. 5, *Law in American History*, ed. Donald Fleming and Bernard Bailyn, 329–402. Cambridge, Mass.: Harvard Univ. Press, 1971.

Shade, William G. "Society and Politics in Antebellum Virginia's Southside." *Journal of Southern History* 53 (1987): 163–93.

Shalhope, Robert E. "Toward a Republican Synthesis: The Emergence of an Understanding of Republicanism in American Historiography." *William and Mary Quarterly*, 3d ser., 29 (1972): 49–80.

———. "Republicanism and Early American Historiography." *William and Mary Quarterly*, 3d ser., 39 (1982): 334–56.

Shaw, Ronald E. "Canals in the Early Republic: A Review of Recent Literature." *Journal of the Early Republic* 4 (1984): 117–42.

Shepard, E. Lee. "Courts in Conflict: Town-County Relations in Post-Revolutionary Virginia." *Virginia Magazine of History and Biography* 85 (1977): 184–99.

———. "George Wythe." In *The Virginia Law Reporters before 1880*, ed. W. Hamilton Bryson, 90–95. Charlottesville: Univ. Press of Virginia, 1977.

———. "Lawyers Look at Themselves: Professional Consciousness and the Virginia Bar, 1770–1850." *American Journal of Legal History* 25 (1981): 1–23.

———. "John Anthony Gardner Davis" and "John Tayloe Lomax." In *Legal Education in Virginia, 1779–1979: A Biographical Approach*, ed. W. Hamilton Bryson, 181–85, 359–66. Charlottesville: Univ. Press of Virginia, 1982.

Sheridan, Richard. "The British Credit Crisis of 1772 and The American Colonies." *Journal of Economic History* 20 (1960): 160–86.

Smelser, Marshall. "The Federalist Period as an Age of Passion." *American Quarterly* 10 (1958): 391–419.

———. "The Jacobin Phrensy: The Menace of Monarchism, Plutocracy, and Anglophobia, 1789–1798." *Review of Politics* 21 (1959): 239–58.

Stourzh, Gerald. "*Constitution:* Changing Meanings of the Term from the Early Seventeenth to the Late Eighteenth Century." In *Conceptual Change and the Constitution,* ed. Terence Ball and J. G. A. Pocock, 35–54. Lawrence: Univ. Press of Kansas, 1988.

Thomas, Robert G. "The Virginia Convention of 1788: A Criticism of Beard's An Economic Interpretation of the Constitution." *Journal of Southern History* 19 (1953): 63–72.

Treon, John Alfred. "*Martin v. Hunter's Lessee:* A Case History." Ph.D. diss., University of Virginia, 1970.

Tucker, J. Randolph. "Henry St. George Tucker." In *Legal Education in Virginia, 1779–1979: A Biographical Approach,* ed. W. Hamilton Bryson, 601–12. Charlottesville: Univ. Press of Virginia, 1982.

Warren, Charles. "Legislative and Judicial Attacks on the Supreme Court of the United States: A History of the Twenty-Fifth Section of the Judiciary Act." *American Law Review* 47 (1913): 1–34.

Washburn, Wilcomb E. "Law and Authority in Colonial Virginia." In *Law and Authority in Colonial America,* ed. George Athan Billias, 116–35. Barre, Mass.: Barre Publishers, 1965.

Waterman, Julius S. "Thomas Jefferson and Blackstone's Commentaries." In *Essays in the History of Early American Law,* ed. David H. Flaherty, 451–88. Chapel Hill: Univ. of North Carolina Press, 1969.

Williams, David Alan. "The Small Farmer in Eighteenth-Century Virginia Politics." In *Colonial America: Essays in Politics and Social Development,* ed. Stanley N. Katz and John M. Murrin, 3d ed., 410–21. New York: Alfred A. Knopf, 1983.

Wood, Gordon S. "Interests and Disinterestedness in the Making of the Constitution." In *Beyond Confederation: Origins of the Constitution and American National Identity,* ed. Richard Beeman, Stephen Botein, and Edward C. Carter, 69–109. Chapel Hill: Univ. of North Carolina Press, 1987.

Wren, J. Thomas. "The Ideology of Court and Country in the Virginia Ratifying Convention of 1788." *Virginia Magazine of History and Biography* 93 (1985): 389–408.

———. "The Role of the District Court in Northern Neck Society, 1789–1807." *Northern Neck of Virginia Historical Magazine* 35 (1985): 3961–77.

Wyatt, Edward A. "George Keith Taylor, 1769–1815, Virginia Federalist And Humanitarian." *William and Mary Quarterly,* 2d ser., 16 (1936): 1–18.

INDEX

Adams, John, 52, 66, 94, 114; midnight appointments by, 58, 78
Adams, John Quincy: election of 1824 and appointment of Clay called a corrupt bargain, 92–94; election of 1828, 94; nationalism, 96–97, 114
Ad quod damnum, 100–106
Agrarian: interests, 7, 55–56, 98, 102–5; independence, 9, 12, 38, 88, 108; rights, 9, 55–56, 119; bias toward indebted farmers, 19; opposition to Hamiltonianism, 47, 52; opposition to state banking, 51–52; politics, 49, 62, 96; society, law in, 106–7, 113. *See also* Country republican ideology; Liberty; Property rights
Alexandria, 30, 51, 93
Alien and Sedition Acts: declared unconstitutional, 11, 53; upheld by Federalist federal judges, 52–53, 57; Republican criticism, 52–54, 114–16
Ambler, John, 76
American Revolution: use of Country, republican ideology, 8–9; resolutions of protest, 10–11, 90; Patriots, 12, 53; courts closed to British and Loyalists, 37, 39; British debt, 37, 39–41, 43, 45; confiscation of British and Loyalist property, 39, 41; proprietary domain of Lord Fairfax, 74, 78
Anti-Federalists: for jury trial, x, 9, 18–21; for common-law rights, liberty as highest goal, 9, 18–20; for constitutional principles, 10, 23–24; demand for a federal bill of rights, 16; debate over the Constitution in the Virginia ratifying convention, 16–20; for limited government, 17–18; view that the Constitution was ratified conditionally, 20–21; view of federal law, 21, 23–24, 37–38, 68, 81; view of the U.S. Bill of Rights, 22–23; call for further amendments, 23; division into moderate and extreme wings, 23; denial of the Constitution as fundamental, 23, 68; view of the federal appellate system, 43, 46; alliance with Republicans, 47, 49, 129n. 7; drawn to Old Republicans, 57–58, 61–62; self-image, 62; tradition, 114
Appeals. *See* Appellate courts; Legal reform
Appellate courts: jurisdiction, federal over state, xi, 1, 11, 60, 69, 73, 116; as an issue in the Virginia ratifying convention, 18; decentralized court system, 22, 30–33, 43, 46, 110, 113–14, 119; jurisdiction, state over county, 24, 25–28, 98; jurisdiction over fact and law, 28, 40–41, 43; results of Virginia district and circuit courts, 32; *Ware v. Hylton*, 43; *Fairfax's Devisee v. Hunter's Lessee*, 81–82; Virginia court of appeals and legislature rejects Supreme Court jurisdiction, 82–83, 86, 90; *Martin v. Hunter's Lessee*, 83–85; Supreme Court upholds jurisdiction, 84–86, 89–90; *Cohens v. Virginia*, 90
Articles of Confederation: 2, 16, 40, 118; seen as a basis for interpreting the Constitution, 23, 50, 54–55

Banking, in Virginia, 51–52, 87, 93, 136n. 10. *See also* Hamilton, Alexander: Hamiltonianism
Barbour, James, 91
Baring v. Reeder, 69–70
Bill of Rights, U.S.: drafted by Madison, 21, 48; First Amendment, 53; view of Anti-Federalists, 21–23
Blue Ridge, 89, 92, 94
Bond. *See* Debt
British debts: creditors, 7, 9, 19, 28; as issue in the Virginia ratifying convention, 18–19; jury trial, 26, 28, 40–41, 43; subtraction of interests, 26, 40–41, 45; courts closed, 37–38;

163

British debts (*cont.*)
  Jones v. Walker, 38–40; *Ware v. Hylton*, 40–43; debt payment into state loan office, 40–43, 128n. 10; *McCall v. Turner*, 41; Anglo-American relations and Jay Treaty commission, 43–45; results, 45–46. *See also* Convention of 1802; Debt; Jury
Brockenbrough, William, 4
Brooke, Francis T., 72, 82

Cabell, William H., 4, 72, 82, 103
Call, Daniel, 98
Carr, Dabney, 4, 103
Carrington, Paul, 70, 79
Chancery. *See* Courts; Equity law
Chase, Samuel, 42, 60–61
Checks and balances: separation of powers, 12, 56, 118; advocated by Madison, 15; criticized by Henry, 17
Chisholm v. Georgia, 42
Circuit court, U.S., district of Virginia: jury trial, 26, 28; British debt cases, 38–43; enforcement of the Sedition Act, 60; Marshall and Tucker as judges, 73; Fairfax litigation, 75
Circuit courts, Virginia. *See* Superior or circuit courts, Virginia
Clay, Henry, 94, 96
Coalter, John, 72, 82, 91, 103
Cohens v. Virginia, 85, 89–90
Coles, Isaac, 13
College of William and Mary, 65, 66, 107
Colston, Raleigh, 76
Commentaries (Tucker), 99–100, 136n. 19
Common law: colonial development, ix, 3, 5, 8, 54, 110–11; as custom, xii, 5, 11, 104, 110–12; as a science, xii, 66, 70, 98; Virginia, xiii, 5, 49, 69–70, 110–11; rights, 3, 18, 104, 111, 116; modification by the legislature, 8, 15, 104, 106; trespass on the case, 35, 36 (table 2), 101 (table 4); assault and battery, 36 (table 2); covenant, 36 (table 2); detinue, 36 (table 2); ejectment, 36 (table 2); slander, 36 (table 2); trespass, 36 (table 2); trover, 36 (table 2); suing a sovereign, 42; English, 54, 69, 115; federal, 54, 114–16, 118; English, as an authority in Virginia, 69–70; legal process in economic development and internal improvements, 97, 100–105; comparison of Virginia common law with that of England and of other states, 99–100, 105–6; determination of law and facts, 99–100, 136n. 19; special motions, 100–101; relation to judicial review, 104; rule of law throughout the realm, 115–16. *See also* Ad quod damnum; Debt; Eminent domain; Inquest of office found; Legal reform; Libel; Plea
Commonwealth v. Caton, 63–64, 66–68
Compromise of 1796: terms of, 77; criticized by Roane, 78; in the Fairfax litigation, 78–82, 85
Congress: Bill of Rights, 21–22; judiciary acts, 21–22, 58, 84; Jay Treaty, 44; Convention of 1802, 45; Alien and Sedition Acts, 52; Chase impeachment trial, 60–61; Missouri crisis, 89; corrupt bargain, 94
Constitutional Whig (Richmond), 93
Constitution, U.S.: seen as a treaty, 2, 23; criticized by Anti-Federalists, 9, 16–20; seen as similar to legislation, not fundamental law, 11, 23–24, 50, 109; and Article Three, 22, 42; and Article Six, Supremacy Clause, 22, 68–69, 83–84; construed strictly, 23, 50; seen as a revised Articles of Confederation, 23, 50; criticized by Old Republicans, 50; construed broadly, 50, 87, 115
Constitution, Virginia: importance of the county courts in, 3, 6, 109–11; revision of, support for calling a convention, 12, 47, 67–68, 87, 91, 97–98, 108–9; preservation of, opposition to calling a convention, 49–50, 98, 109–12; interpretations of, 67–69, 104, 106, 109–12
Convention of 1802, 45
Corbin, Francis, 13, 48, 51–52
Corruption. *See* Country republican ideology
Country gentlemen: appeal of, an ideal romanticized, 3, 88, 107–8; opposed to constitutional reform, 9, 49, 95;

opposed by reformers, 12, 87, 108; government by seen as a model, 17–18, 111; grand juries, members of, 29; geographic area of, 92, 95; state internal improvements, benefiting from, 96; to compromise reform, ability of, 97; dominance of, 106–8, 113–14. *See also* Agrarian

Country republican ideology: Court-Country paradigm, 8; view of the American Revolution, 8; view of the 1780s constitutional debate, 8–9; view of Hamiltonianism, 48; use by Republicans, 48–49; Country opposition or party, 48–49, 52, 57–58, 61–62; Court party and policies, 51–52, 91, 93; view of the 1790s and the election of 1800, 57–58; view of the Jefferson administration and Chase impeachment, 61–62; view of the Era of Good Feelings, 88, 91, 110; use by Old Republicans, 89, 91, 94, 110–11; use by Pleasants's party, 92–93, 96; view of the Republican party caucus as the Richmond junto, 92–94; view of the 1824 election of Adams and appointment of Clay as the corrupt bargain, 94. *See also* Agrarian

County courts: fundamental in Virginia's government, 3, 6, 109–11; model of good government, 17–18, 109–11; court day, 24; courthouse as location for most law and government in decentralized Virginia, 24–25, 32–33, 51, 105, 107–8, 110–11, 114, 119; value of suits, not small-claims courts, 26, 126n. 25; Cumberland County court, 27–28, 36 (table 2), 101 (table 4), 126n. 25, 128n. 24; Campbell County court, 28, 36 (table 2), 101 (table 4), 126n. 25, 27; Frederick County court, 28, 36 (table 2), 101 (table 4), 126nn. 25, 27, 128n. 24; York County court, 28, 36 (table 2), 101 (table 4), 126nn. 25, 27, 128n. 24; clerks, 31; Caroline County court, 36 (table 2), 101 (table 4); internal improvements in legal process, 100–106; common law education for, 107; colonial development, 109, 111–12; Spotsylvania County court, 126n. 25. *See also* Fredericksburg: city hustings court; Justices of the peace; Richmond: city hustings court

Courts: Virginia admiralty court, 25, 64; Virginia court of chancery, 25, 64–65. *See also* Circuit court, U.S., district of Virginia; County courts; District court, U.S., in Virginia; District courts, Virginia; General Court; Superior or circuit courts, Virginia; Supreme Court, U.S.; Virginia Supreme Court of Appeals

Crawford, William, 93–94

Crenshaw and Crenshaw v. Slate River Company, 102–6

Currie's Administrators v. the Mutual Assurance Society, 137n. 22

Cushing, William, 42

Custom. *See* Common law; Fundamental law; Unwritten constitution

The Danger Not Over (Pendleton), 57

Dawson, John, 13

Debt: jury trials and subtraction of interests, x, 3, 7, 26, 28, 35–36, 37 (table 3), 40–41, 46; installment legislation, 25; volume of suits, 34, 128n. 24; indebtedness and view of the law, 34–35, 46; bond, 35, 36 (table 2); debt action, 35, 36 (table 2), 101 (table 4); plaintiff withdrawals, 35–36, 37 (table 3); comparison of defendants and plaintiffs, 35–37; out-of-court settlements, 36, 46; courts closed to creditors, 37, 39, 45; geographic area of indebtedness, 37–38, 44, 127n. 5; relation to British taking slaves, 44. *See also* British debts; Common law: trespass on the case; Convention of 1802; Jury

Demurrer to the evidence. *See* Legal reform

District court, U.S., in Virginia, 40, 73

District courts, Virginia: legislation establishing them, 25–26, 64, 126n. 23; description of how they worked, 26–30, 64; at Prince Edward County, 27 (table 1), 28–30, 36 (table 2), 37 (table 3), 101 (table 4), 126n. 27; at Winchester, 27 (table 1), 75, 78, 85; at

District courts, Virginia (*cont.*)
Fredericksburg, 30–31, 36 (table 2); results, 30–33, 126n. 25; at Dumfries, 76. *See also* General Court

Ejectment. *See* Common law
Elections: of 1800, 57; of 1824, 92–94; of 1828, 92, 94–95
Eleventh Amendment, 42, 76–77, 90
Eminent domain: in internal improvement projects, 101–5; and principle of fair compensation, 103–4
England, 6, 8, 10, 90. *See also* American Revolution; British debts; Common law; Convention of 1802; Jay Treaty; Merchants; Treaty of 1783; Unwritten constitution
Eppes, Francis, 40
Equity law, 19, 21, 36 (table 2), 65, 66–67. *See also* Courts: Virginia court of chancery
Era of Good Feelings: description of, 87; criticism of and reaction against, 88, 110, 114; endorsed by Republican moderates, 91, 102; results, 105

Fairfax, Denny Martin, 75–77, 80
Fairfax, Thomas, 74–75
Fairfax litigation: exemplifying two kinds of law, 73; rents, quitrents, claim to feudal dues, 74, 77–79, 81; state confiscation and selling of the waste and ungranted land, 74–77, 79–81; *Hunter v. Fairfax's Devisee*, 75–77, 79–80; state escheating Fairfax plantations, 75–77, 79–81; *Fairfax v. Commonwealth*, 76–77; land syndicate purchase of plantations, 76–77; *Marshall v. Commonwealth*, 77; compromise of 1796, apparent end to litigation, 77, 79; litigation continued by Marshalls, 78–79; *Fairfax's Devisee v. Hunter's Lessee*, 81–82; *Hunter v. Martin, Devisee of Fairfax*, 82–83; *Martin v. Hunter's Lessee*, 83–85; results in the law, 84–85, 135n. 21
Fairfax's Devisee v. Hunter's Lessee, 81–82
Fairfax v. Commonwealth, 76–77, 80
Farrel and Jones, 39–40
The Federalist, 13, 48, 67, 69

Federalists: criticism of Anti-Federalists, 9–10; supporting the Constitution in the Virginia ratifying convention, 16–20, 118; as a political party, 23, 47, 52–53, 73, 130n. 10; political party in Virginia, 50–53, 57, 59, 77; geographic base and personnel, 51–52, 65; reaction to French Revolution, 52; suppressing the Whiskey Rebellion, 52; popularity during the Quasi-War with France, 52, 57, 59; opposition to Virginia Resolutions of 1798, 53–55
Fleming, William, 70–73, 79, 82
Fredericksburg, 92, 93; location for developing law profession, 30–31, 127n. 34; city hustings court, 31, 36 (table 2), 101 (table 4). *See also* District courts, Virginia; Superior or circuit courts
Fundamental law: and the U.S. Constitution, 11, 24, 57; advocated by Old Republicans, 57, 106, 109–10; and the Virginia constitution, 68–69, 104, 109–10; as the basis for judicial review, 104. *See also* Common law; Unwritten constitution

General Assembly: revision of the state judiciary, 24, 64–65, 70, 72, 79; decentralized state government, 24, 105, 108, 110–11, 114; justices of the peace as members, 25, 29, 49, 96, 110; confiscation of British land and debts and closing courts, 38, 74–77; debate over the Virginia Resolutions of 1798, 53–55; Henry memorial, 55; Compromise of 1796, 77; caucus, 91; dominance of the gentry, 92, 108, 110–11; corporations, 100–101, 137n. 22; internal improvement acts, 100–106; factions of Henry and Madison, 124n. 2. *See also* Resolutions of the General Assembly
General Court: district court system, 25–31, 32–33, 64–65; circuit riding, 27, 31, 64; Superior or circuit court system, 31–33; *Kamper v. Hawkins*, 66–68
Genet, Edmond, 52
Gentry. *See* Country gentlemen

Giles, William Branch: leadership among Old Republicans, 2, 4, 96–97, 109–10; Republican party formation, 47–48; Virginia Resolutions of 1798, 53; impeachment of Federalist federal judges, 59–61; countering Pleasants's party and constitutional reform, 96, 109; liberty as the most valuable goal, 110; defense of the county-court system and power of the local gentry, 110–11; view of the Virginia constitution, 110–11

Gilmer, Francis Walker, 107–8

Gilmer, Peachy, 108

Grayson, William, 21

Great Valley: northern Valley, 13, 32, 48, 50, 52, 75, 92, 93, 94–95; southern Valley, 28, 32, 92, 94–95, 97; Fairfax proprietary area, 74; the support for or against legal, judicial, and constitutional reform and government centralization, 95, 97

Green, John W., 103

Griffin, Cyrus, 40

Hamilton, Alexander: Hamiltonianism, 11, 47–52, 57, 87, 114; Federalist party, 23; opposed by Republicans, 23, 47–48; *The Federalist*, 48

Hening, William Waller, 6

Henry, Patrick: British debt cases, 3, 7, 38–39, 45–46, 127n. 7; model country lawyer, 3–4; liberty as greatest goal, 9, 18, 55, 62, 118; criticized for preference for an unwritten constitution, 9–10; leads opposition to the Constitution in the Virginia ratifying convention, 9–10, 16–20, 48; view of the law, 15; Virginia district court system, 24, 29; Resolutions of 1790, 48; memorial bill and criticism by Republicans, 55; Virginia Resolutions of 1798, 55; against outside interference, 55, 81; tradition and legacy, 55–56, 61–62, 96–97, 117–18; criticized as a model for lawyers, 107–8. *See also* Henry's party

Henry's party: pro-debtor, 7, 9, 25–27, 38–39, 45–46; liberty as highest goal, 9; geographic base and personnel, 13, 37–39, 46, 49, 52, 124n. 2; against state judicial and constitutional reform, 24–29, 38, 47; ambivalence toward Republicans, 47–49, 51–52; power center at county level, 51; against the Fairfax claims, for state confiscation, 75, 80–81. *See also* Henry, Patrick

Hook, John, 35, 46

Horwitz, Morton J., ix, 98, 101–2, 103

House of Delegates. *See* General Assembly

Hunter, David, 75, 77, 79

Hunter v. Fairfax's Devisee: U.S. circuit court in Virginia, 75; Virginia district court at Winchester, St. George Tucker's opinion, 75; court of appeals, Fleming's opinion, 79; court of appeals, Roane's opinion, 80; record of appeal before the Supreme Court, 81

Hunter v. Martin, Devisee of Fairfax, 82–83, 113, 116; reviving Virginia's states' rights movement, 85, 88; confirmed by legislature, 90

Hylton, Daniel, & Company, 40

Impeachment movement, 59–61. *See also* Giles, William Branch; Marshall Court; Randolph, John

Injunction. *See* Equity law

Innes, James, 51

Inquest of office found, 75, 79–80

Internal improvements: federal, 87, 89, 91, 97, 114; Virginia, 87, 91, 95–97, 136n. 10; Roanoke–Dismal Swamp canal, 96; counties, 96, 105–6

Interposition: defined, 1, 56; as a protection for liberty, 62; to prevent the appellate jurisdiction of the Supreme Court, 83, 84–86, 89–90. *See also* Virginia Doctrine; Virginia Resolutions of 1798

Iredell, James, 40–43

Jackson, Andrew, 93–94

James River: valley, 13, 28, 32, 34, 38, 49, 106; canal and navigation improvement, 95–97

Jay, John, 40–41, 44, 76

Jay Treaty: and British debt, 44–45, 128n. 20; and the Fairfax litigation, 76, 81–82, 85

Jefferson, Thomas: for state legal and constitutional reform and against local elite rule, 12, 30, 49–50, 67–68, 108; strict construction of the Constitution, 23; formation of the Republican party, 23, 47–49; British debt, 40, 43, 45; Kentucky and Virginia Resolutions, 53–57; election of 1800, 57; moderate course as president, 57–58; his presidency criticized, 58, 61–62; possible appointment of Roane, 66, 132n. 6; criticism of Marshall Court, 90

Johnson, Chapman, 91
Johnson, Zachariah, 13
Jones, Joseph, 13
Jones v. Walker, 38–40, 127n. 7
Jones, William, 39–40

Judicial review: federal review of state acts, 43, 60, 81–84; federal review of federal acts, 59, 69, 83–84, 87; interpretations of, 60, 63–64, 67, 69, 73, 104; state review of state acts, 63–68, 104; state review of federal acts, 82–83. *See also Commonwealth v. Caton; Crenshaw and Crenshaw v. Slate River Company; Fairfax's Devisee v. Hunter's Lessee; Hunter v. Martin, Devisee of Fairfax; Kamper v. Hawkins; McCulloch v. Maryland; Marbury v. Madison; Martin v. Hunter's Lessee;* "Remonstrance of the Judges"; *Ware v. Hylton*

Judiciary act of 1789, 21–22; section twenty-five, 22, 81, 83–84, 89–90, 116; and circuit riding, 58–59
Judiciary act of 1793, 39
Judiciary act of 1801, 58–59; repealed, 58
Judiciary act of 1802, 58–59; and circuit riding, 58–59

Jury: check in an appellate court system, x, xiii, 7, 28, 41, 46; protection from tyranny, 3, 6–7, 111; jurisdiction over law and fact, 6–7, 28, 40–41, 43, 98–100, 136n. 19; protection of local interests, 7, 20, 27–28, 35–37, 43, 85, 100–106, 110–11; not secured in the Constitution, 9, 18–20; fundamental right, 11, 111, 124n. 11; familiarity, 20, 30; petit and grand, 29–30, 35; judges' instructions, 41, 98–99; in Fairfax litigation, 75–76, 78–80; rights of, against judges, 98–103; in eminent domain proceedings, 100–106; steady rate of trials, 126n. 27. *See also* British debts; Debt

Justices of the peace: use of law manuals, 5–6; role, 6; against the Constitution, 13, 15; model of good government, 17–18, 110–11; administrative jurisdiction, 24–25, 31, 50, 105, 110; members of the House of Delegates, 25, 29, 49, 96, 110; judicial jurisdiction, 25, 35; grand jurors in the state courts, 29–30; against state constitutional reform, 49; local rule, 98, 108, 110–11; criticized, 108; defended, 109–12. *See also* County courts

Kamper v. Hawkins, 66–69, 104
Kentucky and Virginia Resolutions. *See* Virginia Resolutions of 1798

Law: means for economic development, ix, xii, 97–98, 100–106, 119; interpretations of, xi, xii, 15, 25, 34–35, 46, 70, 97–99, 101–3, 114, 117; uniform and centralized or diverse and decentralized, 69–70, 73, 83–86, 113, 116–17, 119; slow development in Virginia, 106–8, 113–14; reflection of society, 113; relation to the separation and division of powers, 118–19. *See also* Common law; Equity law; Fundamental law; Lawyers; Legal reform

Lawyers: country, ix, xii, 3, 5, 28, 32–33, 34–35, 66, 98–99; professionalism, ix, xii, 30–31, 34–35, 66, 98, 103, 127n. 34; education, 5–6, 107–8; effect on, by Virginia district and circuit courts, 32; kind of practice, 32, 107–8; relation to Virginia society, 106–8, 113–14; circuit riding, 107; criticism of country lawyers, 107–8. *See also* Law; Legal reform

Lee, Henry: in Madison's party, 48; advocate of state banking, 51; in Federalist party, 51–52; as Virginia governor, 51–52, 76; in opposition to the Virginia Resolutions of 1798, 53–55; in syndicate to purchase Fairfax plantations, 76
Lee, Richard Bland, 48
Lee, Richard Henry, 21
Legal reform: appeals and appellate court system, 24–25, 28–29, 36–38, 99–100; beneficial to defendants or plaintiffs, 36–37, 99–101, 102–6; judges instructing juries, 98–99; judges summing up the evidence, 99; new trials, 100–101; in eminent domain for internal improvements, 100–107; demurrer to the evidence, 101 (table 4); special verdict, 101 (table 4); results, 113–14; connection of reforms with nationalism, 114; court reports, 114. *See also* Law; Lawyers
Leigh, Benjamin Watkins, 109–12
Libel, 53–54
Liberty: protected through juries and the common law, 3, 6–7, 124n. 11; as greatest goal, 4, 9, 18, 38, 55, 62, 110; secured in Virginia's government, 17–18, 109–11; secured by weak and limited government, 17–18, 110–11; protected by watching government, 62; opposite to uniformity and centralization, 83, 119. *See also* Agrarian; Country gentlemen; Property rights
Localism: juries as protection of locals and their community, x, xii–xiii, 3, 7, 19–20, 27–28; law as a foreign threat, xi, xiii, 7, 12, 15, 34–35, 37, 46, 53, 61, 81, 85, 89, 116; interests and power, xii–xiii, 17, 81, 89; law as protection of locals and their community, xii–xiii, 9, 34–35, 46, 69, 73, 80, 85, 98, 114, 116; community consensus, 5, 19, 20; Constitution creating a foreign threat, 16–20; defense of local rule, 25, 49–50, 110–11, 113; resistance to outside interference, 55, 81; Supreme Court as a foreign threat, 68–69, 73, 81, 87, 89–91, 96–97; national government as a foreign threat, 89–91, 114; internal improvements, 96–97, 100–106; decentralized government, 105–6, 110–11, 117; relation to provincialism, 117. *See also* Country gentlemen; County courts; Jury; Justices of the peace
Lynchburg, 92, 93
Lyons, Peter, 70, 79

McCall v. Turner, 41, 65, 106, 113
McCulloch v. Maryland, 85, 87, 88, 116
Madison, James: pro-creditor, 7; value of a written constitution, 11; for legal and constitutional reform in Virginia and against local elite rule, 12–13, 30, 67–68, 108; "Vices of the Political System of the United States," 13; in the drafting of the Constitution, 13, 15; constitutional theory, 13, 15, 56, 116, 119; supporting the Constitution in the Virginia ratifying convention, 16–17; strict construction of the Constitution, 23; leadership in forming the Republican party, 23, 47–49, 130n. 10; *The Federalist*, 48, 56; Virginia Resolutions of 1798 and interpretation of them, 53–57; *Virginia Report*, 56. *See also* Madison's party
Madison's party: pro-creditor, 7, 9, 25–26; geographic base and personnel, 13, 124n. 2; for judicial and constitutional reform in Virginia, 24–27, 30, 38, 47; Resolutions of 1790, 48; in formation of and drawn to Republican party, 48–49. *See also* Madison, James
Marbury v. Madison, xi, 59–60, 69, 84
Marshall Court: acting in a vacuum, xi, 1, 84–85; judicial nationalism, 1, 60, 69, 84–86, 87–90, 118–19; contest with Republicans over *Marbury*, 59–60; criticized by Republicans and Old Republicans as a threat to Virginia, 68–69, 73, 81–82, 85, 87, 89–91, 96–97, 114; broad construction of the Constitution, 87. *See also* Marshall, John; Supreme Court, U.S.
Marshall, James: lawyer for the Fairfax family, 76; in the syndicate to purchase Fairfax plantations, 76–77; *Marshall v. Commonwealth*, 76–77; in Federalist party, 77–78; suits to collect rents, 77–79, 85; *Marshall v.*

Marshall, James (cont.)
   Conrad, 78; continuation of Fairfax litigation, 78–81, 85
Marshall, John: view of and antagonism with Roane, xii, 69, 73, 85–86, 116–19; advocate of legal uniformity and nationalism, 2, 85–86, 88, 116–19; value of a written constitution, 11, 69; in Madison's party, 13; "Gracchus" and "Aristides," 51; against the Country opposition and the Resolutions of 1790, 51; Federalist party leader, 51–52, 65, 73, 130n. 10; appointment as chief justice, 58; *Marbury v. Madison*, 59–60, 69; view of the law, 73; circuit court duties, 73, 77–78; on Fairfax claims in the Virginia ratifying convention, 75; lawyer for the Fairfax family, 75, 76; in the syndicate to purchase Fairfax plantations, 76; *Marshall v. Commonwealth*, 76–77; managing the Compromise of 1796, 77; suits to collect rents, 77–79, 85; *Marshall v. Conrad*, 78; continuation of Fairfax litigation, 78–81, 85; concurrence in Story's opinion in *Martin v. Hunter's Lessee*, 84; *McCulloch v. Maryland*, 85; *Cohens v. Virginia*, 85, 89–90; "Friend of the Union" and "A Friend of the Constitution," 88; role for the Supreme Court, 88; view of and opposition to states' rights, 88, 90; Federalist or nationalist goals, 118. *See also* Marshall Court
Marshall v. Commonwealth, 77
Marshall v. Conrad, 78–79
Martin v. Hunter's Lessee, xi, 1, 79, 83–86, 116; beginning the Marshall Court nationalist era, 85, 87
Mason, George, 13, 16
Merchants: to benefit from state legal and constitutional reform, 25–26, 36–37, 98, 103; problems in the Virginia courts, 27–28, 30, 35–38, 41, 43, 46, 106–7; relation to law profession, 98, 103. *See also* British debts; Debt; Jury
Missouri crisis and Compromise, x, 11, 89, 91, 96
Monroe, James, 13, 48, 91, 130n. 10

Moore, Andrew, 48
Morris, Robert, 76

National Gazette, 48
Nationalism, advocacy of: by the Federalist party, 52; by the Marshall Court, 84–86, 87–88; by Pleasants's party, 94, 96, 114
Natural law. *See* Fundamental law
Newmyer, R. Kent, 101–2, 103
New trials. *See* Legal reform
New Views of the Constitution (Taylor), 2
Nicholas, Wilson Cary, 13, 53
Norfolk, 30, 51–52, 93
Northern Neck, 13, 32, 48–50, 52, 57, 92, 106; location for developing law profession, 30–31, 127n. 34; Fairfax proprietary area, 74, 77–78; support for legal, judicial, constitutional reform and government centralization, 95
Northwest (or West) Virginia, 92, 93; on support for legal, judicial, constitutional reform and government centralization, 95
Nullification, 1, 54–55, 85

Old Republicans: view of the Constitution and federalism, 2, 57, 117; preference for principle and unwritten constitution, 3, 50, 109–12; conservatism, 3, 89, 109–12, 117; liberty as greatest goal, 4; self-image, 4, 62; view of the Virginia Resolutions of 1798, 47–48, 54–57; contrast with moderate Republicans on interpreting the Constitution, 50; geographic base and personnel, 50, 61, 65, 92, 95–96, 109, 132n. 32; view of the election of 1800 and criticism of Jefferson presidency, 57–58, 61–62; criticism of Federalists and the Marshall Court, 57–59, 85, 91; view of the Chase impeachment, 61; appeal of the Country, republican ideology, 88–89, 91, 110; opposition to the national government, 90–91; relation with Republican party, 91, 93, 95–96, 105; election of 1824, 93; countering Pleasants's reform movement, 96, 109; criticized for preference for an unwritten constitution, 111; view of Virginia, 118

Page, John, 4, 23, 48
Panic of 1819, x, 3, 89, 91, 96; and depression in Virginia, 46, 88, 96, 107
Parker, Josiah, 13, 48
Parliament, 8, 10, 11, 88
Paterson, William, 42
Pendleton, Edmund: *McCall v. Turner*, 41, 65; role for juries, 41, 65, 98–99; *The Danger Not Over*, 57; view of the Constitution, 57; *Commonwealth v. Caton*, 63, 68; view on judicial review, 63–64, 69; leadership in Virginia judiciary, 63–65, 73; "Remonstrance of the Judges," 64–65; beginning of Old Republicans, 65; formation of Republican party, 65; president of Virginia ratifying convention, 65; similarity with John Taylor, 65; view of common law, 65, 70; role of state judges, 65–66; rivalry with Wythe, 65–66, 73; similarity with Roane, 65–66, 70; tradition, legacy, 96, 104, 106, 113
Petersburg, 92, 93
Philadelphia Convention, 9, 11, 13, 15, 16, 22
Pickering, John, 60
Piedmont, 13, 28, 32, 38, 49–50, 106; on support for or against legal, judicial, and constitutional reform and government centralization, 95
Plea: of *non assumpsit*, 35; of payment, 35, 40; special, in British debt cases, 38, 40
Pleasants, James, 91
Pleasants, John Hampden, 91–93. *See also* Pleasants's party
Pleasants's party: for federal internal improvements, 87, 91; for legal and constitutional reform and against local elite rule, 87, 91, 97–100, 108–9; for democratic reapportionment in Virginia and elections of local and state officials, 87, 92, 95, 108; leadership, 91; against the Virginia Republican party caucus and Richmond junto, 91, 93; geographic base and personnel, 91–92, 95; against states' rights and the continuous opposition to the federal government, 91–93; compromising reform, 92, 96; drawing upon, but problems with using, Country, republican rhetoric, 92–94, 96; foundation for the Virginia Whig party, 92–97; election of 1824, 93–94; election of 1828, 94–95
Practice in the Courts (Robinson), 135n. 21, 136n. 19
Prince Edward County, 29–30. *See also* District courts, Virginia; Superior or circuit courts, Virginia
Property rights: relation to liberty and independence, 6–7, 9; between debtors and creditors, 7; law as a protection of, 37, 119; in internal improvements, 100–105; fundamental, 104, 111. *See also* Agrarian; Country gentlemen; Liberty
Protective tariffs, 89, 91, 114
Provincialism, xii, 12, 46, 85, 97; and court reform, 24, 30, 33; and relation to localism, 117. *See also* States' rights

Quitrent, 77–78

Randolph, Edmund, 13, 16
Randolph, John: leader among the Old Republicans and advocate of the Virginia Doctrine, 2–4, 47–48, 61–62, 96–97; impeachment of Federalist federal judges, 59–61; view of Jefferson, 61–62
"Remonstrance of the Judges": 64–66; status of the Virginia constitution, 68; similarity to Tucker's letter of resignation, 72
Republicans: formation, 23, 47–49, 130n. 10; opposition to Jay Treaty, 44, 128n. 20; alliance with Anti-Federalists, 47–49; use of Country, republican ideology to gain Anti-Federalists and Old Republicans, 48–49, 51, 91; geographic base and personnel, 48–49, 57, 65, 95–96; differences with Anti-Federalists, 49–50, 54–57, 129n. 7; compromising reform, 49–50, 105;

Republicans (cont.)
view of the Constitution, 50; contest with Federalists in Virginia, 50–52; power center at state level, 51; opposition from Henry, 51–52; state banking and internal improvements, 51–52, 87, 91, 93, 97, 105; opposition to Alien and Sedition Acts and passage of Virginia Resolutions of 1798, 53–55; opposition to a federal common law, 54, 114–16; criticism of Henry, 55; repeal of the Judiciary Act of 1801, 55; predominance in Virginia, 57, 77; division after the election of 1800, 58, 61–62; opposition from Old Republicans, 61–62; Virginia party caucus, 91, 93; alliance with Old Republicans, 91, 93, 95–97, 105; election of 1824, 93–94; election of 1828, 94–95

Resolutions of 1790. *See* Resolutions of the General Assembly

Resolutions of the General Assembly: colonial and American Revolution precedents, 10–11, 90; against Hamiltonianism, the Resolutions of 1790, 11, 48, 51; on the Missouri crisis and against the Compromise, 11, 89, 135n. 4; against the appellate jurisdiction of the Supreme Court, 11, 90, 113; for constitutional amendments, 23, 44, 50; to suspend the treaty of 1783, 43; against the Jay Treaty, 44; against a federal common law, 54; against *McCulloch v. Maryland*, 88; against *Cohens v. Virginia*, 90. *See also* General Assembly; Virginia Resolutions of 1798

Richmond: 32, 38, 51–52, 72, 73, 93; lawyers, 30, 106–9; city hustings court, 36 (table 2), 126n. 25; Richmond junto, 92–94

Richmond Enquirer, 87–88, 92

Ritchie, Thomas, 88, 90, 97

Roane, Spencer: relation to Henry, xii, 4, 13, 29; similarity to Pendleton, xii, 65–66; contrast and rivalry with St. George Tucker, xii, 65–73; views on the common law, xii, 66, 69–70, 99, 106; leader of the court of appeals, xii, 62, 72–73, 87; advocate of the Virginia Doctrine, 2, 47, 96–97, 116; role of state judges, 66, 69, 80, 106, 113; on an appointment by Jefferson, 66, 132n. 6; *Kamper v. Hawkins*, 67–68; view of judicial review, 67, 69; view of the Virginia constitution, 68, 106; value of an unwritten constitution, 68–69; appointment to the court of appeals, 69; *Baring v. Reeder*, 69–70; proposals on seriatim opinions, 70–71; contrast and antagonism with Marshall, 73, 78, 80, 85–86, 116–19; view of the law, 73, 106, 117, 119; *Marshall v. Conrad*, 78; criticism of the Compromise of 1796, 78, 80; *Hunter v. Fairfax's Devisee*, 79–80; common law in the Fairfax litigation, 80; view of juries, 80, 85, 99–100, 102, 106; criticized by Story, 82; *Hunter v. Martin, Devisee of Fairfax*, 83; interpretation of the Supremacy Clause and advocate of state concurrent jurisdiction on constitutionality, 83, 85, 116–17; "Hampden," 87; drawing upon the Country, republican ideology, 88; advocate of interposition, 88, 119; "Algernon Sidney," 90; relation to the Old Republicans, 96; countering Pleasants's party, 96; tradition, legacy 104, 113; view of Virginia, 118; Virginia's mission, liberty, 118; view of America, 118–19; dissenting opinions, 133n. 15; *Currie's Administrators v. the Mutual Assurance Society*, 137n. 22

Robertson, David, 127n. 7

Robinson, Conway, *Practice in the Courts*, 135n. 21, 136n. 19

Romanticizing the past: Henry as a model country lawyer, 3, 107; in the face of decline, 88; preserving the Virginia constitution, 109–12; Virginia Resolutions of 1798, 114–15

Ross, David, 35, 46

Ruffin, Edmund, 13

Secession, 1, 53, 115

Seriatim opinions, 42–43, 70–72, 104
Slavery, x, 89, 92, 95; in British debt cases, 38, 43–44
Smith, Meriwether, 13
Southern jurisprudence, ix–x, xii–xiii, 5; Virginia as a model, 119–20
Southside, 13, 20, 28, 31, 34, 38, 48–50, 51–52, 56, 97, 106; support for Old Republicans, 61, 94, 97, 109; support against legal, judicial, constitutional reform, and government centralization, 95, 97; benefiting from state internal improvement, 96–97
Southwest Virginia, 92, 93; support against legal, judicial, and constitutional reform and government centralization, 95, 97
Sovereignty, 56, 67–68, 116–18; in each state, 1, 2, 21, 54–55, 88, 118; and relation to common law, 114–16
Special plea. *See* Plea
Special verdict. *See* Legal reform
Starke, Richard, 6
States' rights, xiii, 1, 10, 47, 85, 114, 120; and division of power, 56, 118–19; opposition to, 87–88, 90, 91, 93
Story, Joseph: *Martin v. Hunter's Lessee*, 1, 84–85; *Fairfax's Devisee v. Hunter's Lessee*, 81–82; criticism of Roane's opinions, 82, 84; criticism of localism, 84; interpretation of the Supremacy Clause, for uniformity, 84, 116
Strother, French, 13
Stuart, Archibald, 13, 91
Stuart v. Laird, 59
Superior or circuit courts, Virginia: description and location, 31–33; results, 32–33; Fredericksburg, 36 (table 2); Prince Edward County, 36 (table 2), 101 (table 4), 126n. 25. *See also* General Court
Supreme Court, U.S.: *Martin v. Hunter's Lessee*, 1, 73, 83–86, 87; *Chisholm v. Georgia*, 42; *Ware v. Hylton*, 42–43; *Stuart v. Laird*, 59; *Marbury v. Madison*, 59–60; *Fairfax's Devisee v. Hunter's Lessee*, 73, 81–83; *McCulloch v. Maryland*, 85, 87; *Cohens v. Virginia*, 85, 89–90. *See also* Marshall Court

Taylor, Creed, 71, 107
Taylor, George Keith, 53
Taylor, John: *New Views of the Constitution*, 2; leader among the Old Republicans, 2–3, 61–62, 96; advocate of the Virginia Doctrine, 2–3, 96–97; in Henry's party, 9, 13; test of constitutional principles, 10, 62; formation of Republican party, 47–48, 65, 130n. 10; Virginia Resolutions of 1798, 53–55, 115; similarity to Pendleton, 65; *Construction Construed and Constitutions Vindicated*, 90
Tazewell, Henry, 29
Tazewell, Littleton Waller, 4, 96
Tidewater, 13, 32, 48–49, 61; support against legal, judicial, and constitutional reform and government centralization, 95, 97
Tobacco planters: indebtedness, 3, 7, 34, 38, 46, 88; influence in Virginia, 95–96; benefiting from state internal improvements, 96; and lawyers, 106–7. *See also* Country gentlemen
Toler, Richard, 91
Treaty of 1783: confiscation of British property, 38–39, 75–76, 79; British debt, 38–44; terms not carried out, 38–44; not binding until the Constitution, 41–43, 75; in the Fairfax litigation, 75–76, 79 82, 85
Trespass on the case. *See* Common law; Debt
Tucker, Henry St. George: *Commentaries*, 99–100, 136n. 19; his law school, 107
Tucker, St. George: similarity with Wythe, xii, 65–66; contrast and rivalry with Roane, xii, 65–73, 106; legal professionalism, xii, 66; appointment to the court of appeals, 66; edition of *Blackstone's Commentaries*, 66; views on the common law, xii, 66, 69–70; professor of law, College of William and Mary, 66, 107; advocate of judicial review, 67; *Kamper v. Hawkins*, 67–68; view of the Virginia constitution, 67–68; value of a written constitution, 68; *Baring v. Reeder*, 69–70; resignation from the

Tucker, St. George (*cont.*)
court of appeals, 72; appointment to the U.S. district court in Virginia, and on the U.S. circuit court in Richmond, 73; view of the law, 73; *Hunter v. Fairfax's Devisee*, 75, 79
Tyler, John, 4, 29
Tyranny, 57, 62, 89, 111; from uniformity and centralization, 90, 116–17. *See also* Liberty

Unwritten constitution: Virginia, xii, 2, 3, 5, 9–11, 15, 18, 24; English, xii, 8, 9–10, 68, 111; fundamental character of the county court system, 49, 109–12; relation to the Virginia constitution of 1776, 68–69, 109–12; basis for judicial review, 104; the test of time, 104, 110. *See also* Common law; Fundamental law

Virginia: economic decline, x, 3, 34, 46, 88, 92, 105; decline in influence, x, 3, 88, 92, 114; migration out, 88, 89; political economy, 105; decentralized government and society, 105–6, 113–14; relation of law and society, 106–7. *See also* Constitution, Virginia; Courts; General Assembly
Virginia Doctrine: 1–2, 4–5, 120; origins, 23–24, 48; political dogma, 96–97, 116
Virginia Dynasty, x, 3, 91–92
Virginian (Lynchburg), 91, 93
Virginia Plan, 13, 15
Virginia ratifying convention: debate over the ratification of the Constitution, 9, 16–20; ratify then recommend amendments compromise, 20–21; recommended amendments, 21–22; Pendleton as president, 65; issue of the Fairfax claims, 75, 78, 81; votes, 124n. 2
Virginia Report, 56, 96–97, 116
Virginia Resolutions of 1798: Alien and Sedition Acts declared unconstitutional, 11, 53; debate over, 53–56; division among Republicans, 54–57; answer from Virginia Federalists, 55; response from other states, 55; as propaganda for election of 1800, 57; part of the Virginia Doctrine, 96–97, 116; myth, 114–15
Virginia Supreme Court of Appeals: on appeals from state courts, 32, 99–101; rejects appellate jurisdiction of Supreme Court, 62, 82–83; *Commonwealth v. Caton*, 63–64; leadership on the court, 63–65, 72–73, 106; "Remonstrance of the Judges," 64–65; legislative changes in the judiciary, 64–65, 70, 72, 79; personnel, 65, 66, 69, 70, 72, 82, 106; rivalry between Roane and Tucker, 70–72; Tucker's resignation, 72; *Fairfax v. Commonwealth*, 76–77; *Marshall v. Conrad*, 78; *Hunter v. Fairfax's Devisee*, 79–81; criticism of Story, 82; *Hunter v. Martin, Devisee of Fairfax*, 82–83; rejects Supreme Court reversal of *Hunter v. Fairfax's Devisee*, 82–83; the highest court on state common law, 82–83, 85; declares section twenty-five of the Judiciary Act of 1789 unconstitutional, 83; on changing Virginia's common law, 98–101; *Whitacre v. M'Ilhaney*, 99; *Crenshaw and Crenshaw v. Slate River Company*, 102–6
Virtue, 9, 12, 110

Ware, John Tyndal, 40
Ware v. Hylton: enters docket as *Jones v. Hylton*, 40; U.S. circuit court opinion by James Iredell, 40–42, 43; Supreme Court, 42–43
War interests. *See* British debts
Washington, George, 13, 20, 44, 51–52, 65
Wayles, John, 40
Webb, George, 5–6
Whigs. *See* England; Pleasants's party
Whitacre v. M'Ilhaney, 99, 113
White, Alexander, 13, 48
Wickham, John, 107
Williamsburg, 72
Williams v. Price, 135n. 21
Wilson, James, 42
Winchester, 78, 93. *See also* District courts, Virginia
Wirt, William, 4, 107–8, 127n. 7
Worcester v. Georgia, xi

Wythe, George: legal professionalism, xii, 65; similarity with Tucker, xii, 65–66, 70; view of the law, xii, 70, 73; view on judicial review, 63–64; *Commonwealth v. Caton*, 63–64, 68; court of chancery, 65; professor of law, College of William and Mary, 65, 107; formation of the Virginia Federalist party, 65, 130n. 10; contrast and rivalry with Pendleton, 65–66, 73, 106